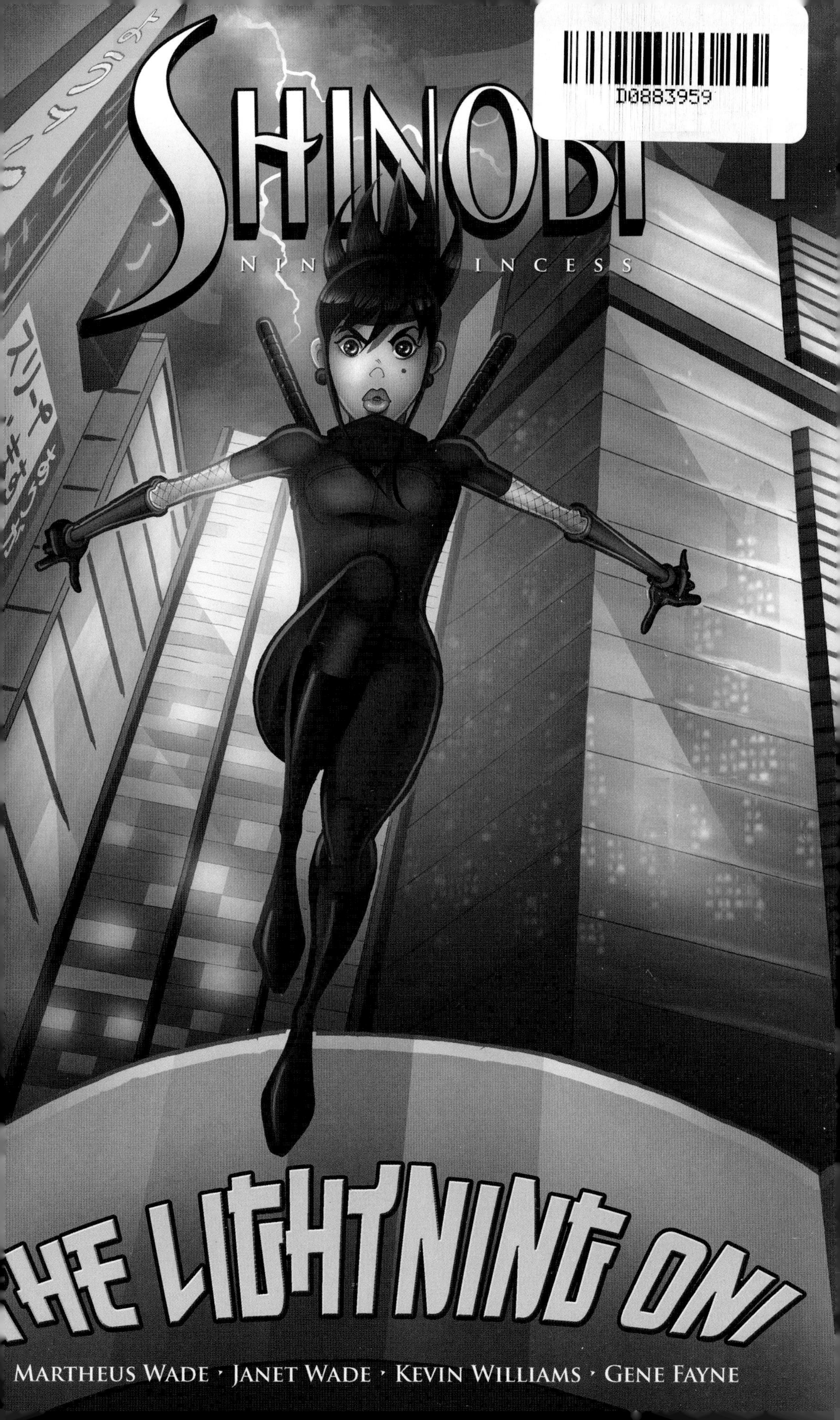
SHINOBI
NIN INCESS
THE LIGHTNING ONI
MARTHEUS WADE · JANET WADE · KEVIN WILLIAMS · GENE FAYNE

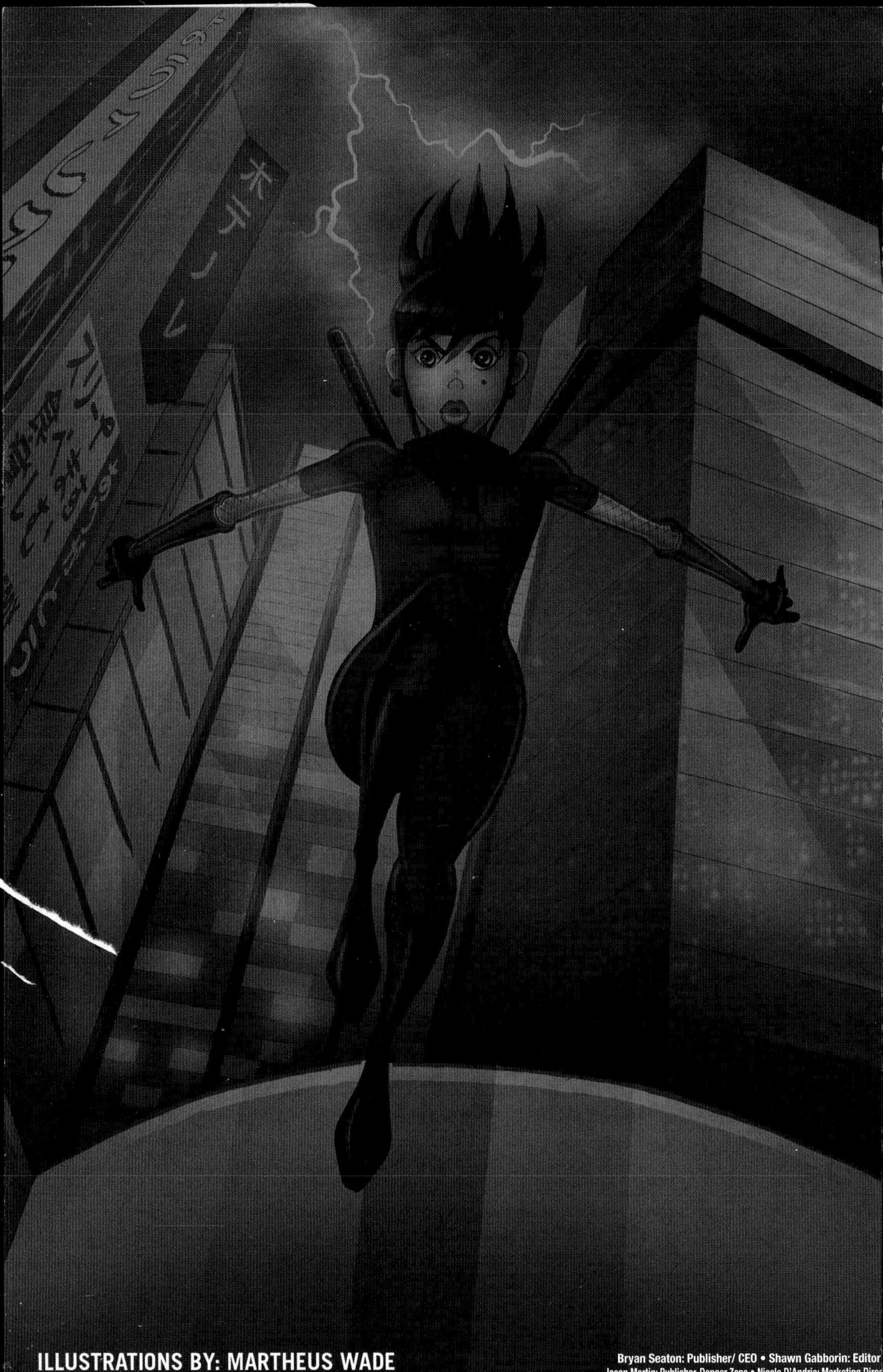

ILLUSTRATIONS BY: MARTHEUS WADE
WRITEN BY: MARTHEUS AND JANET WADE
INTERIOR COLORS BY: MARTHEUS WADE AND GENE FAYNE
COVER BY: MARTHEUS WADE & GENE FAYNE

Bryan Seaton: Publisher/ CEO • Shawn Gabborin: Editor
Jason Martin: Publisher-Danger Zone • Nicole D'Andria: Marketing Direc
Jim Dietz: Social Media Manager • Danielle Davison: Executive Adm
Chad Cicconi: Noodle Oni • Shawn Pryor: President of Creator

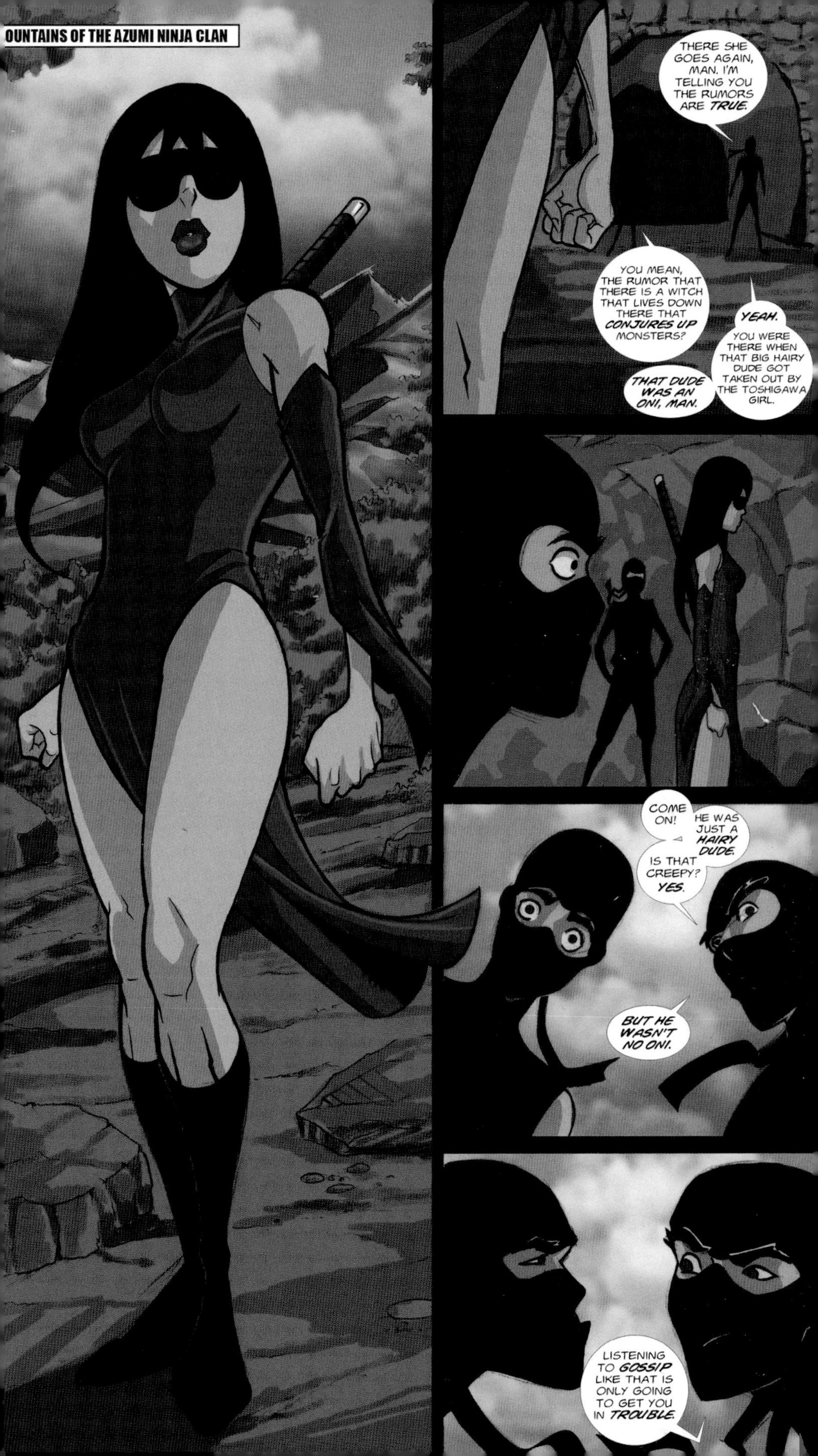
OUNTAINS OF THE AZUMI NINJA CLAN
THERE SHE GOES AGAIN, MAN. I'M TELLING YOU THE RUMORS ARE *TRUE*.
YOU MEAN, THE RUMOR THAT THERE IS A WITCH THAT LIVES DOWN THERE THAT *CONJURES UP* MONSTERS?
YEAH. YOU WERE THERE WHEN THAT BIG HAIRY DUDE GOT TAKEN OUT BY THE TOSHIGAWA GIRL.
THAT DUDE WAS AN ONI, MAN.
COME ON!
HE WAS JUST A *HAIRY DUDE.*
IS THAT CREEPY? *YES*.
BUT HE WASN'T NO ONI.
LISTENING TO *GOSSIP* LIKE THAT IS ONLY GOING TO GET YOU IN *TROUBLE*.

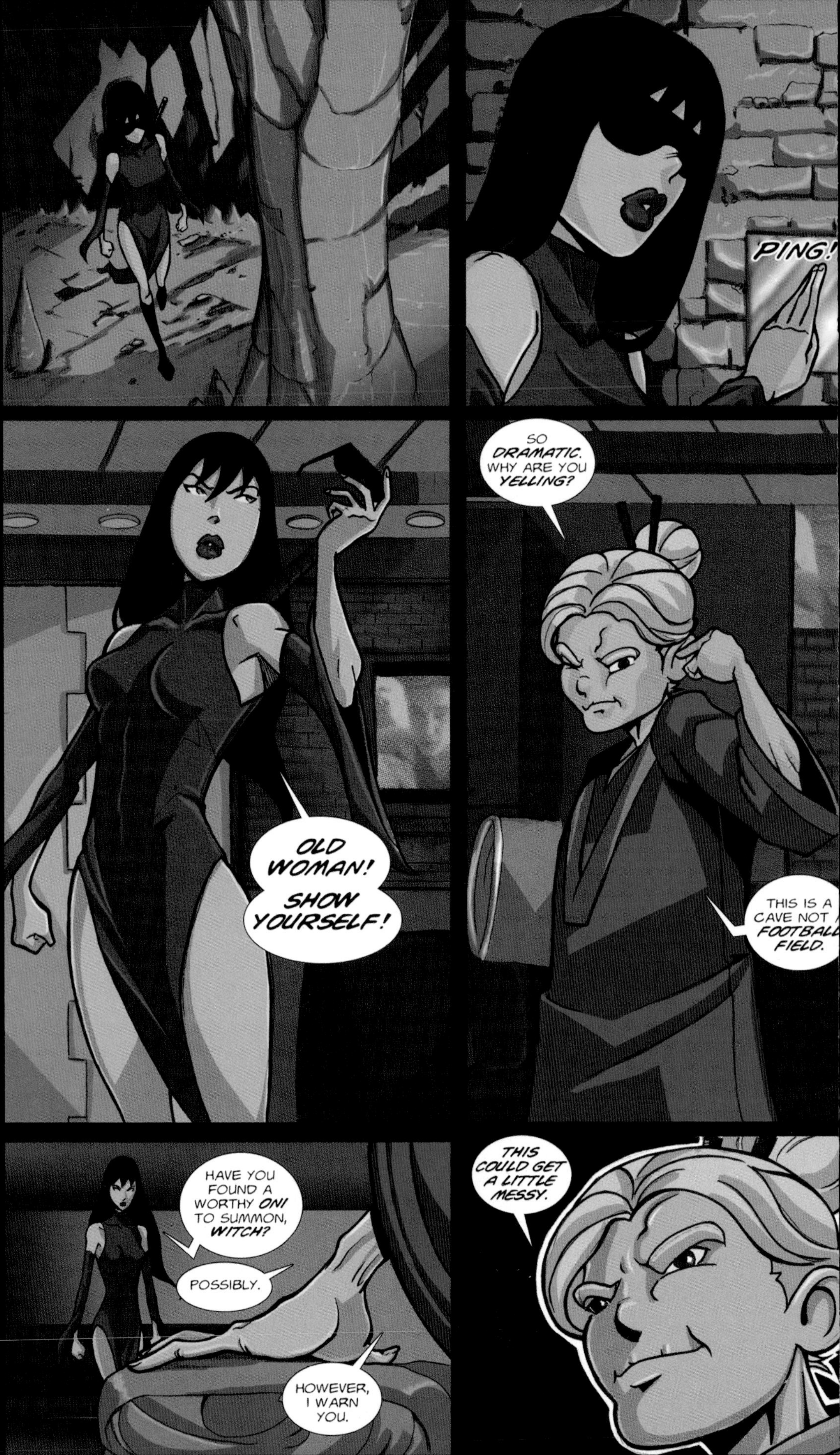
PING!
OLD WOMAN! SHOW YOURSELF!
SO DRAMATIC. WHY ARE YOU YELLING?
THIS IS A CAVE NOT A FOOTBALL FIELD.
HAVE YOU FOUND A WORTHY ONI TO SUMMON, WITCH?
POSSIBLY.
HOWEVER, I WARN YOU.
THIS COULD GET A LITTLE MESSY.

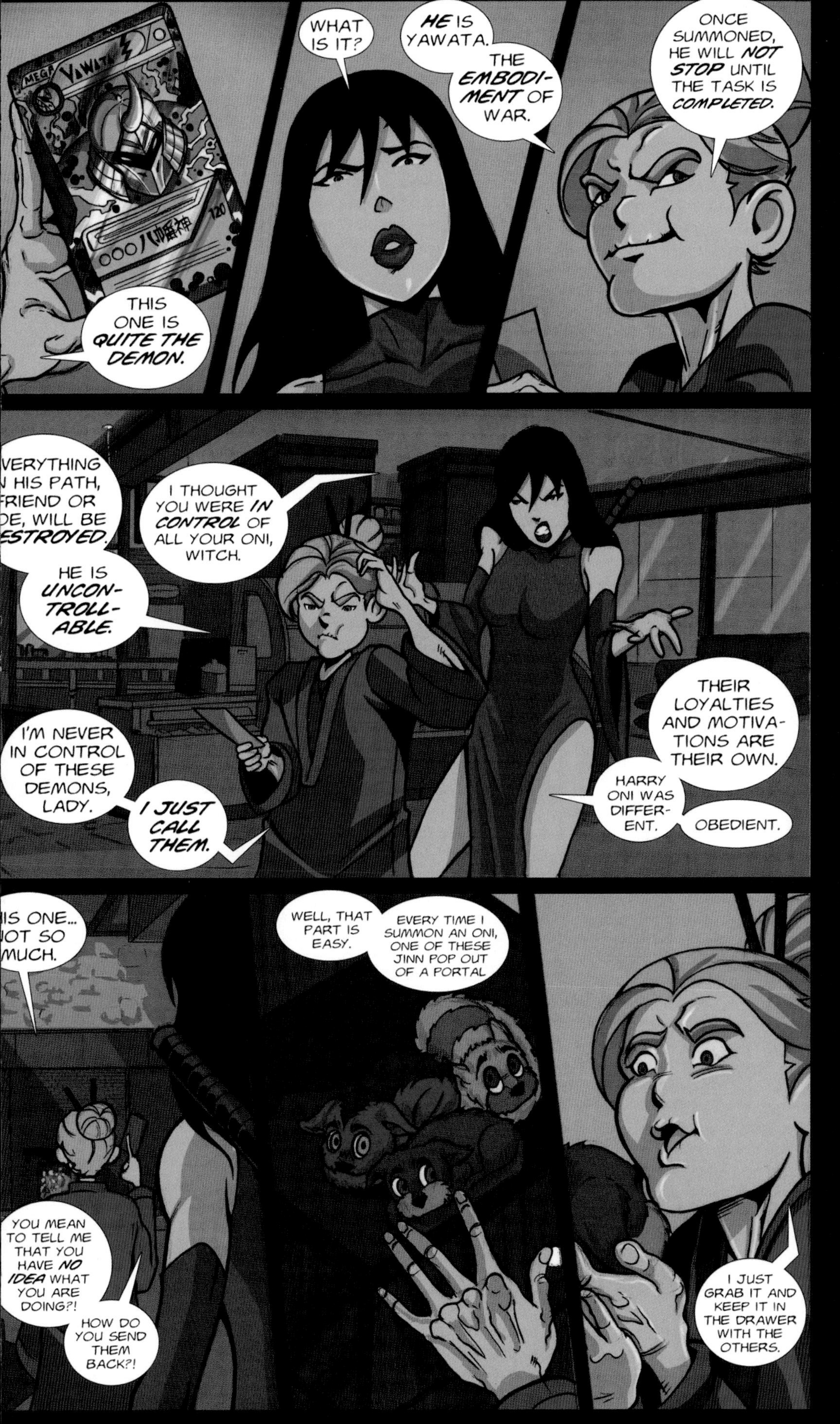
MEGA YAWATA
120
THIS ONE IS QUITE THE DEMON.
WHAT IS IT?
HE IS YAWATA.
THE EMBODIMENT OF WAR.
ONCE SUMMONED, HE WILL NOT STOP UNTIL THE TASK IS COMPLETED.
VERYTHING N HIS PATH, FRIEND OR DE, WILL BE ESTROYED.
HE IS UNCONTROLLABLE.
I THOUGHT YOU WERE IN CONTROL OF ALL YOUR ONI, WITCH.
I'M NEVER IN CONTROL OF THESE DEMONS, LADY.
I JUST CALL THEM.
THEIR LOYALTIES AND MOTIVATIONS ARE THEIR OWN.
HARRY ONI WAS DIFFERENT.
OBEDIENT.
IS ONE... NOT SO MUCH.
YOU MEAN TO TELL ME THAT YOU HAVE NO IDEA WHAT YOU ARE DOING?!
HOW DO YOU SEND THEM BACK?!
WELL, THAT PART IS EASY.
EVERY TIME I SUMMON AN ONI, ONE OF THESE JINN POP OUT OF A PORTAL
I JUST GRAB IT AND KEEP IT IN THE DRAWER WITH THE OTHERS.

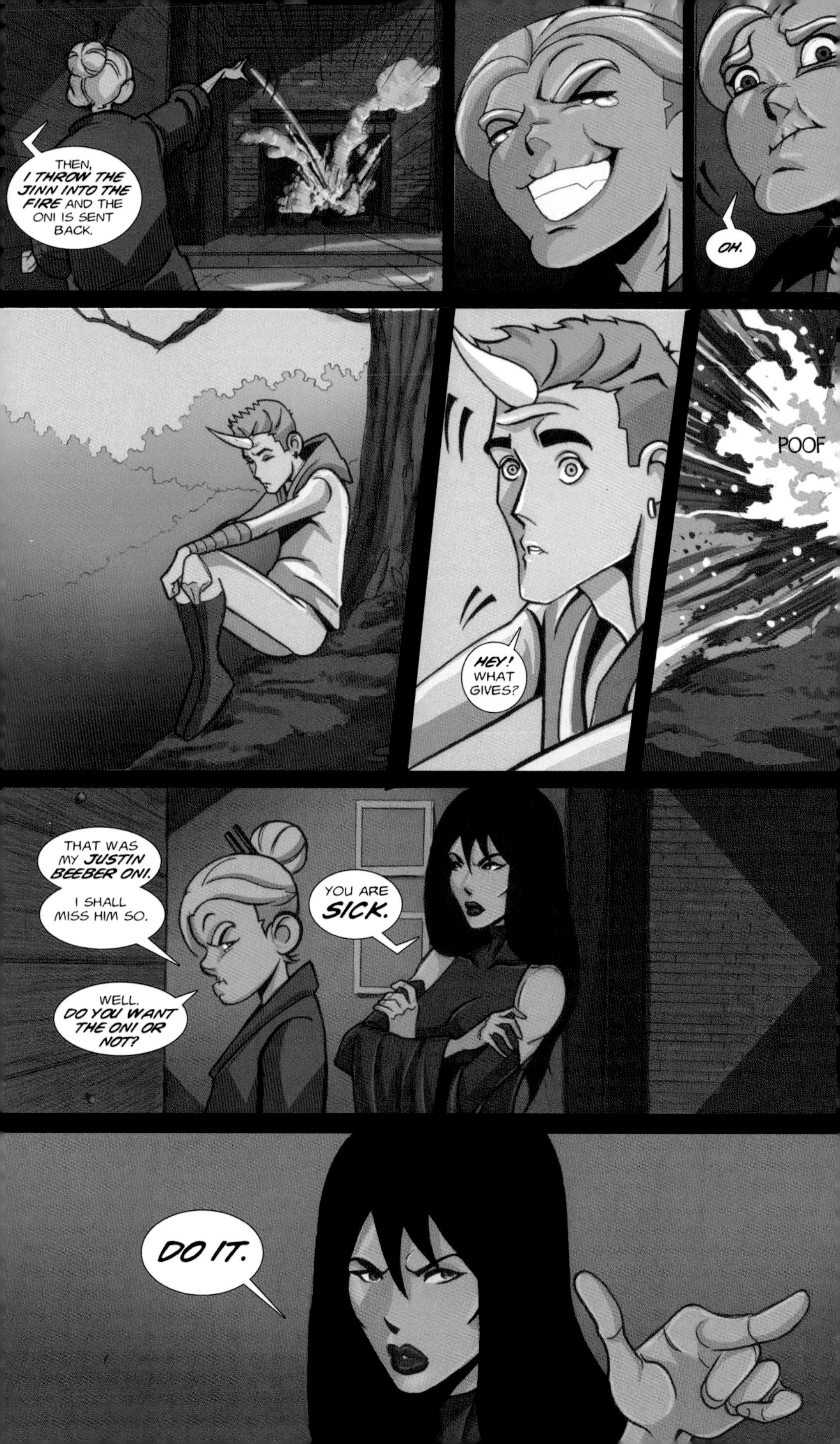
THEN, *I THROW THE JINN INTO THE FIRE* AND THE ONI IS SENT BACK.
OH.
HEY! WHAT GIVES?
POOF
THAT WAS MY *JUSTIN BEEBER ONI.*
I SHALL MISS HIM SO.
YOU ARE *SICK.*
WELL. *DO YOU WANT THE ONI OR NOT?*
DO IT.

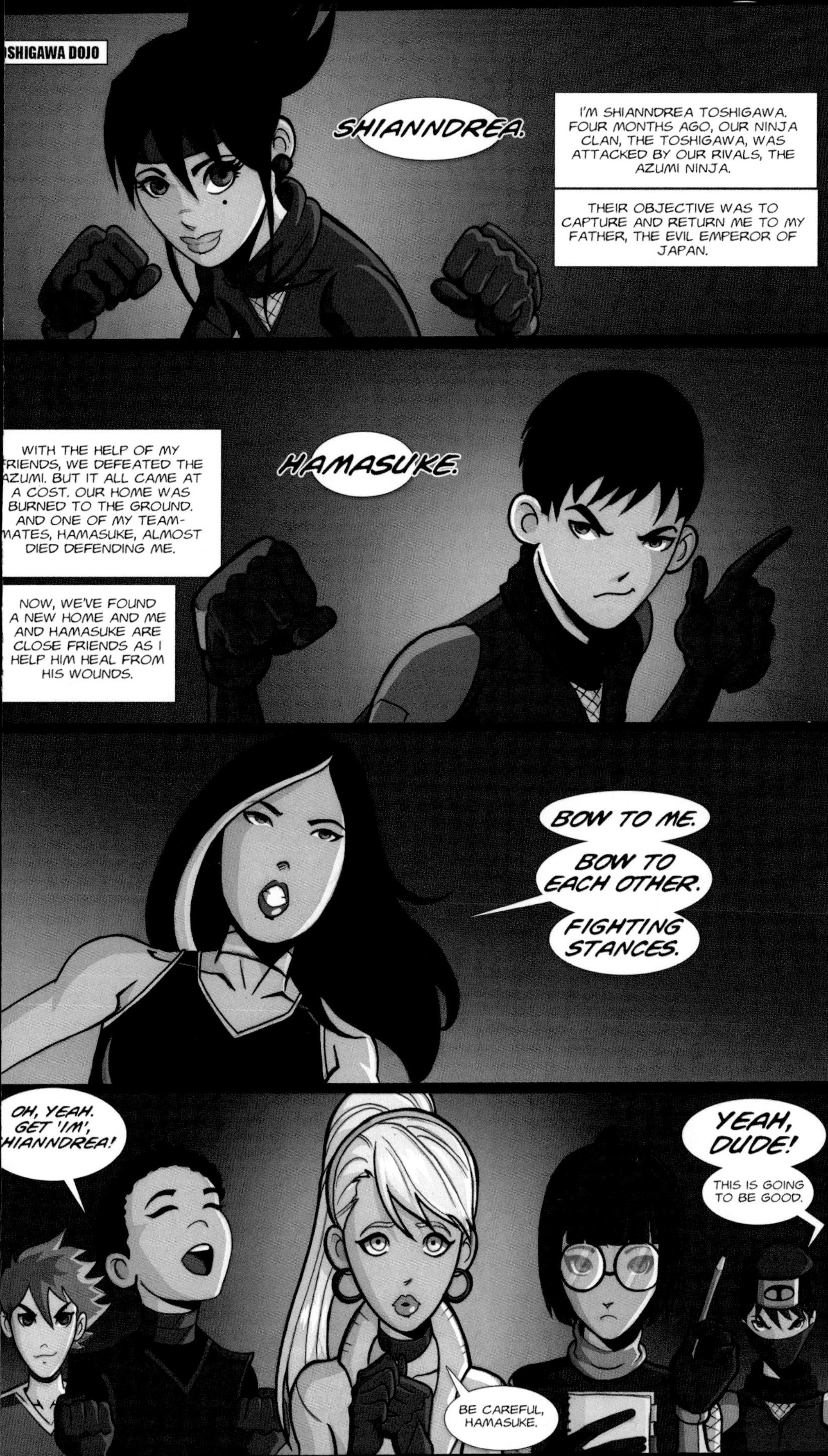

OSHIGAWA DOJO
SHIANNDREA.
I'M SHIANNDREA TOSHIGAWA. FOUR MONTHS AGO, OUR NINJA CLAN, THE TOSHIGAWA, WAS ATTACKED BY OUR RIVALS, THE AZUMI NINJA.
THEIR OBJECTIVE WAS TO CAPTURE AND RETURN ME TO MY FATHER, THE EVIL EMPEROR OF JAPAN.
WITH THE HELP OF MY FRIENDS, WE DEFEATED THE AZUMI. BUT IT ALL CAME AT A COST. OUR HOME WAS BURNED TO THE GROUND. AND ONE OF MY TEAM-MATES, HAMASUKE, ALMOST DIED DEFENDING ME.
NOW, WE'VE FOUND A NEW HOME AND ME AND HAMASUKE ARE CLOSE FRIENDS AS I HELP HIM HEAL FROM HIS WOUNDS.
HAMASUKE.
BOW TO ME.
BOW TO EACH OTHER.
FIGHTING STANCES.
OH, YEAH. GET 'IM', HIANNDREA!
BE CAREFUL, HAMASUKE.
YEAH, DUDE!
THIS IS GOING TO BE GOOD.

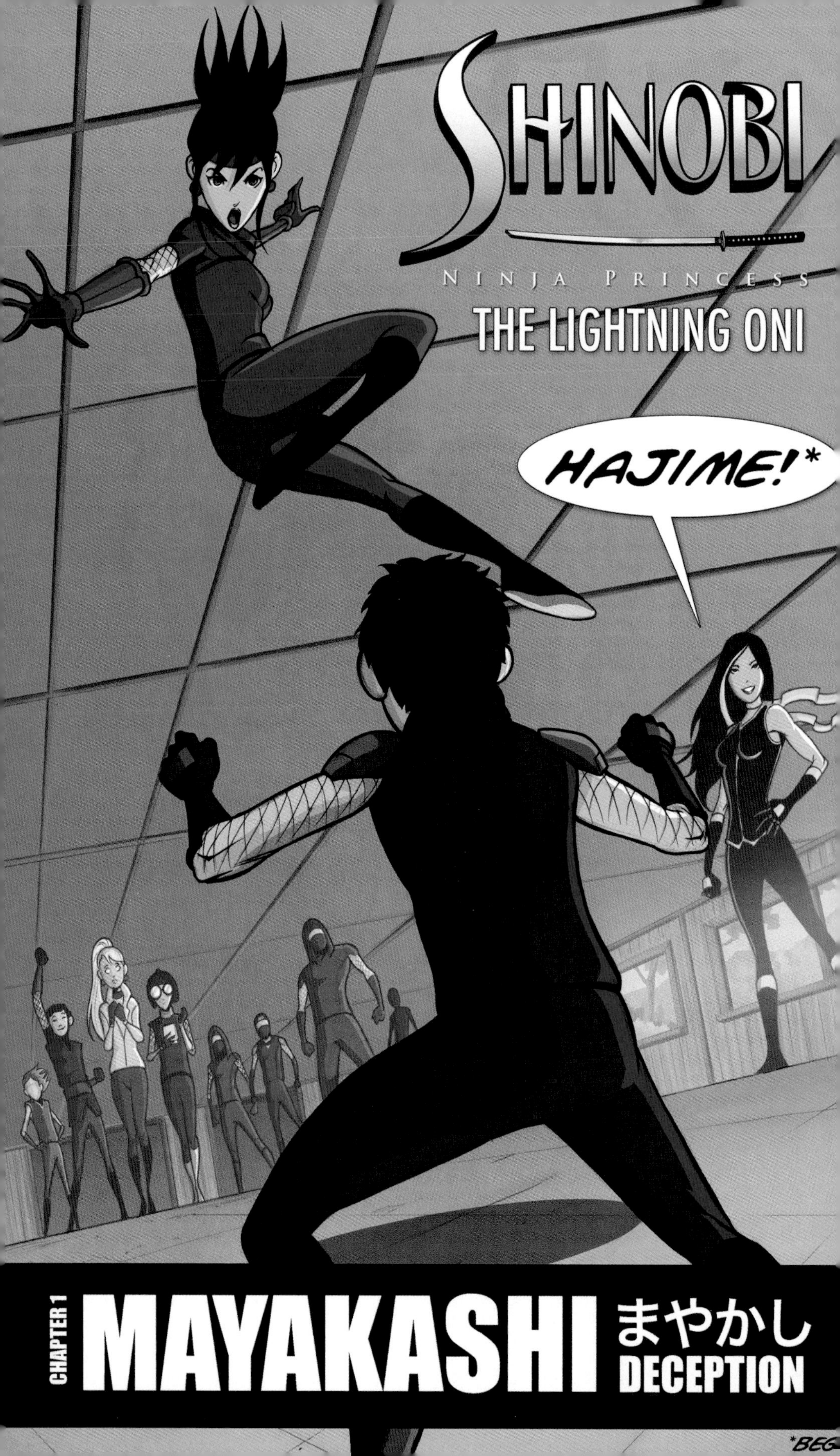
SHINOBI
NINJA PRINCESS
THE LIGHTNING ONI
HAJIME!*

CHAPTER 1 MAYAKASHI まやかし DECEPTION

*BEG

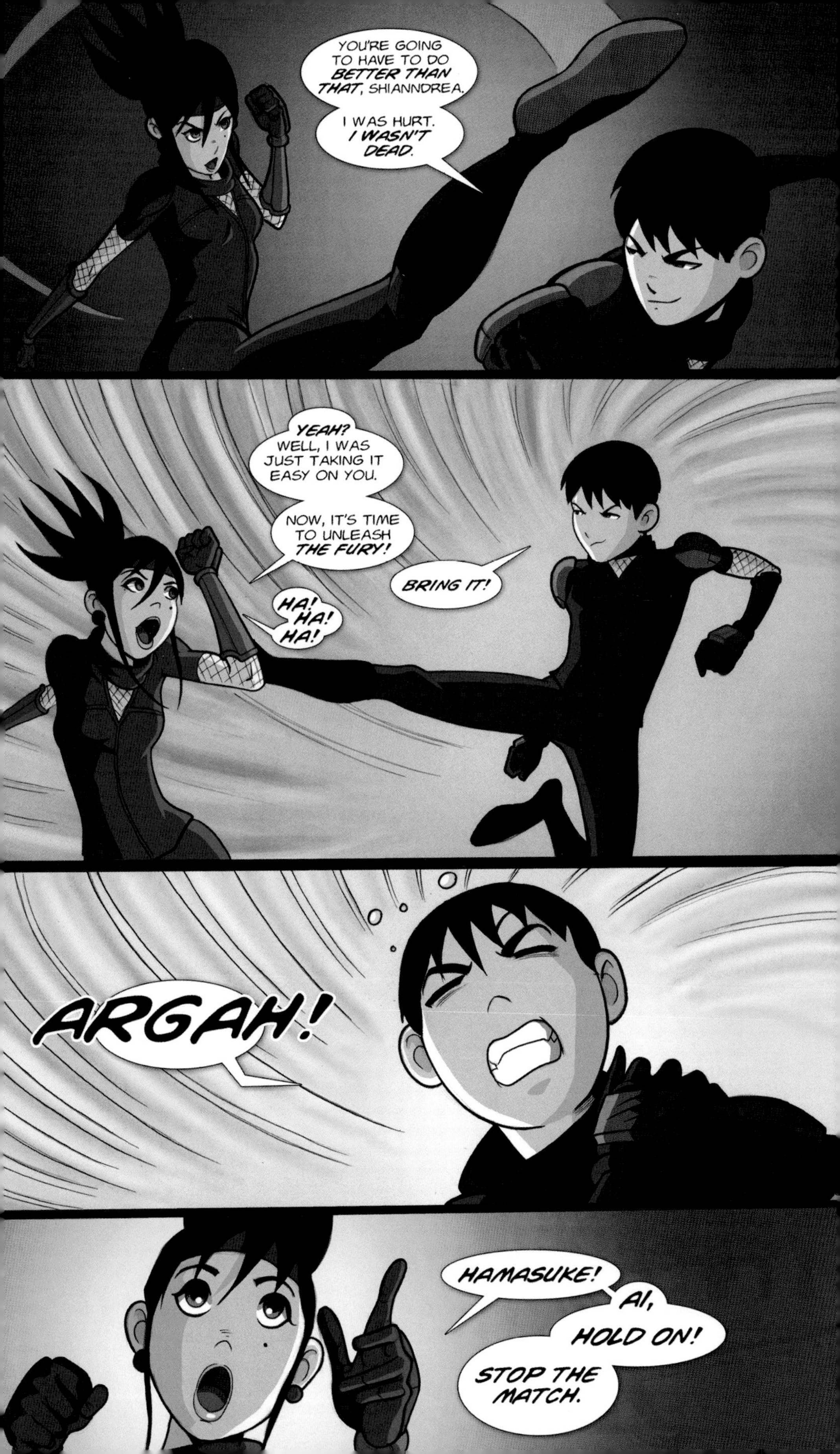
YOU'RE GOING TO HAVE TO DO BETTER THAN THAT, SHIANNDREA.
I WAS HURT. I WASN'T DEAD.
YEAH? WELL, I WAS JUST TAKING IT EASY ON YOU.
NOW, IT'S TIME TO UNLEASH THE FURY!
BRING IT!
HA! HA! HA!
ARGAH!
HAMASUKE!
AI, HOLD ON!
STOP THE MATCH.

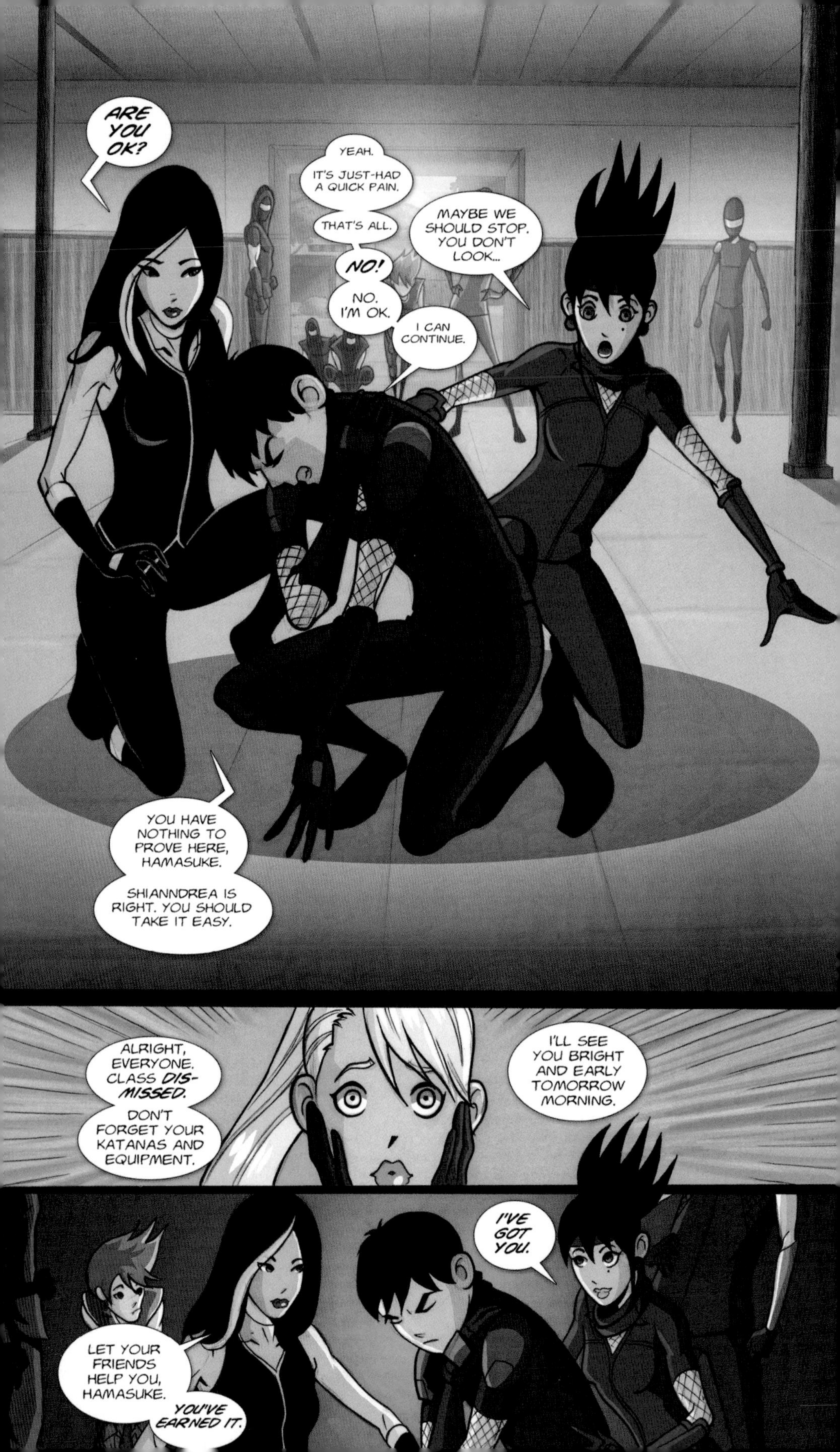
ARE YOU OK?
YEAH.
IT'S JUST-HAD A QUICK PAIN.
THAT'S ALL.
NO!
NO. I'M OK.
I CAN CONTINUE.
MAYBE WE SHOULD STOP. YOU DON'T LOOK...
YOU HAVE NOTHING TO PROVE HERE, HAMASUKE.
SHIANNDREA IS RIGHT. YOU SHOULD TAKE IT EASY.
ALRIGHT, EVERYONE. CLASS DIS-MISSED.
DON'T FORGET YOUR KATANAS AND EQUIPMENT.
I'LL SEE YOU BRIGHT AND EARLY TOMORROW MORNING.
LET YOUR FRIENDS HELP YOU, HAMASUKE.
YOU'VE EARNED IT.
I'VE GOT YOU.

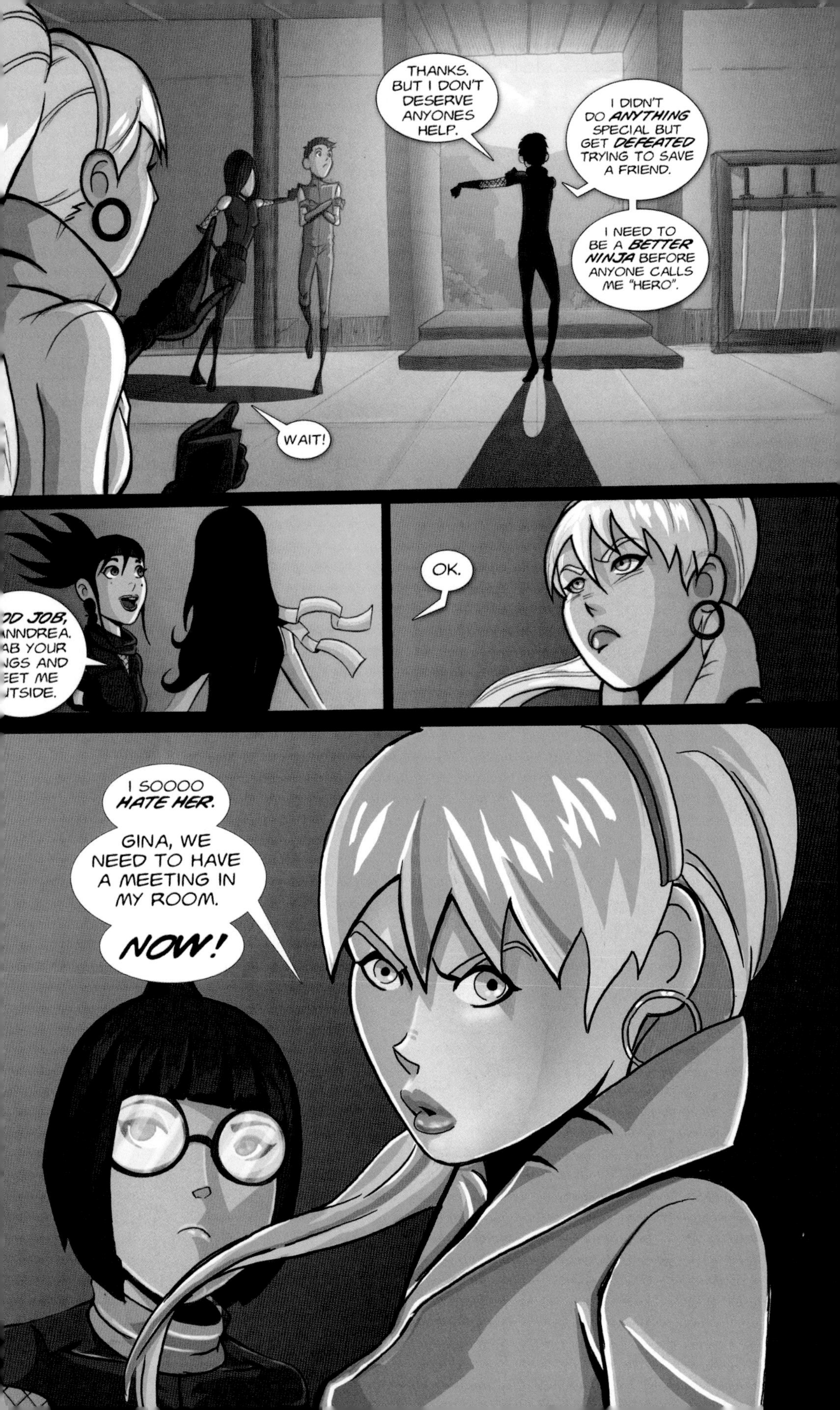
THANKS. BUT I DON'T DESERVE ANYONES HELP.
I DIDN'T DO ANYTHING SPECIAL BUT GET DEFEATED TRYING TO SAVE A FRIEND.
I NEED TO BE A BETTER NINJA BEFORE ANYONE CALLS ME "HERO".
WAIT!
OD JOB, ANNDREA. AB YOUR NGS AND EET ME TSIDE.
OK.
I SOOOO HATE HER.
GINA, WE NEED TO HAVE A MEETING IN MY ROOM.
NOW!

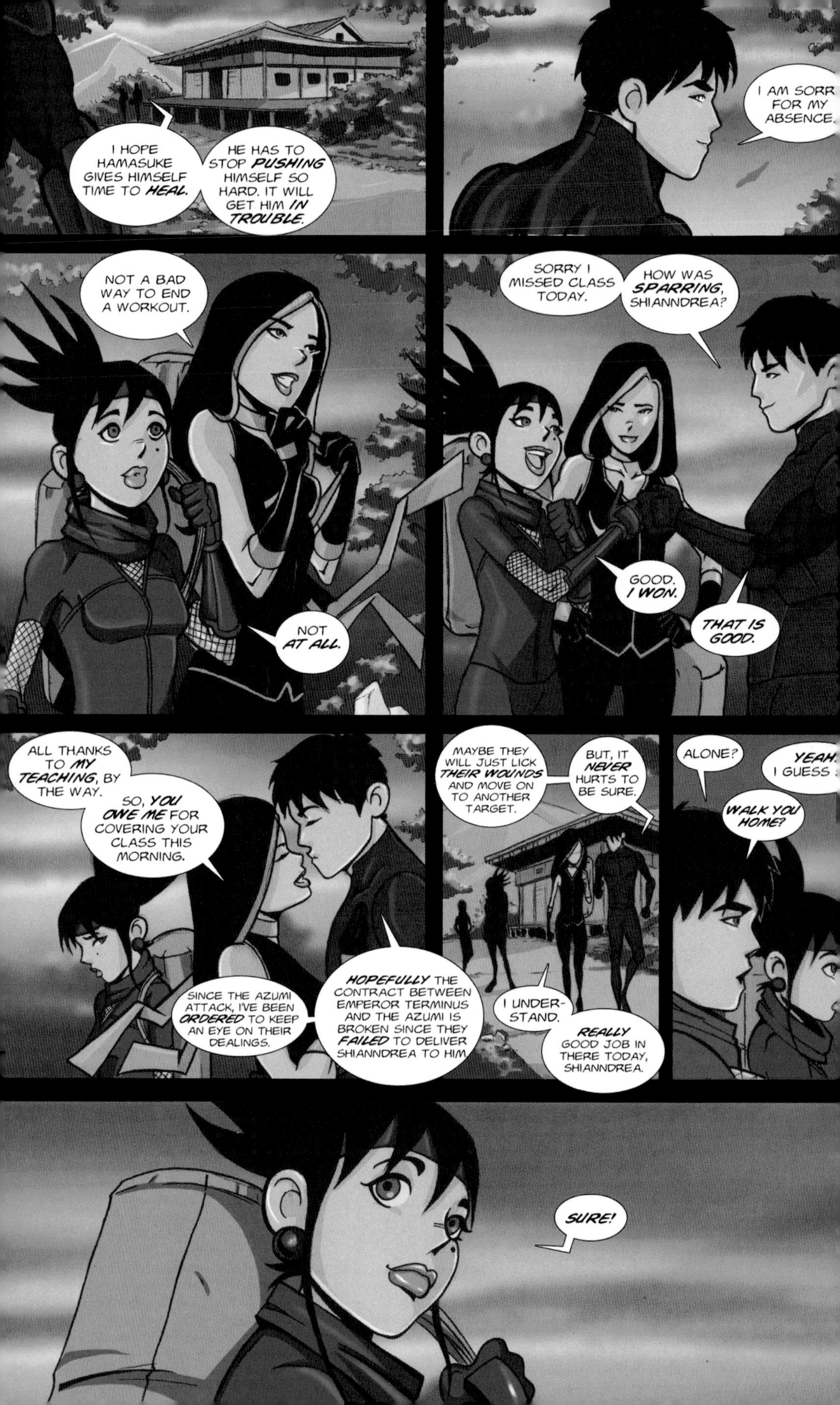
I HOPE HAMASUKE GIVES HIMSELF TIME TO HEAL.
HE HAS TO STOP PUSHING HIMSELF SO HARD. IT WILL GET HIM IN TROUBLE.
I AM SORR FOR MY ABSENCE.
NOT A BAD WAY TO END A WORKOUT.
NOT AT ALL.
SORRY I MISSED CLASS TODAY.
HOW WAS SPARRING, SHIANNDREA?
GOOD. I WON.
THAT IS GOOD.
ALL THANKS TO MY TEACHING, BY THE WAY.
SO, YOU OWE ME FOR COVERING YOUR CLASS THIS MORNING.
SINCE THE AZUMI ATTACK, I'VE BEEN ORDERED TO KEEP AN EYE ON THEIR DEALINGS.
HOPEFULLY THE CONTRACT BETWEEN EMPEROR TERMINUS AND THE AZUMI IS BROKEN SINCE THEY FAILED TO DELIVER SHIANNDREA TO HIM
MAYBE THEY WILL JUST LICK THEIR WOUNDS AND MOVE ON TO ANOTHER TARGET.
BUT, IT NEVER HURTS TO BE SURE.
I UNDER-STAND.
REALLY GOOD JOB IN THERE TODAY, SHIANNDREA.
ALONE?
YEAH. I GUESS
WALK YOU HOME?
SURE!

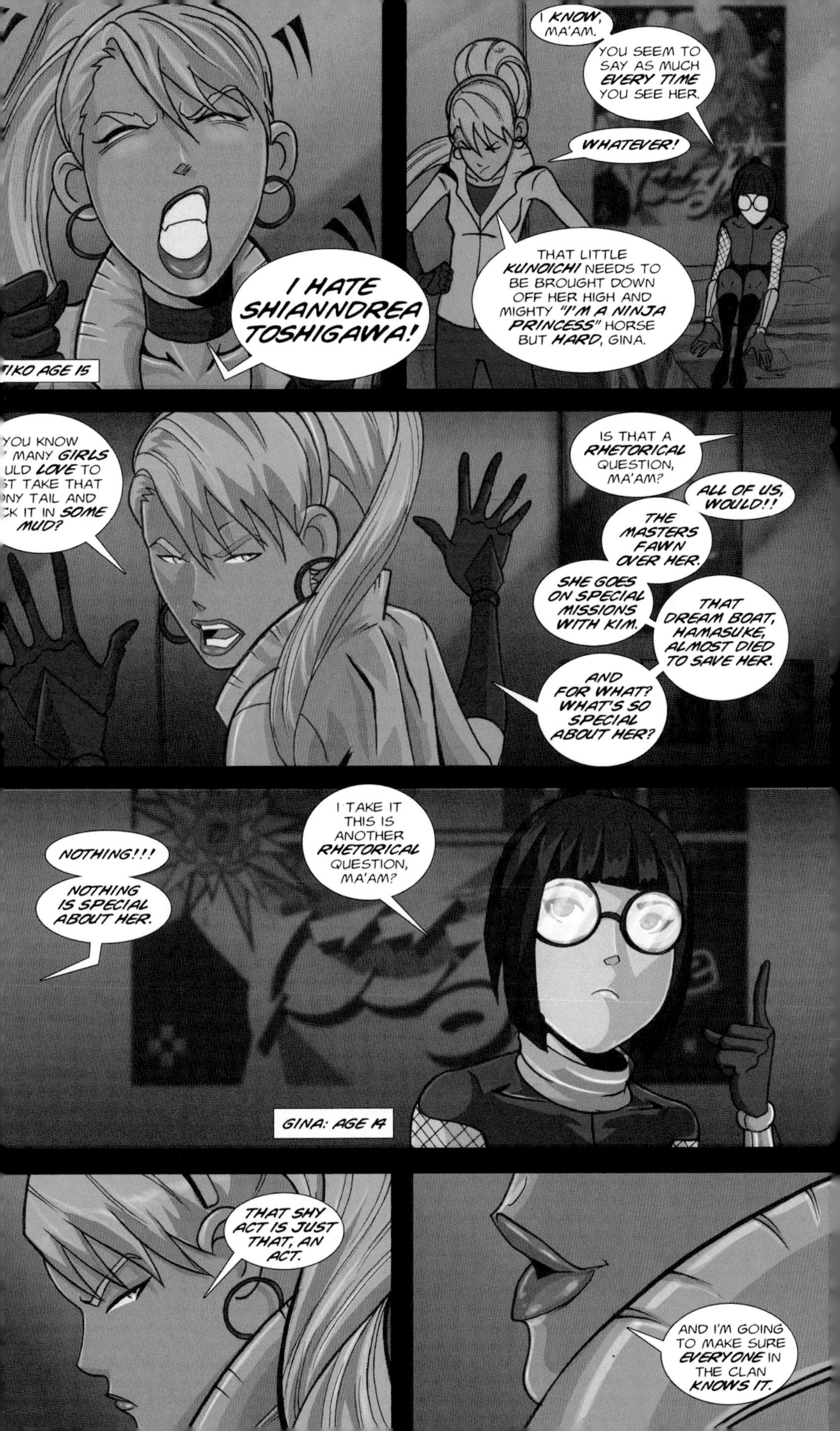
TIKO AGE 15
I HATE SHIANNDREA TOSHIGAWA!
I KNOW, MA'AM.
YOU SEEM TO SAY AS MUCH EVERY TIME YOU SEE HER.
WHATEVER!
THAT LITTLE KUNOICHI NEEDS TO BE BROUGHT DOWN OFF HER HIGH AND MIGHTY "I'M A NINJA PRINCESS" HORSE BUT HARD, GINA.
YOU KNOW ' MANY GIRLS ULD LOVE TO ST TAKE THAT NY TAIL AND CK IT IN SOME MUD?
IS THAT A RHETORICAL QUESTION, MA'AM?
ALL OF US, WOULD!!
THE MASTERS FAWN OVER HER.
SHE GOES ON SPECIAL MISSIONS WITH KIM.
THAT DREAM BOAT, HAMASUKE, ALMOST DIED TO SAVE HER.
AND FOR WHAT? WHAT'S SO SPECIAL ABOUT HER?
NOTHING!!!
NOTHING IS SPECIAL ABOUT HER.
I TAKE IT THIS IS ANOTHER RHETORICAL QUESTION, MA'AM?
GINA: AGE 14
THAT SHY ACT IS JUST THAT, AN ACT.
AND I'M GOING TO MAKE SURE EVERYONE IN THE CLAN KNOWS IT.

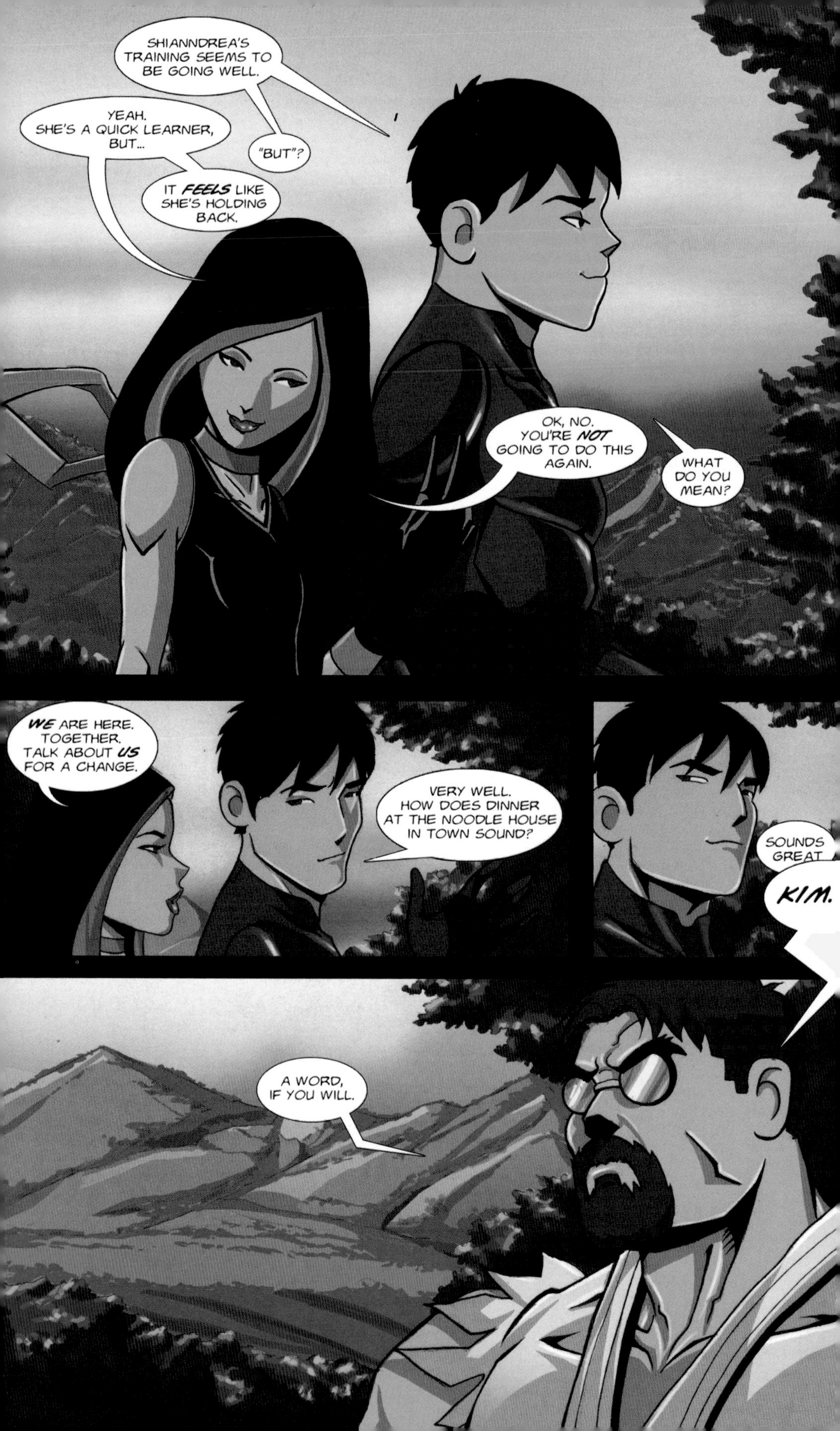
SHIANNDREA'S TRAINING SEEMS TO BE GOING WELL.
YEAH. SHE'S A QUICK LEARNER, BUT...
"BUT"?
IT *FEELS* LIKE SHE'S HOLDING BACK.
OK, NO. YOU'RE *NOT* GOING TO DO THIS AGAIN.
WHAT DO YOU MEAN?
WE ARE HERE. TOGETHER. TALK ABOUT *US* FOR A CHANGE.
VERY WELL. HOW DOES DINNER AT THE NOODLE HOUSE IN TOWN SOUND?
SOUNDS GREAT
KIM.
A WORD, IF YOU WILL.

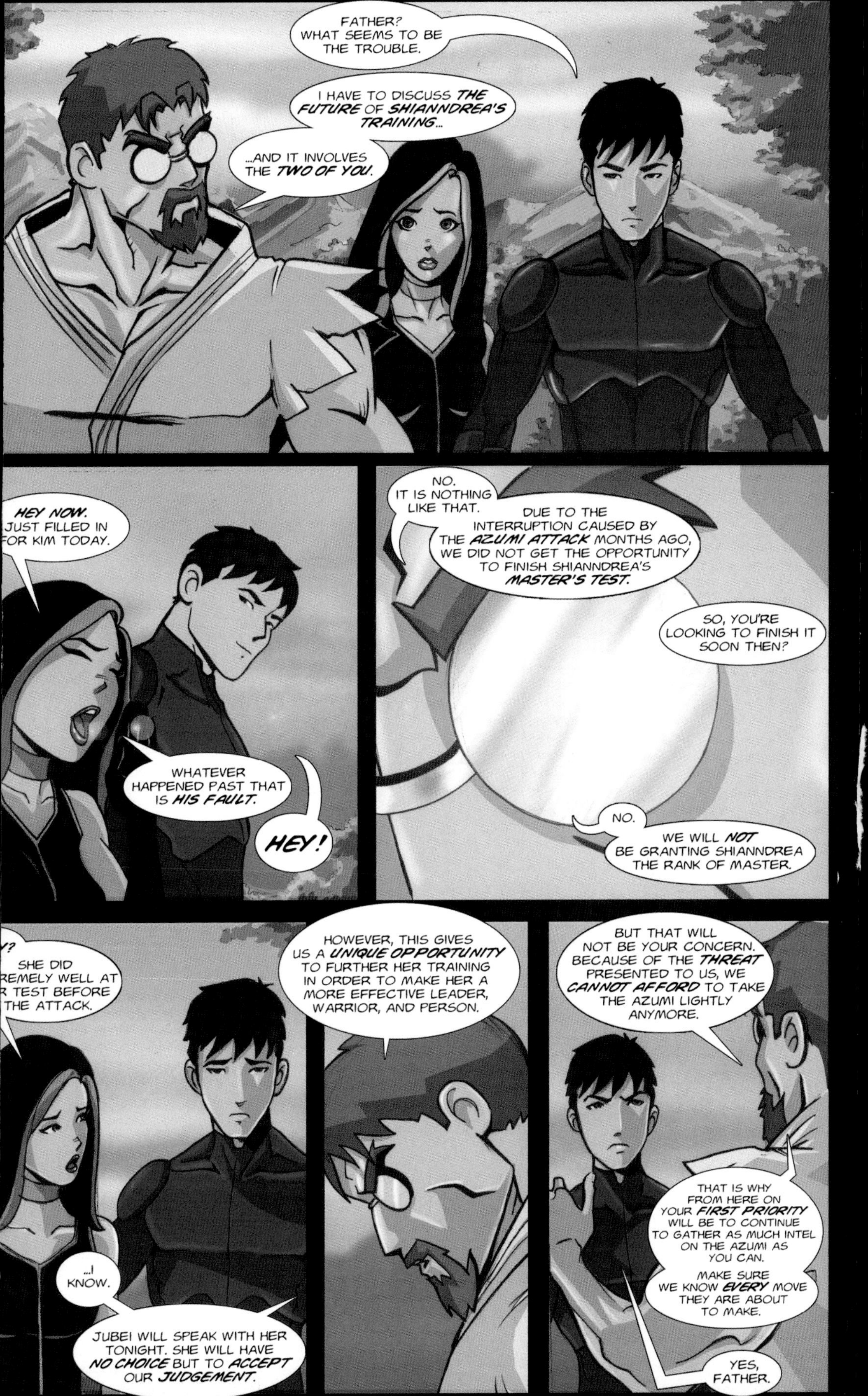
FATHER? WHAT SEEMS TO BE THE TROUBLE.
I HAVE TO DISCUSS *THE FUTURE* OF *SHIANNDREA'S TRAINING*...
...AND IT INVOLVES THE *TWO OF YOU*.
HEY NOW. JUST FILLED IN FOR KIM TODAY.
WHATEVER HAPPENED PAST THAT IS *HIS FAULT*.
HEY!
NO. IT IS NOTHING LIKE THAT.
DUE TO THE INTERRUPTION CAUSED BY THE *AZUMI ATTACK* MONTHS AGO, WE DID NOT GET THE OPPORTUNITY TO FINISH SHIANNDREA'S *MASTER'S TEST*.
SO, YOU'RE LOOKING TO FINISH IT SOON THEN?
NO.
WE WILL *NOT* BE GRANTING SHIANNDREA THE RANK OF MASTER.
SHE DID
REMELY WELL AT
R TEST BEFORE
THE ATTACK.
...I KNOW.
JUBEI WILL SPEAK WITH HER TONIGHT. SHE WILL HAVE *NO CHOICE* BUT TO *ACCEPT* OUR *JUDGEMENT*.
HOWEVER, THIS GIVES US A *UNIQUE OPPORTUNITY* TO FURTHER HER TRAINING IN ORDER TO MAKE HER A MORE EFFECTIVE LEADER, WARRIOR, AND PERSON.
BUT THAT WILL NOT BE YOUR CONCERN. BECAUSE OF THE *THREAT* PRESENTED TO US, WE *CANNOT AFFORD* TO TAKE THE AZUMI LIGHTLY ANYMORE.
THAT IS WHY FROM HERE ON YOUR *FIRST PRIORITY* WILL BE TO CONTINUE TO GATHER AS MUCH INTEL ON THE AZUMI AS YOU CAN.
MAKE SURE WE KNOW *EVERY* MOVE THEY ARE ABOUT TO MAKE.
YES, FATHER.

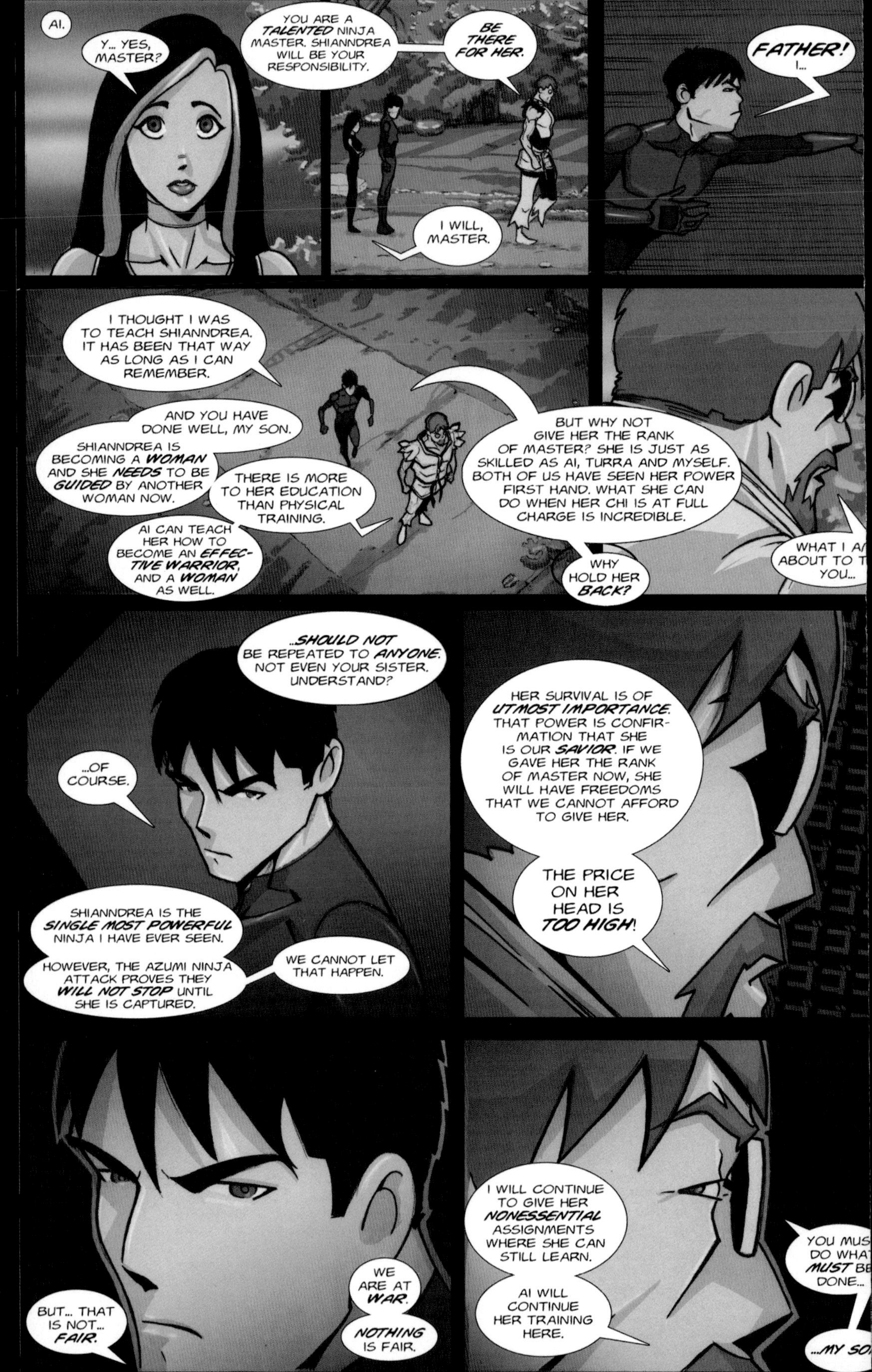
AI.
Y... YES, MASTER?
YOU ARE A TALENTED NINJA MASTER. SHIANNDREA WILL BE YOUR RESPONSIBILITY.
BE THERE FOR HER.
I WILL, MASTER.
FATHER! I...
I THOUGHT I WAS TO TEACH SHIANNDREA. IT HAS BEEN THAT WAY AS LONG AS I CAN REMEMBER.
AND YOU HAVE DONE WELL, MY SON.
SHIANNDREA IS BECOMING A WOMAN AND SHE NEEDS TO BE GUIDED BY ANOTHER WOMAN NOW.
THERE IS MORE TO HER EDUCATION THAN PHYSICAL TRAINING.
AI CAN TEACH HER HOW TO BECOME AN EFFECTIVE WARRIOR, AND A WOMAN AS WELL.
BUT WHY NOT GIVE HER THE RANK OF MASTER? SHE IS JUST AS SKILLED AS AI, TURRA AND MYSELF. BOTH OF US HAVE SEEN HER POWER FIRST HAND. WHAT SHE CAN DO WHEN HER CHI IS AT FULL CHARGE IS INCREDIBLE.
WHY HOLD HER BACK?
WHAT I A ABOUT TO T YOU...
...SHOULD NOT BE REPEATED TO ANYONE. NOT EVEN YOUR SISTER. UNDERSTAND?
...OF COURSE.
SHIANNDREA IS THE SINGLE MOST POWERFUL NINJA I HAVE EVER SEEN.
HOWEVER, THE AZUMI NINJA ATTACK PROVES THEY WILL NOT STOP UNTIL SHE IS CAPTURED.
WE CANNOT LET THAT HAPPEN.
HER SURVIVAL IS OF UTMOST IMPORTANCE. THAT POWER IS CONFIRMATION THAT SHE IS OUR SAVIOR. IF WE GAVE HER THE RANK OF MASTER NOW, SHE WILL HAVE FREEDOMS THAT WE CANNOT AFFORD TO GIVE HER.
THE PRICE ON HER HEAD IS TOO HIGH!
BUT... THAT IS NOT... FAIR.
WE ARE AT WAR.
NOTHING IS FAIR.
I WILL CONTINUE TO GIVE HER NONESSENTIAL ASSIGNMENTS WHERE SHE CAN STILL LEARN.
AI WILL CONTINUE HER TRAINING HERE.
YOU MUS DO WHA MUST BE DONE...
...MY SO

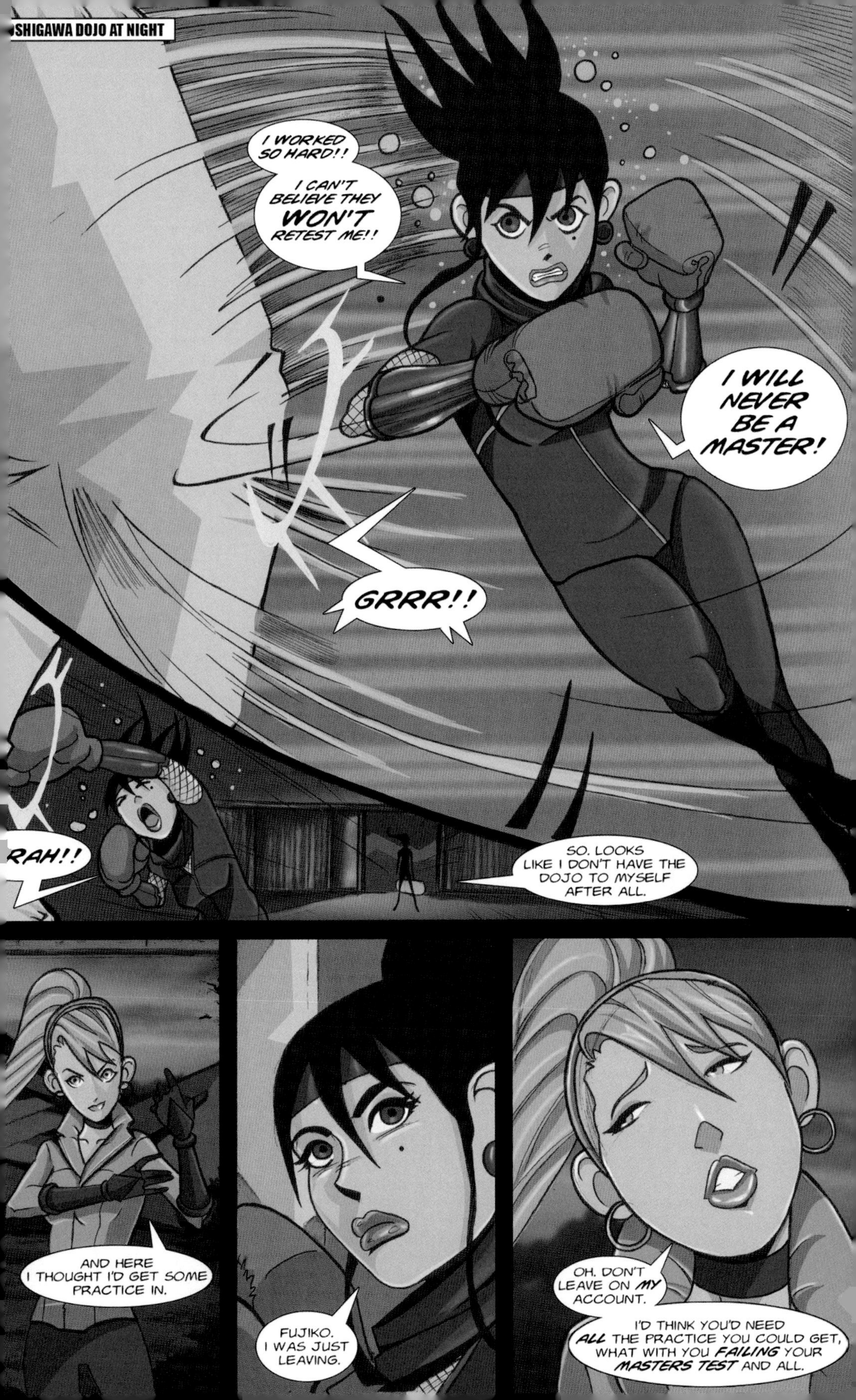

SHIGAWA DOJO AT NIGHT
I WORKED SO HARD!!
I CAN'T BELIEVE THEY WON'T RETEST ME!!
I WILL NEVER BE A MASTER!
GRRR!!
RAH!!
SO. LOOKS LIKE I DON'T HAVE THE DOJO TO MYSELF AFTER ALL.
AND HERE I THOUGHT I'D GET SOME PRACTICE IN.
FUJIKO. I WAS JUST LEAVING.
OH. DON'T LEAVE ON MY ACCOUNT.
I'D THINK YOU'D NEED ALL THE PRACTICE YOU COULD GET, WHAT WITH YOU FAILING YOUR MASTERS TEST AND ALL.

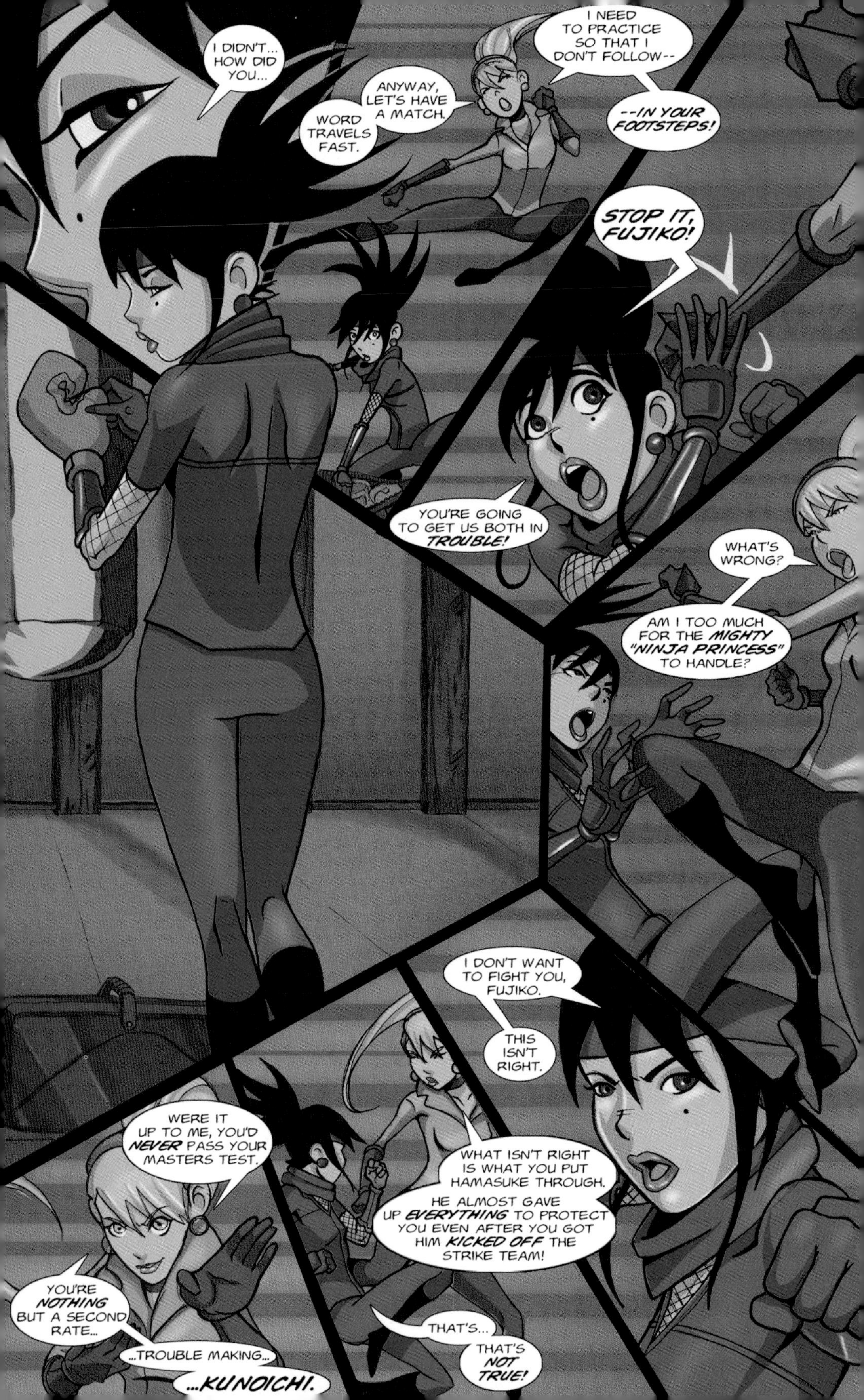
I DIDN'T... HOW DID YOU...
WORD TRAVELS FAST.
ANYWAY, LET'S HAVE A MATCH.
I NEED TO PRACTICE SO THAT I DON'T FOLLOW--
--IN YOUR FOOTSTEPS!
STOP IT, FUJIKO!
YOU'RE GOING TO GET US BOTH IN TROUBLE!
WHAT'S WRONG?
AM I TOO MUCH FOR THE MIGHTY "NINJA PRINCESS" TO HANDLE?
I DON'T WANT TO FIGHT YOU, FUJIKO.
THIS ISN'T RIGHT.
WHAT ISN'T RIGHT IS WHAT YOU PUT HAMASUKE THROUGH.
HE ALMOST GAVE UP EVERYTHING TO PROTECT YOU EVEN AFTER YOU GOT HIM KICKED OFF THE STRIKE TEAM!
THAT'S...
THAT'S NOT TRUE!
WERE IT UP TO ME, YOU'D NEVER PASS YOUR MASTERS TEST.
YOU'RE NOTHING BUT A SECOND RATE...
...TROUBLE MAKING...
...KUNOICHI.

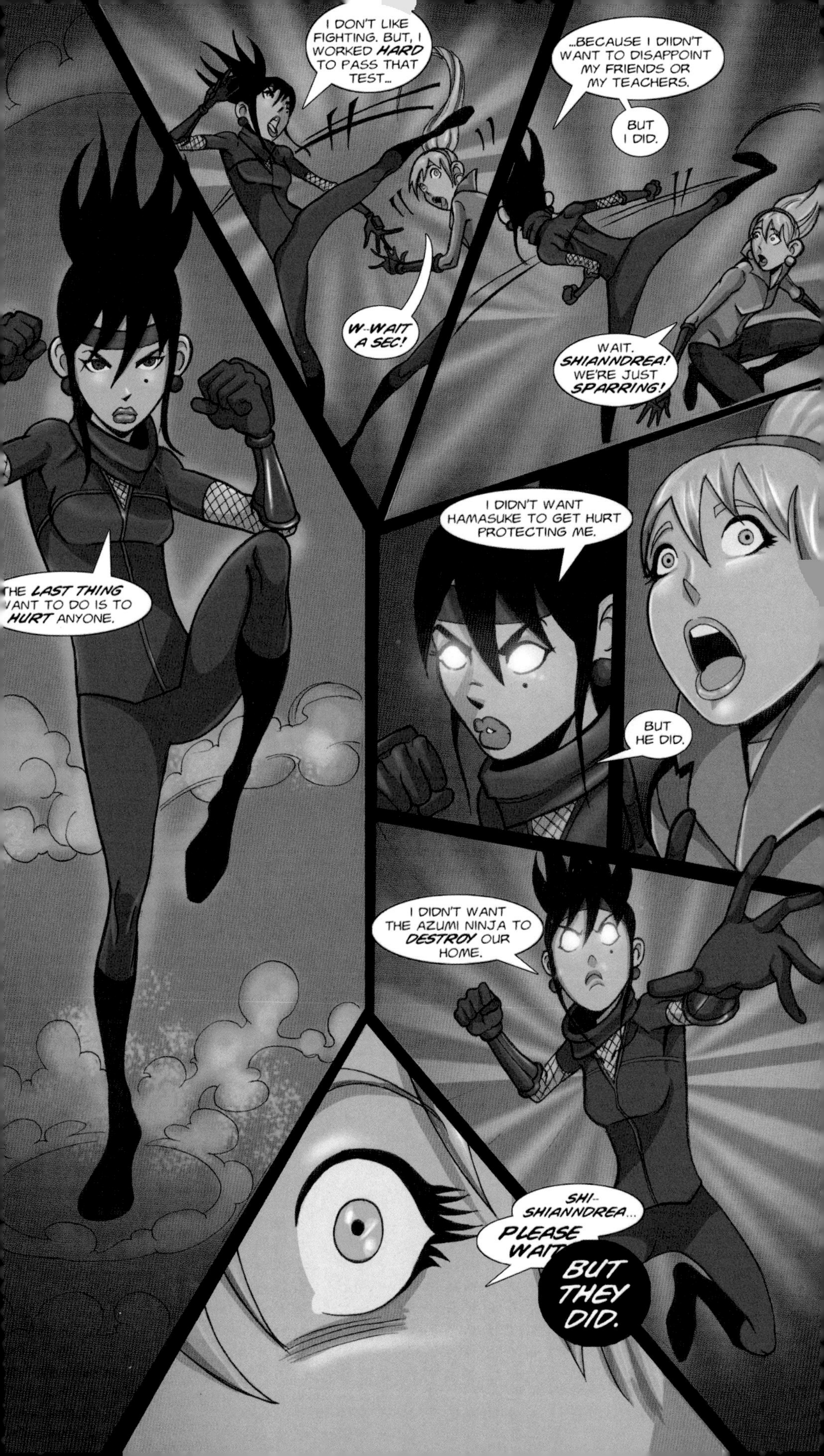

THE LAST THING VANT TO DO IS TO HURT ANYONE.
I DON'T LIKE FIGHTING. BUT, I WORKED HARD TO PASS THAT TEST...
W--WAIT A SEC!
...BECAUSE I DIIDN'T WANT TO DISAPPOINT MY FRIENDS OR MY TEACHERS.
BUT I DID.
WAIT. SHIANNDREA! WE'RE JUST SPARRING!
I DIDN'T WANT HAMASUKE TO GET HURT PROTECTING ME.
BUT HE DID.
I DIDN'T WANT THE AZUMI NINJA TO DESTROY OUR HOME.
SHI-- SHIANNDREA... PLEASE WAIT
BUT THEY DID.

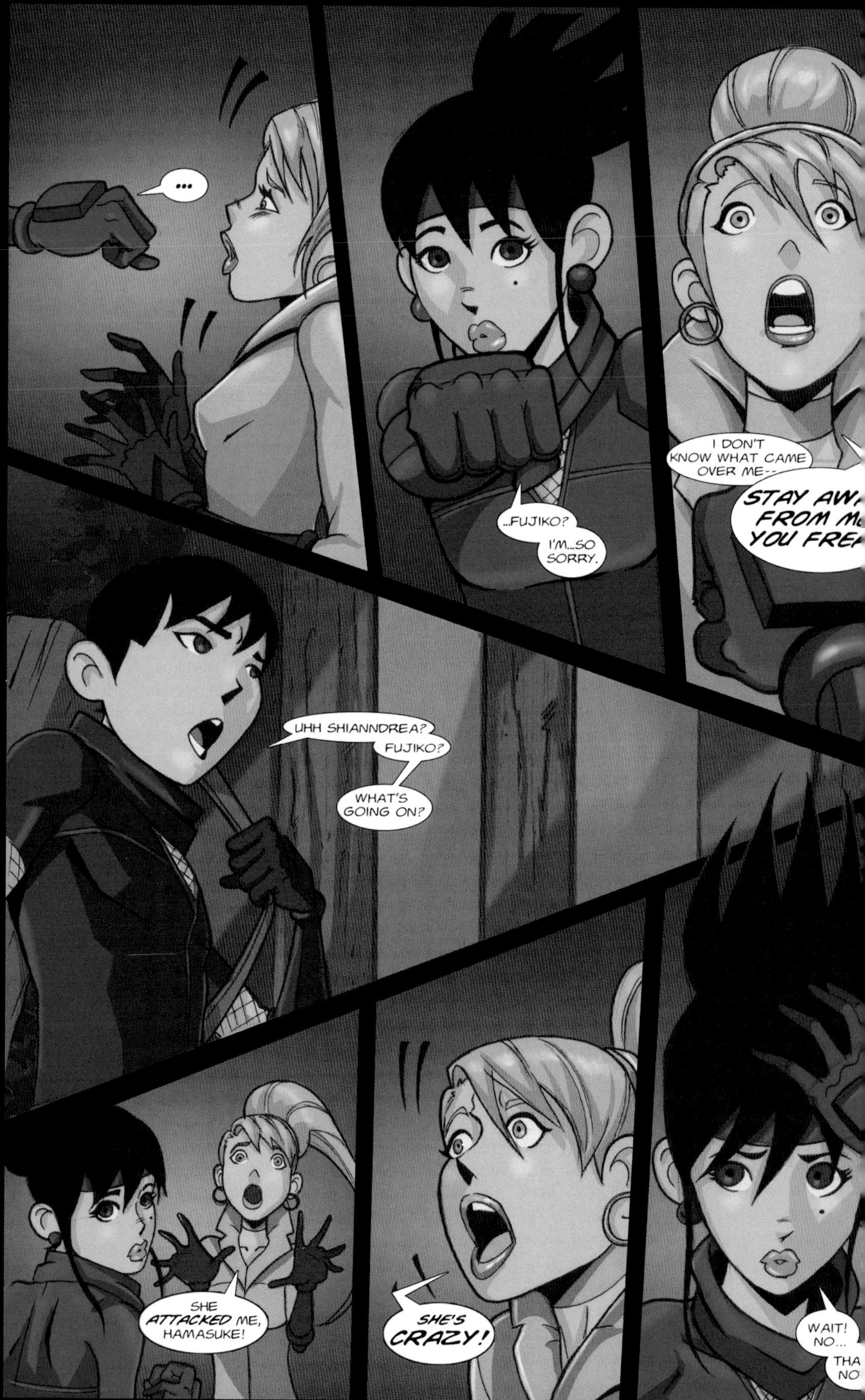

...
...FUJIKO?
I'M...SO SORRY.
I DON'T KNOW WHAT CAME OVER ME--
STAY AW FROM M YOU FRE
UHH SHIANNDREA?
FUJIKO?
WHAT'S GOING ON?
SHE *ATTACKED* ME, HAMASUKE!
SHE'S CRAZY!
WAIT! NO...
THA NO

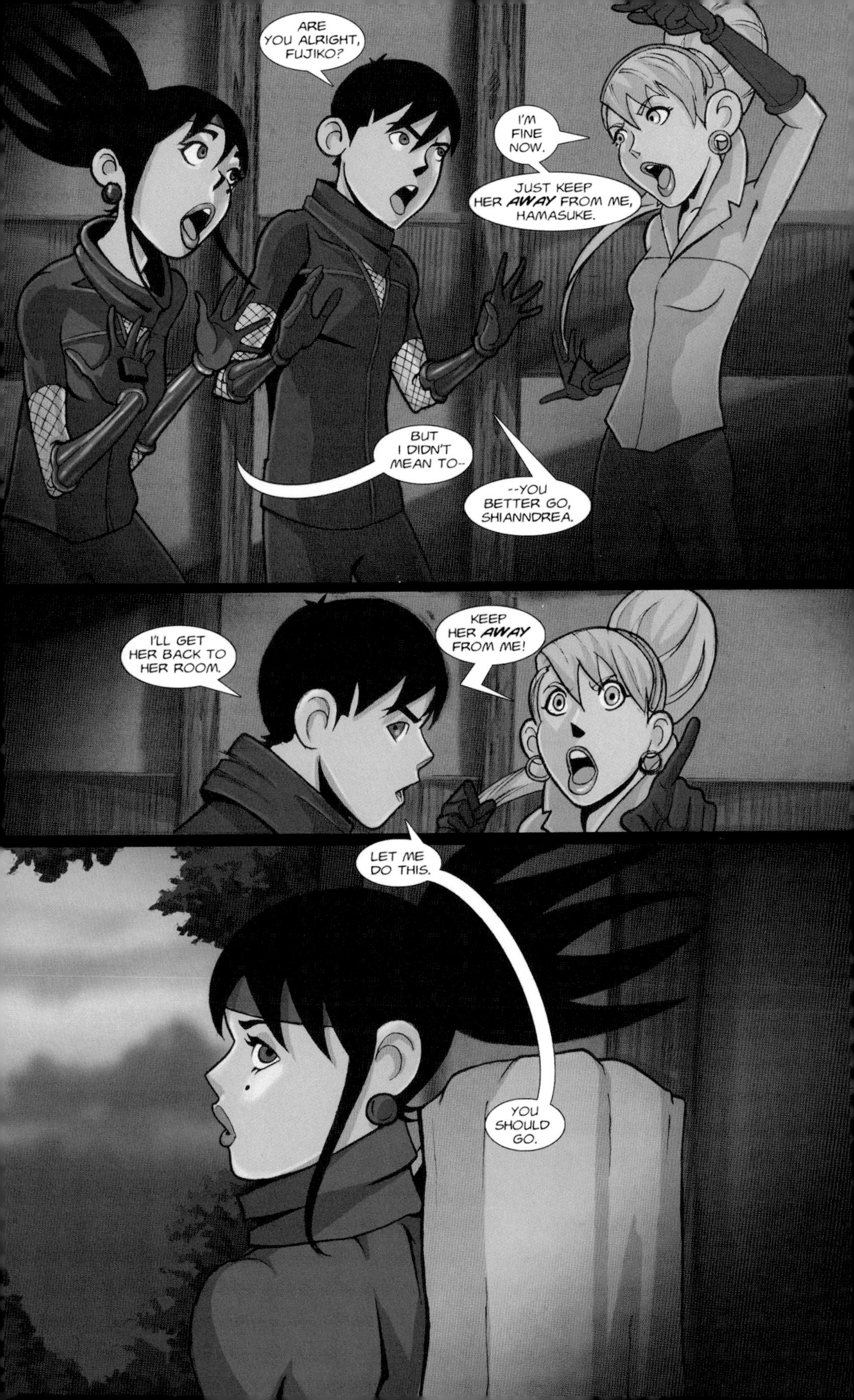
ARE YOU ALRIGHT, FUJIKO?
I'M FINE NOW.
JUST KEEP HER *AWAY* FROM ME, HAMASUKE.
BUT I DIDN'T MEAN TO--
--YOU BETTER GO, SHIANNDREA.
I'LL GET HER BACK TO HER ROOM.
KEEP HER *AWAY* FROM ME!
LET ME DO THIS.
YOU SHOULD GO.

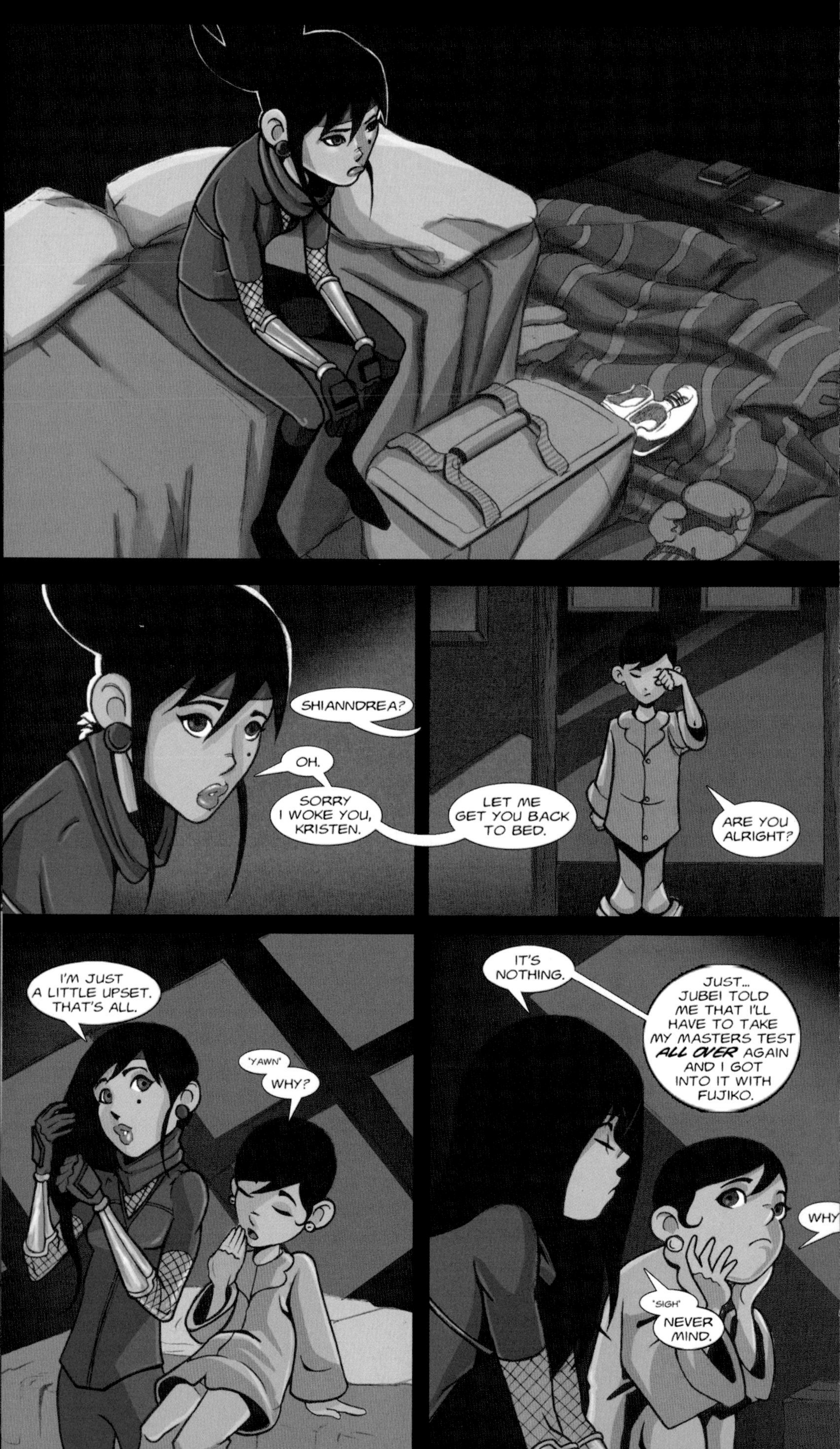
SHIANNDREA?
OH.
SORRY I WOKE YOU, KRISTEN.
LET ME GET YOU BACK TO BED.
ARE YOU ALRIGHT?
I'M JUST A LITTLE UPSET. THAT'S ALL.
YAWN
WHY?
IT'S NOTHING.
JUST... JUBEI TOLD ME THAT I'LL HAVE TO TAKE MY MASTERS TEST ALL OVER AGAIN AND I GOT INTO IT WITH FUJIKO.
SIGH
NEVER MIND.

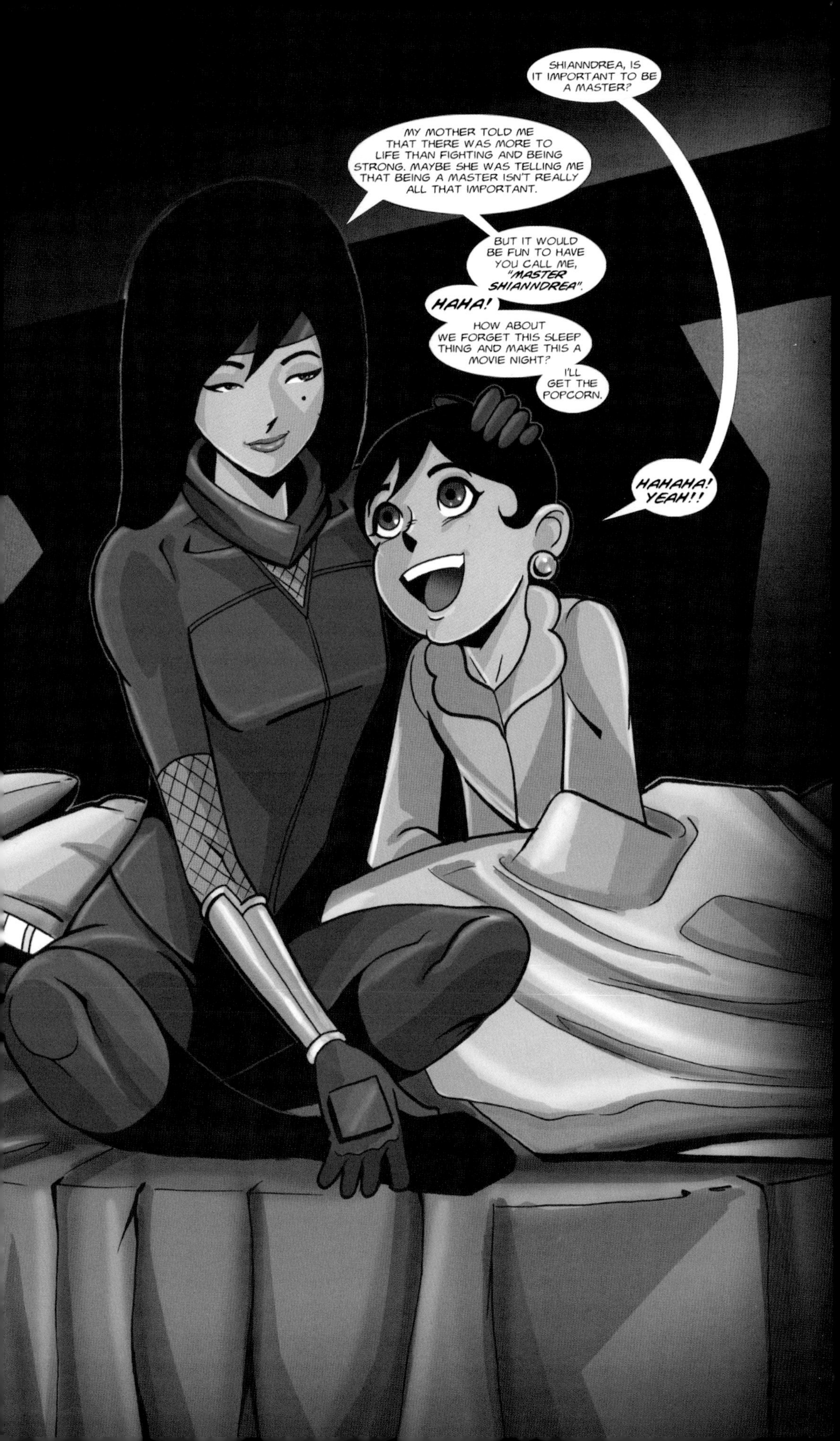
SHIANNDREA, IS IT IMPORTANT TO BE A MASTER?
MY MOTHER TOLD ME THAT THERE WAS MORE TO LIFE THAN FIGHTING AND BEING STRONG. MAYBE SHE WAS TELLING ME THAT BEING A MASTER ISN'T REALLY ALL THAT IMPORTANT.
BUT IT WOULD BE FUN TO HAVE YOU CALL ME, "MASTER SHIANNDREA".
HAHA!
HOW ABOUT WE FORGET THIS SLEEP THING AND MAKE THIS A MOVIE NIGHT?
I'LL GET THE POPCORN.
HAHAHA! YEAH!!

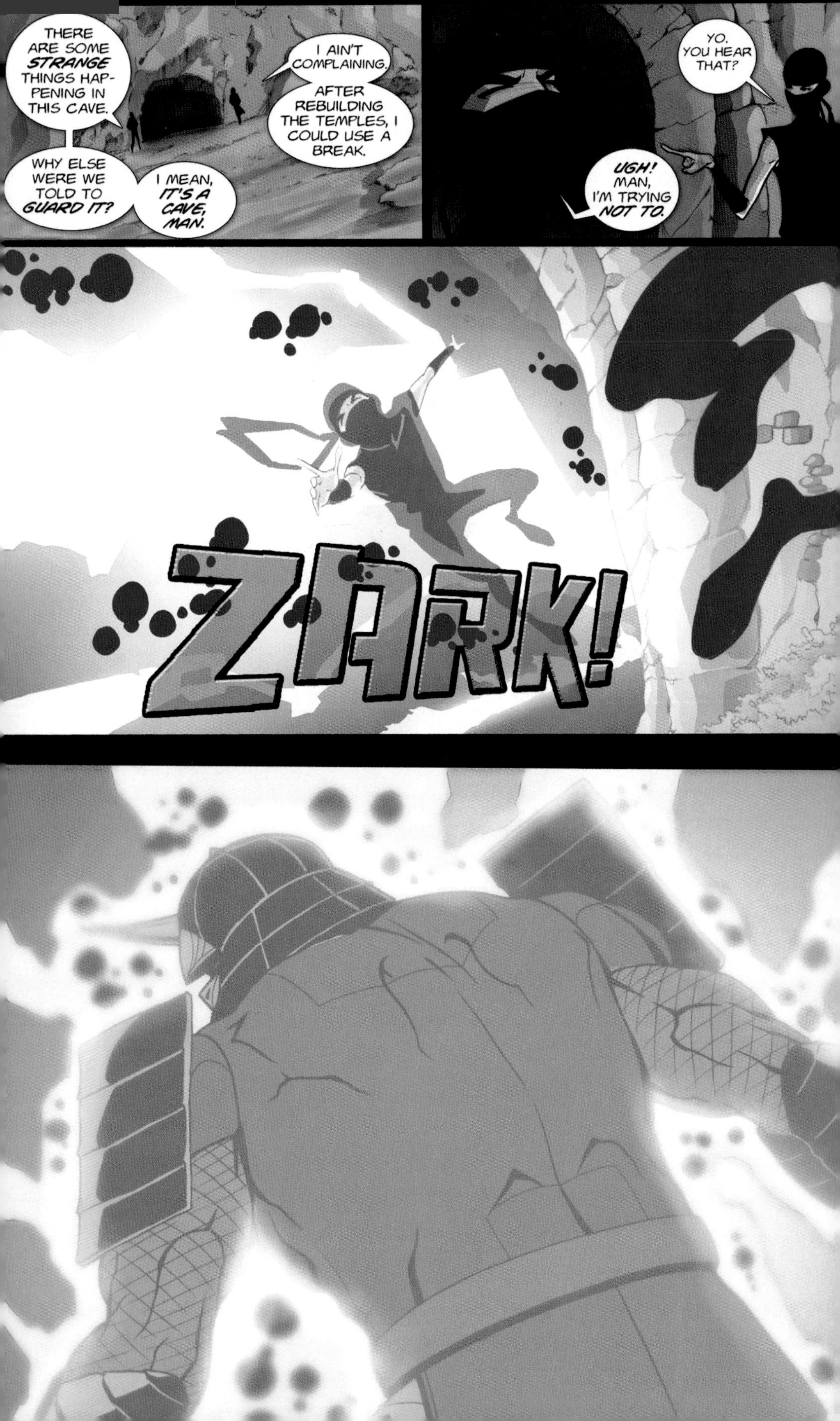
THERE ARE SOME STRANGE THINGS HAP-PENING IN THIS CAVE.
WHY ELSE WERE WE TOLD TO GUARD IT?
I MEAN, IT'S A CAVE, MAN.
I AIN'T COMPLAINING.
AFTER REBUILDING THE TEMPLES, I COULD USE A BREAK.
YO. YOU HEAR THAT?
UGH! MAN, I'M TRYING NOT TO.
ZARK!

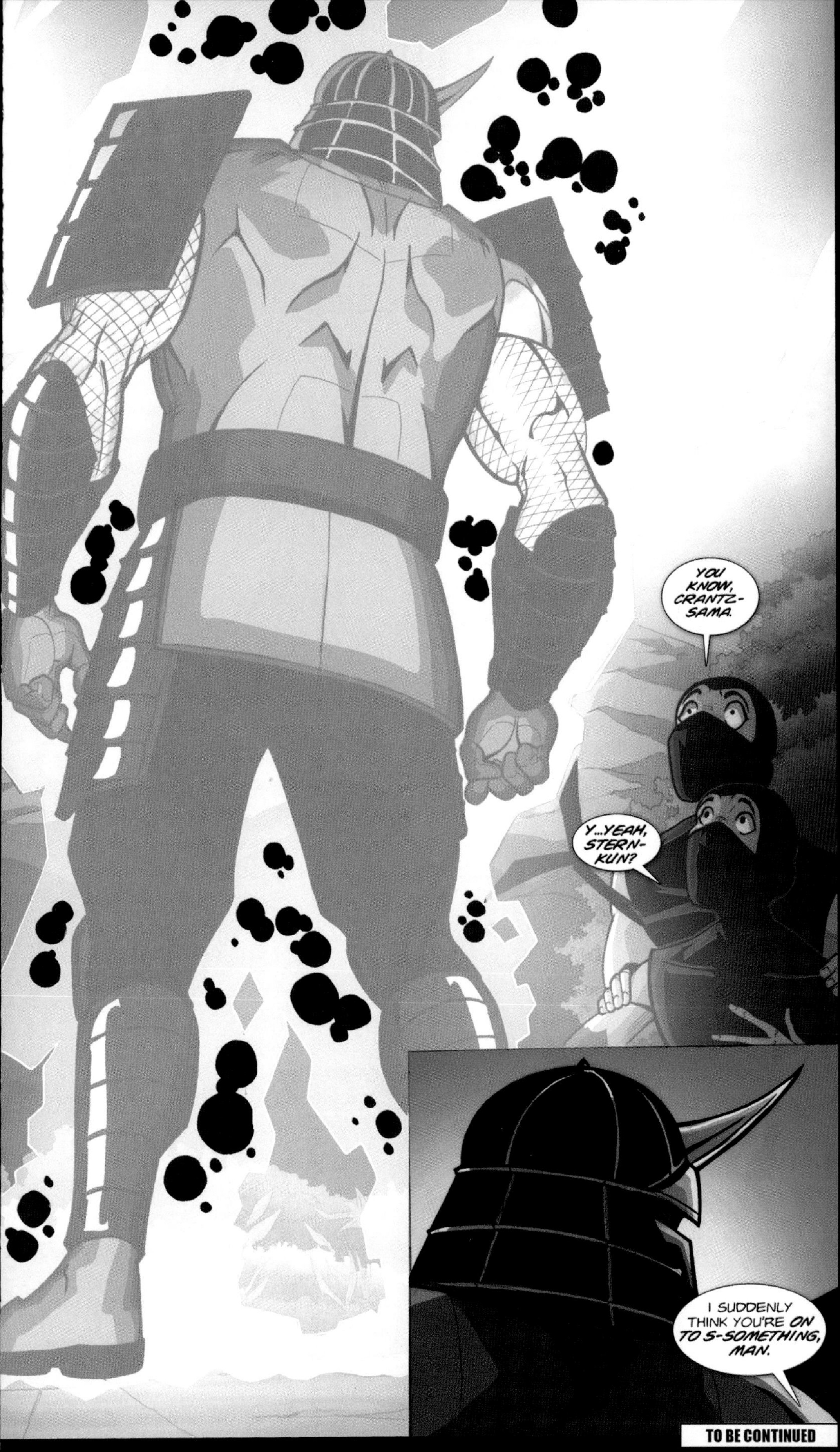

YOU KNOW, CRANTZ-SAMA.
Y...YEAH, STERN-KUN?
I SUDDENLY THINK YOU'RE *ON TO S-SOMETHING,* MAN.
TO BE CONTINUED

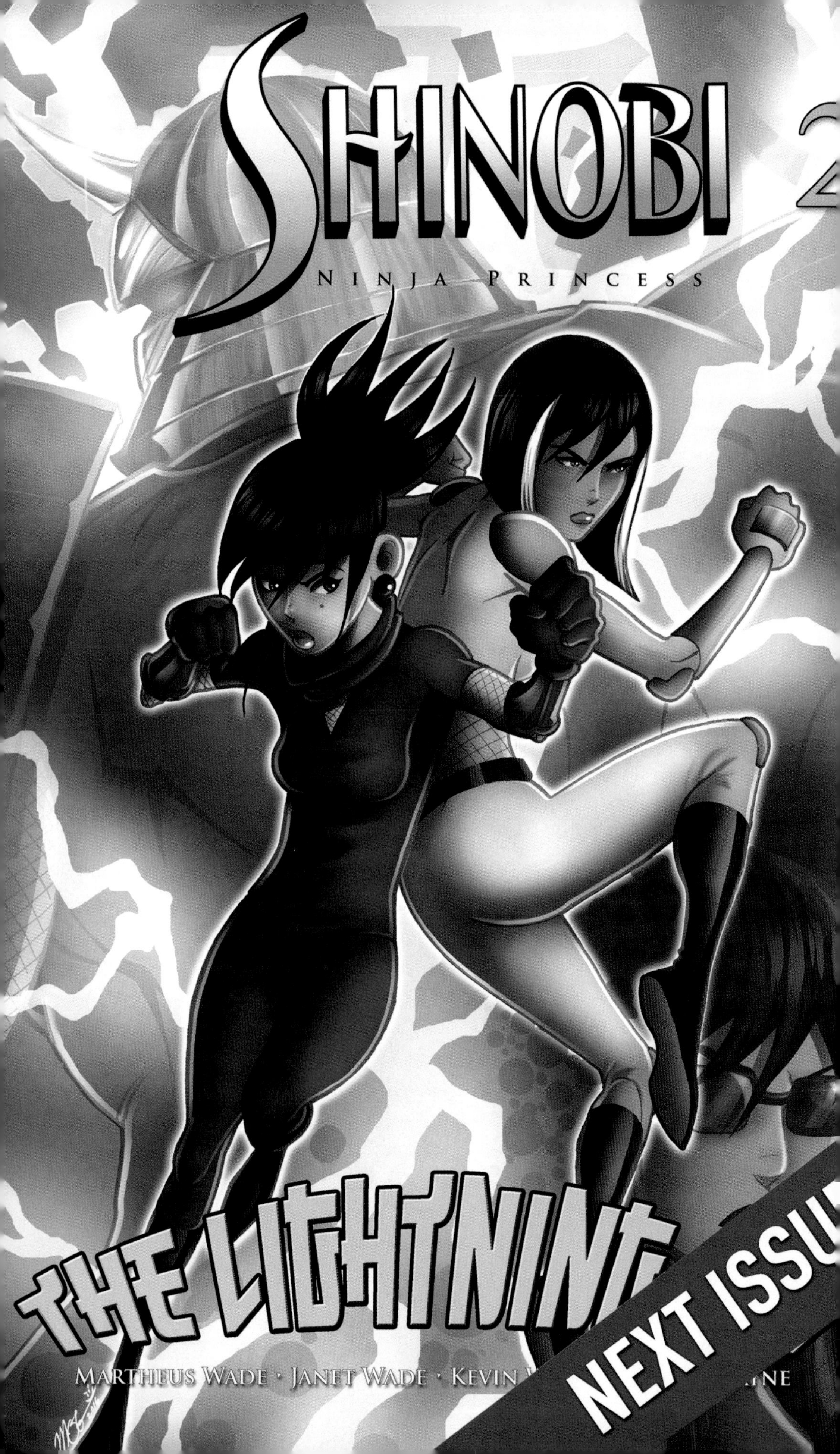
SHINOBI 2
NINJA PRINCESS
THE LIGHTNING
NEXT ISSUE
MARTHEUS WADE · JANET WADE · KEVIN

THE WORLD OF THE SHINOBI

This is the first time you have been to New Tokyo, isn't it?
-Kim

world is an untrusting place after Wolrd War III. ın suffered greatly and Tokyo was destroyed. The ntry was devastated. After the war, Terminus ‹ control of the country and made Japan a finan- power once again by creating Mecha that were l anywhere from domestic labor to military use. ›ugh his new found popularity as a proficient ler, and his unworldly god-like power, Emperor ninus closed off all borders into Japan. He then ›nstructed Japan and rebuilt Tokyo. Under his , Japan is divided into many different provinces wing him to micro-manage the country and ch for his daughter, Shianndrea Toshigawa, the to Japan and the only other person with super- ıral power that can stop him.

ause of this, there are only two ninja clans left: Azumi Ninja Clan and the Toshigawa Ninja ı. Though hunted by the new government and thriving in secret, the Toshigawa are the richer of the two clans due to the cultivation of various ancient financial contracts.

The Azumi, being the younger and poorer of the two clans, have had to scrape for contracts to get by. Their major contractor has been the Yakuza. It has been the dream of Kokoro, head of the Azumi Ninja, to be free of the Yakuza's hold. Out of the blue, the mysterious ninja calling herself The Red Dragon brought Kokoro word of a contract with the Emperor himself. The assignment: Capture Shianndrea Toshigawa and return her to the Emperor at all costs.

Kokoro and his Azumi Ninja will do anything, even tamper with dark magic, to see this end a reality.

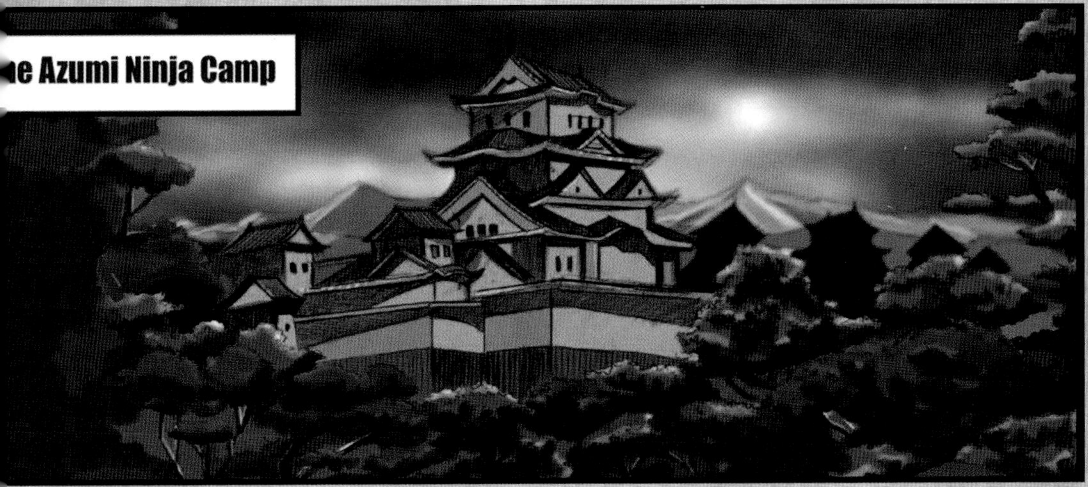
ıe Azumi Ninja Camp

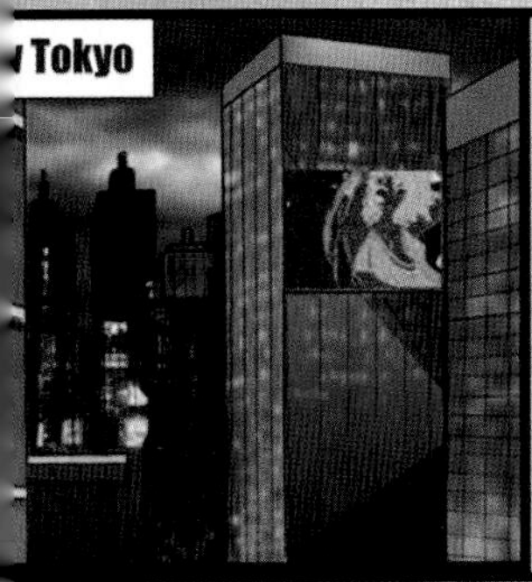
ı Tokyo

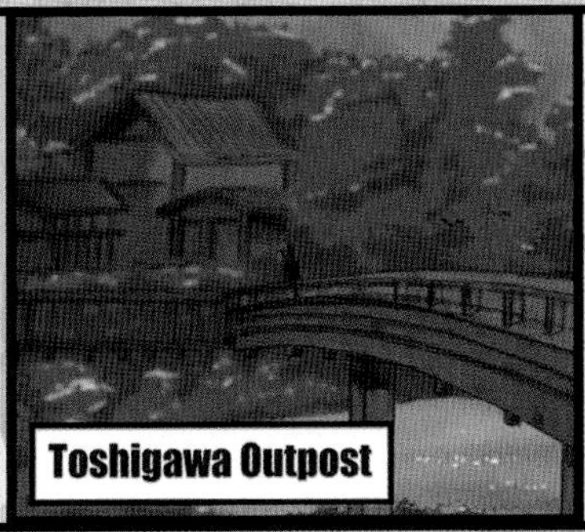
Toshigawa Outpost

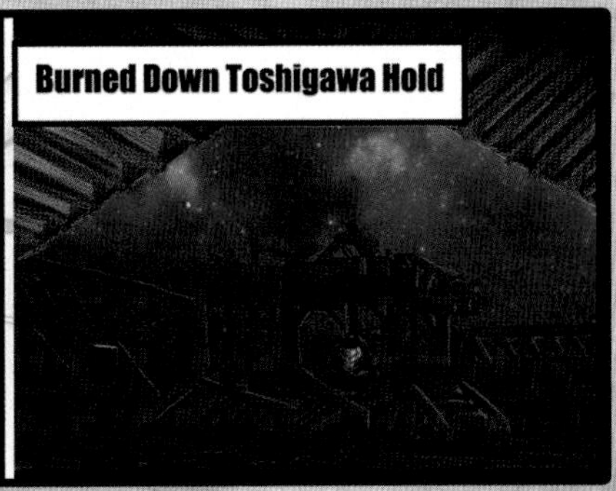
Burned Down Toshigawa Hold

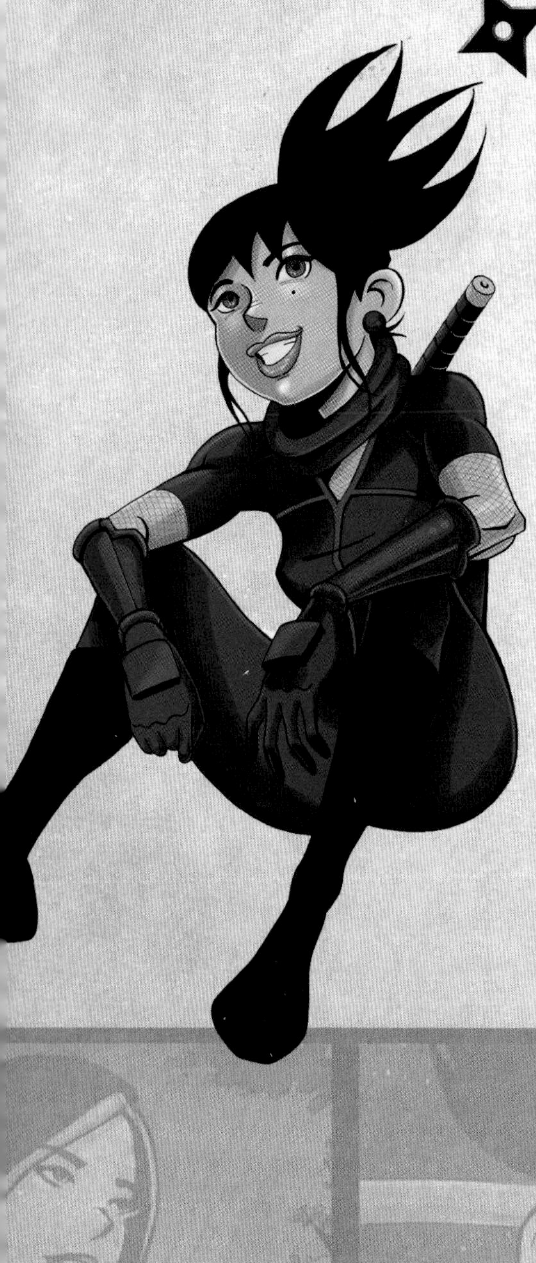

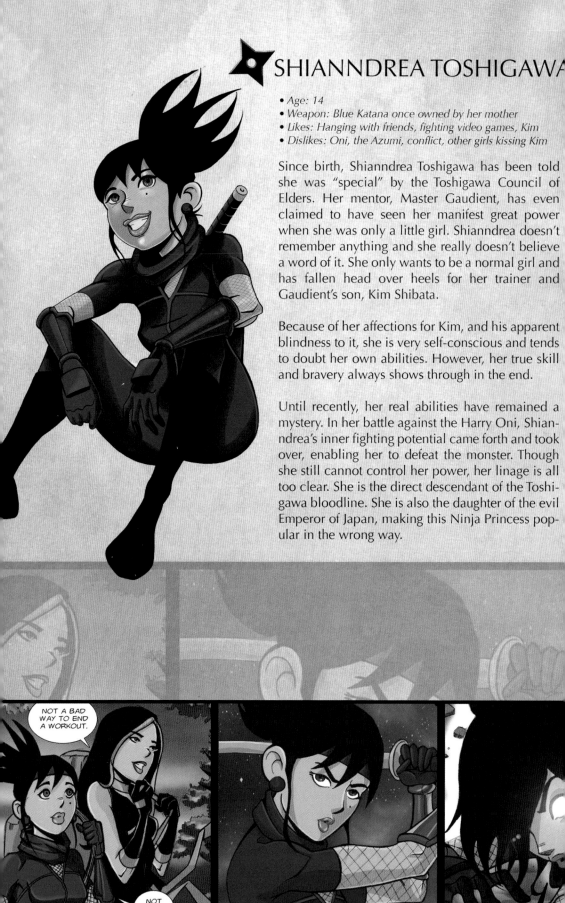

SHIANNDREA TOSHIGAWA

- *Age: 14*
- *Weapon: Blue Katana once owned by her mother*
- *Likes: Hanging with friends, fighting video games, Kim*
- *Dislikes: Oni, the Azumi, conflict, other girls kissing Kim*

Since birth, Shianndrea Toshigawa has been told she was "special" by the Toshigawa Council of Elders. Her mentor, Master Gaudient, has even claimed to have seen her manifest great power when she was only a little girl. Shianndrea doesn't remember anything and she really doesn't believe a word of it. She only wants to be a normal girl and has fallen head over heels for her trainer and Gaudient's son, Kim Shibata.

Because of her affections for Kim, and his apparent blindness to it, she is very self-conscious and tends to doubt her own abilities. However, her true skill and bravery always shows through in the end.

Until recently, her real abilities have remained a mystery. In her battle against the Harry Oni, Shiandrea's inner fighting potential came forth and took over, enabling her to defeat the monster. Though she still cannot control her power, her linage is all too clear. She is the direct descendant of the Toshigawa bloodline. She is also the daughter of the evil Emperor of Japan, making this Ninja Princess popular in the wrong way.

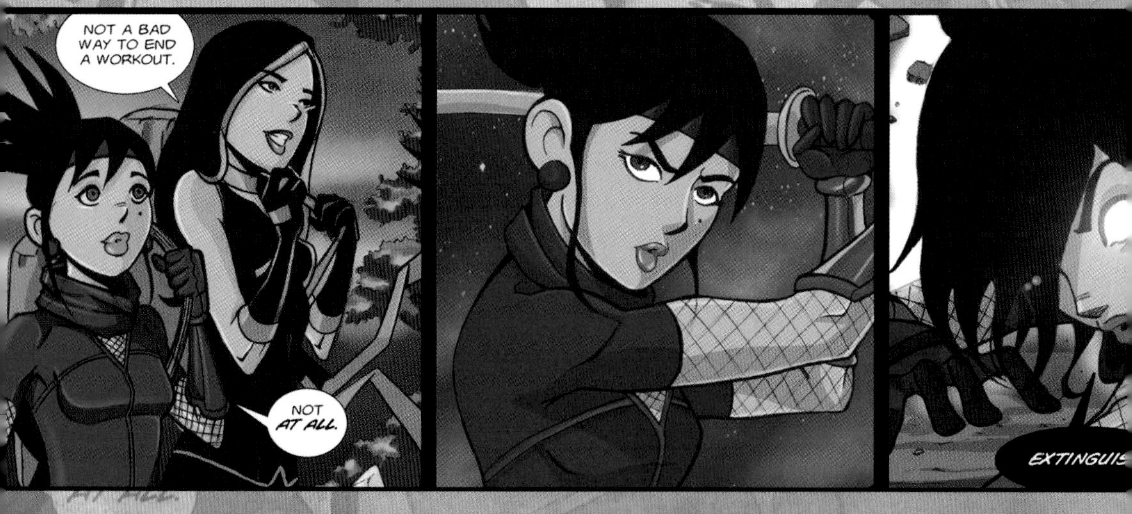
NOT A BAD WAY TO END A WORKOUT.
NOT AT ALL.
EXTINGUIS

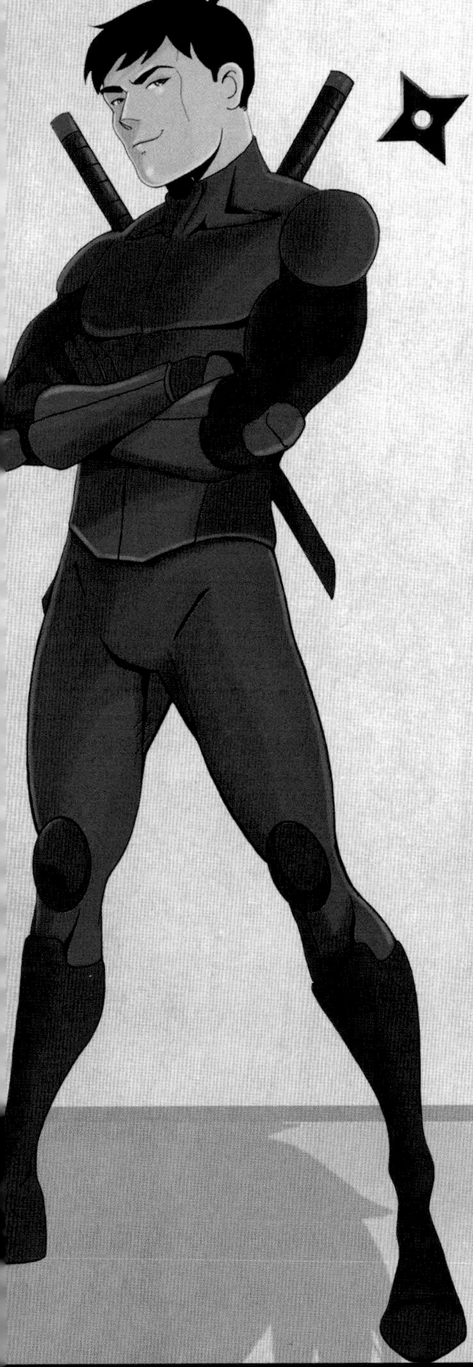

KIM SHIBATA

- *Age: 16*
- *Weapon: Twin Red Katana*
- *Likes: Training, teaching, family, Ai, Shianndrea, loyalty*
- *Dislikes: The Azumi, Oni, betrayal, laziness*

Kim Shibata is the definition of the handsome, duty-bound warrior. He is the trainer of the younger Toshigawa ninja, those who are on the verge of attaining the rank of Master.

His father, Gaudient, trusts his abilities beyond any other. He is the first one The Council of Elders call upon to lead important missions.

A master ninja himself, he takes his responsibilities as a leader very seriously. Training is his life. Every girl in the clan wants to call him their boyfriend. Even though he is the most sought after ninja in the clan, Kim is awkward around girls. But his awkwardness only adds to his appeal, and he has caught the eye of one of the most popular girls in the clan: Ai Ishikawa. Being in a relationship with Ai is a big change for Kim, and he is working hard to "come out of his shell."

This will be no easy task. I have fought this Oni before and he is nearly indestructible. Our only hope is to contain him in some way. When I call your name, please step forward.
-Kim

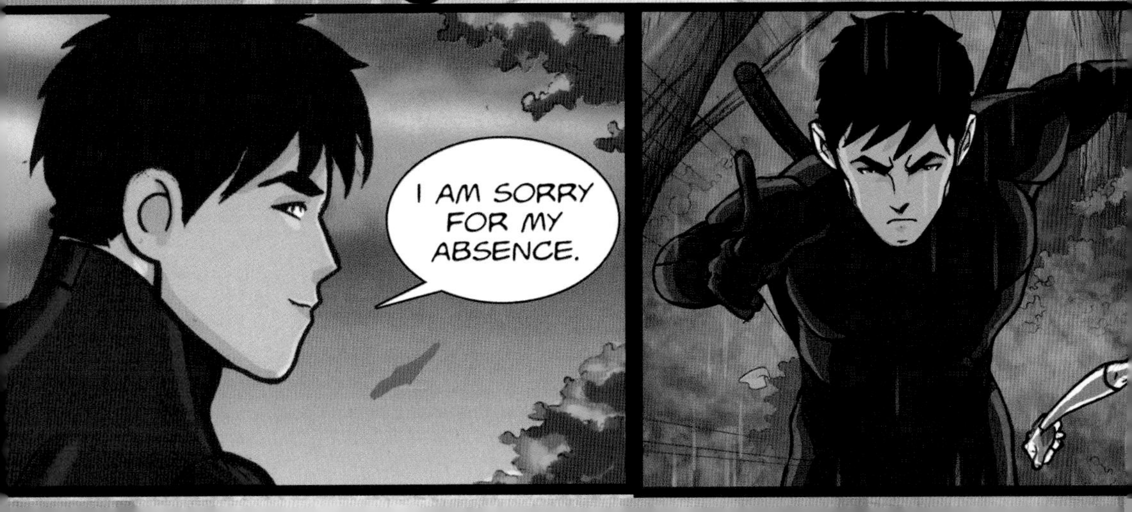
I AM SORRY FOR MY ABSENCE.

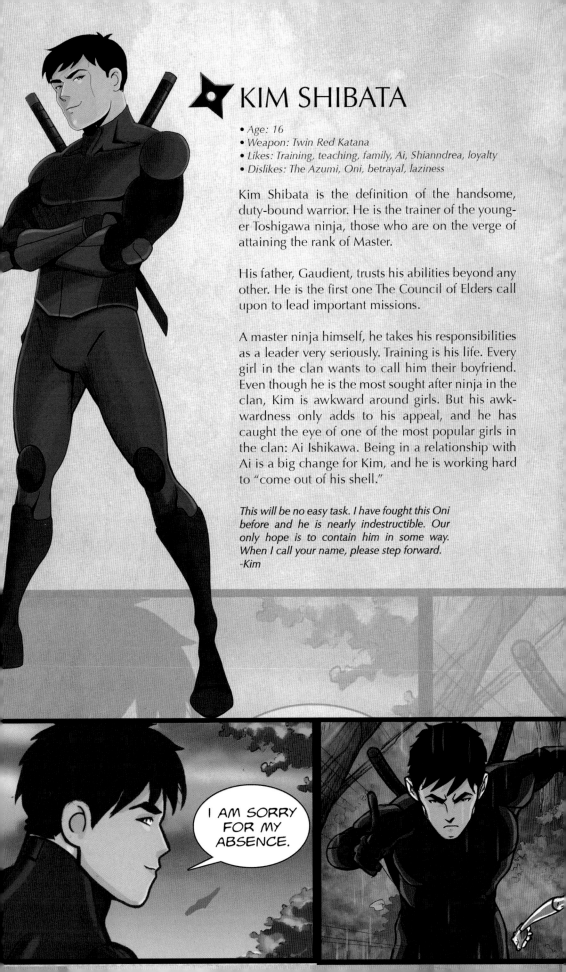

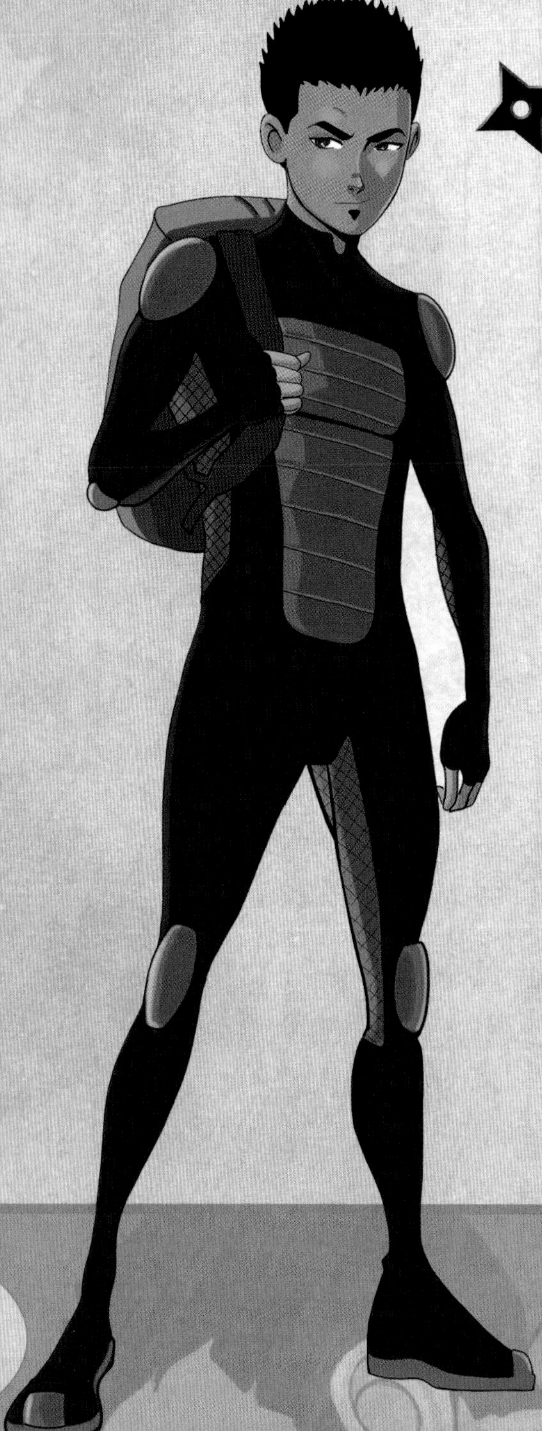

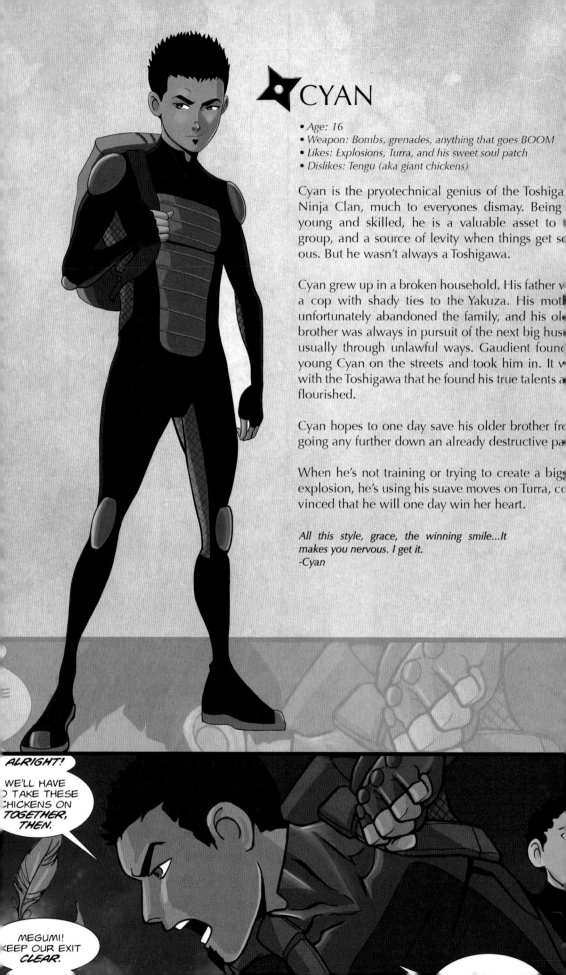

CYAN

- *Age: 16*
- *Weapon: Bombs, grenades, anything that goes BOOM*
- *Likes: Explosions, Turra, and his sweet soul patch*
- *Dislikes: Tengu (aka giant chickens)*

Cyan is the pryotechnical genius of the Toshiga Ninja Clan, much to everyones dismay. Being young and skilled, he is a valuable asset to group, and a source of levity when things get s ous. But he wasn't always a Toshigawa.

Cyan grew up in a broken household. His father a cop with shady ties to the Yakuza. His mot unfortunately abandoned the family, and his ol brother was always in pursuit of the next big hus usually through unlawful ways. Gaudient foun young Cyan on the streets and took him in. It with the Toshigawa that he found his true talents flourished.

Cyan hopes to one day save his older brother fr going any further down an already destructive pa

When he's not training or trying to create a big explosion, he's using his suave moves on Turra, c vinced that he will one day win her heart.

All this style, grace, the winning smile...It makes you nervous. I get it.
-Cyan

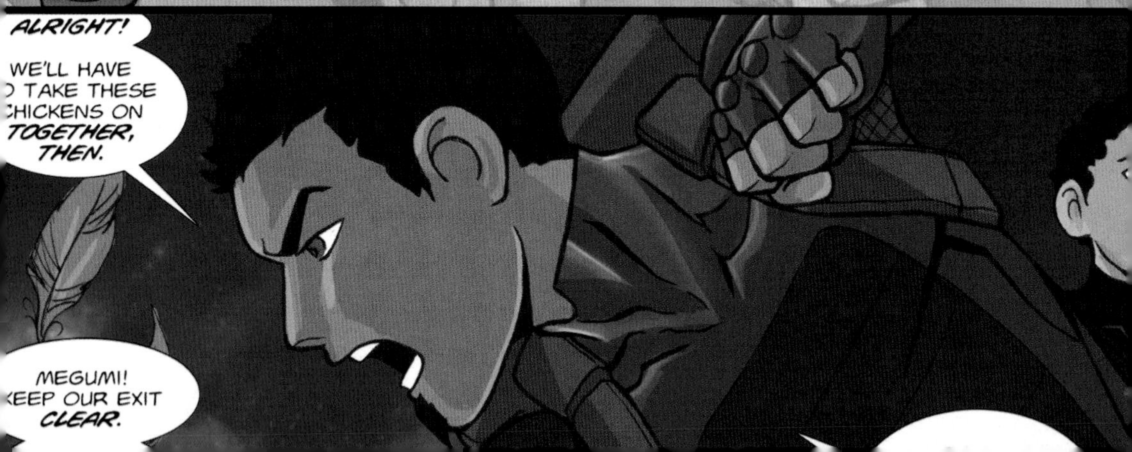
ALRIGHT!
WE'LL HAVE TAKE THESE HICKENS ON TOGETHER, THEN.
MEGUMI! EEP OUR EXIT CLEAR.

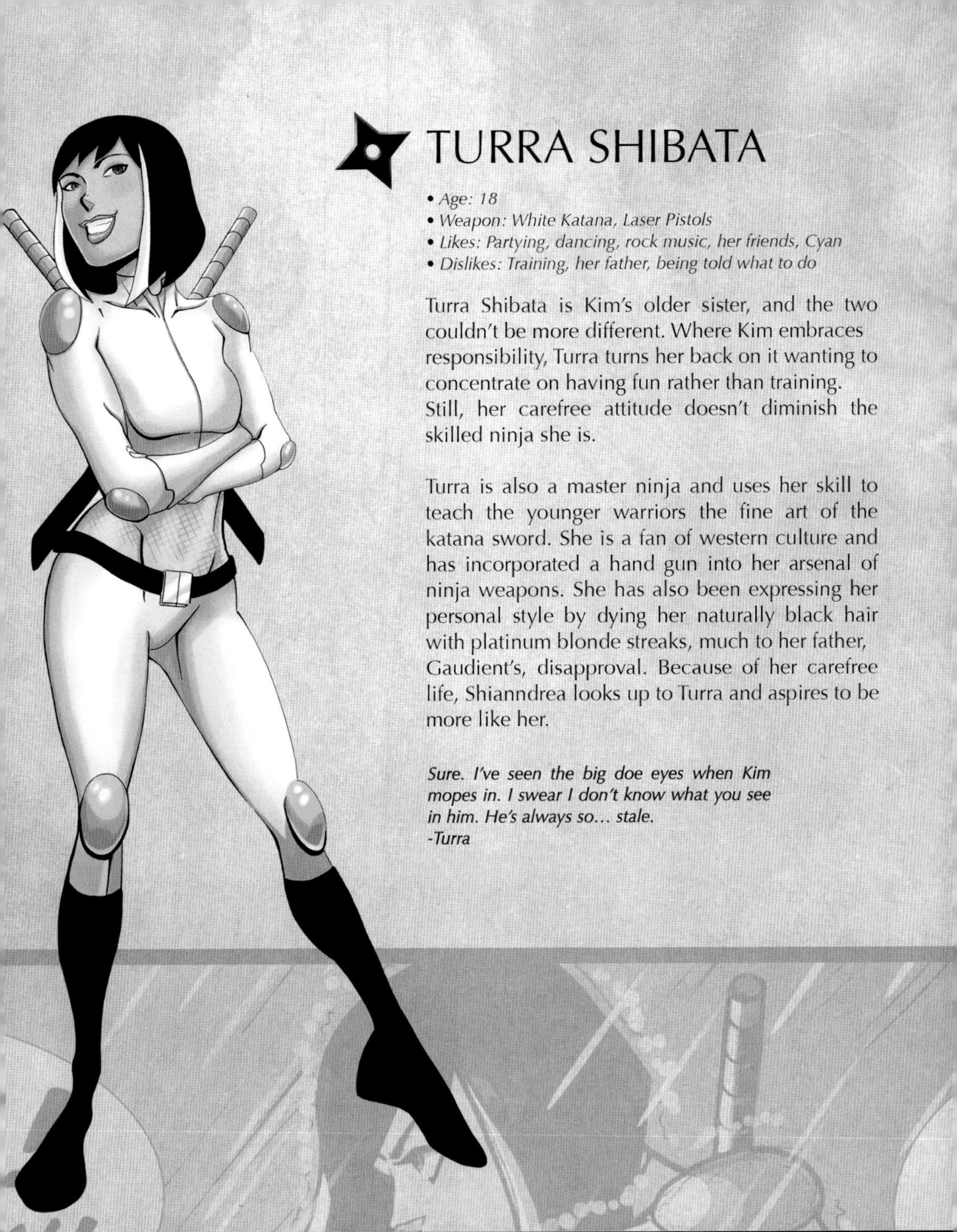

TURRA SHIBATA

- *Age: 18*
- *Weapon: White Katana, Laser Pistols*
- *Likes: Partying, dancing, rock music, her friends, Cyan*
- *Dislikes: Training, her father, being told what to do*

Turra Shibata is Kim's older sister, and the two couldn't be more different. Where Kim embraces responsibility, Turra turns her back on it wanting to concentrate on having fun rather than training. Still, her carefree attitude doesn't diminish the skilled ninja she is.

Turra is also a master ninja and uses her skill to teach the younger warriors the fine art of the katana sword. She is a fan of western culture and has incorporated a hand gun into her arsenal of ninja weapons. She has also been expressing her personal style by dying her naturally black hair with platinum blonde streaks, much to her father, Gaudient's, disapproval. Because of her carefree life, Shianndrea looks up to Turra and aspires to be more like her.

Sure. I've seen the big doe eyes when Kim mopes in. I swear I don't know what you see in him. He's always so… stale.
-Turra

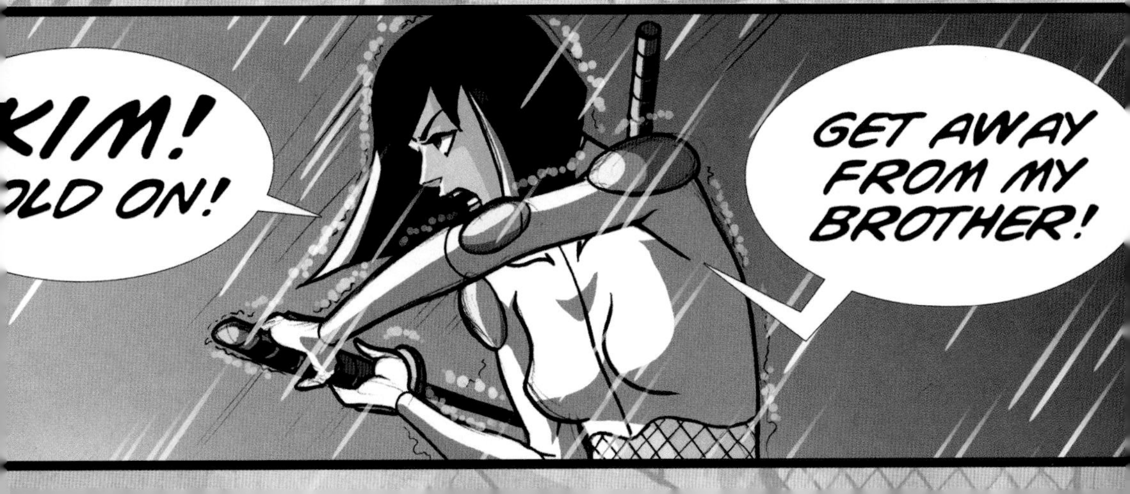
KIM!
OLD ON!
GET AWAY FROM MY BROTHER!

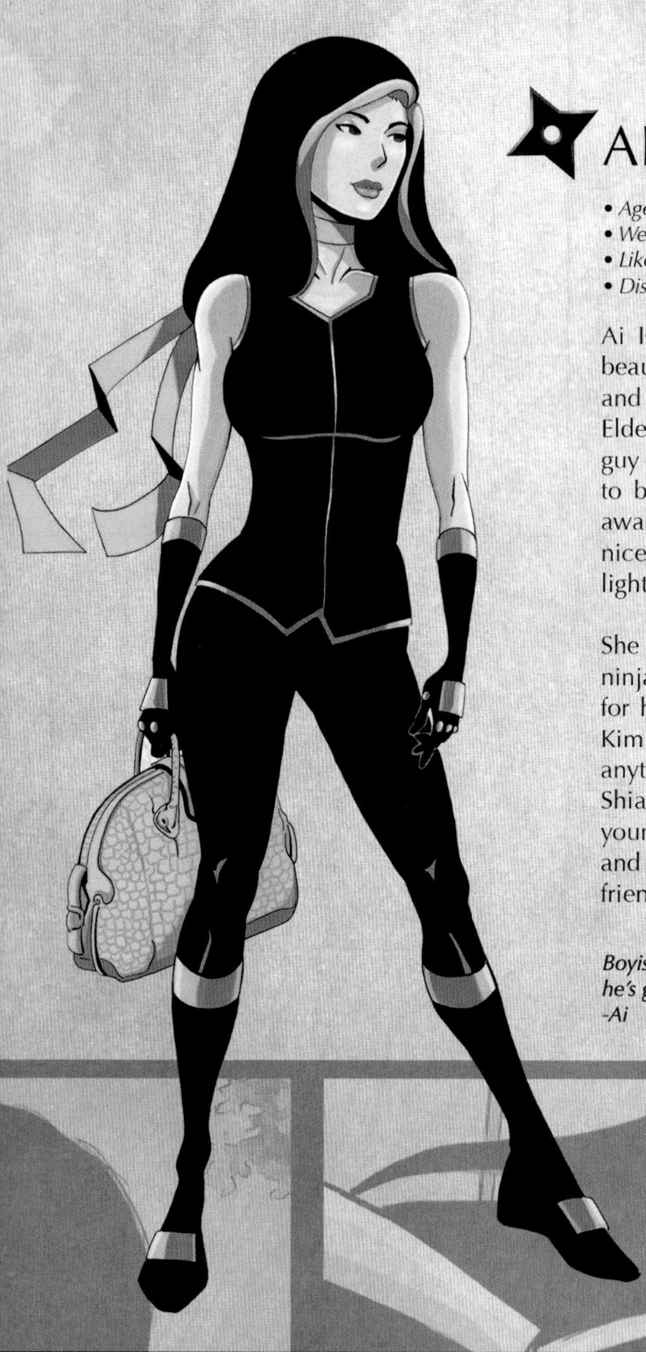

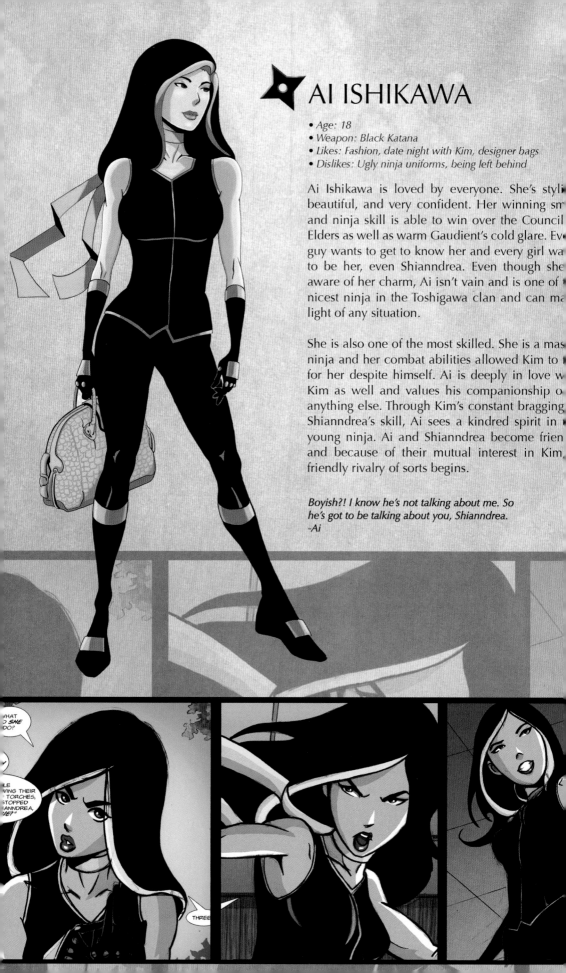

AI ISHIKAWA

- *Age: 18*
- *Weapon: Black Katana*
- *Likes: Fashion, date night with Kim, designer bags*
- *Dislikes: Ugly ninja uniforms, being left behind*

Ai Ishikawa is loved by everyone. She's styli beautiful, and very confident. Her winning sm and ninja skill is able to win over the Council Elders as well as warm Gaudient's cold glare. Ev guy wants to get to know her and every girl wa to be her, even Shianndrea. Even though she aware of her charm, Ai isn't vain and is one of nicest ninja in the Toshigawa clan and can ma light of any situation.

She is also one of the most skilled. She is a mas ninja and her combat abilities allowed Kim to for her despite himself. Ai is deeply in love w Kim as well and values his companionship o anything else. Through Kim's constant bragging Shianndrea's skill, Ai sees a kindred spirit in young ninja. Ai and Shianndrea become frien and because of their mutual interest in Kim, friendly rivalry of sorts begins.

Boyish?! I know he's not talking about me. So he's got to be talking about you, Shianndrea.
-Ai

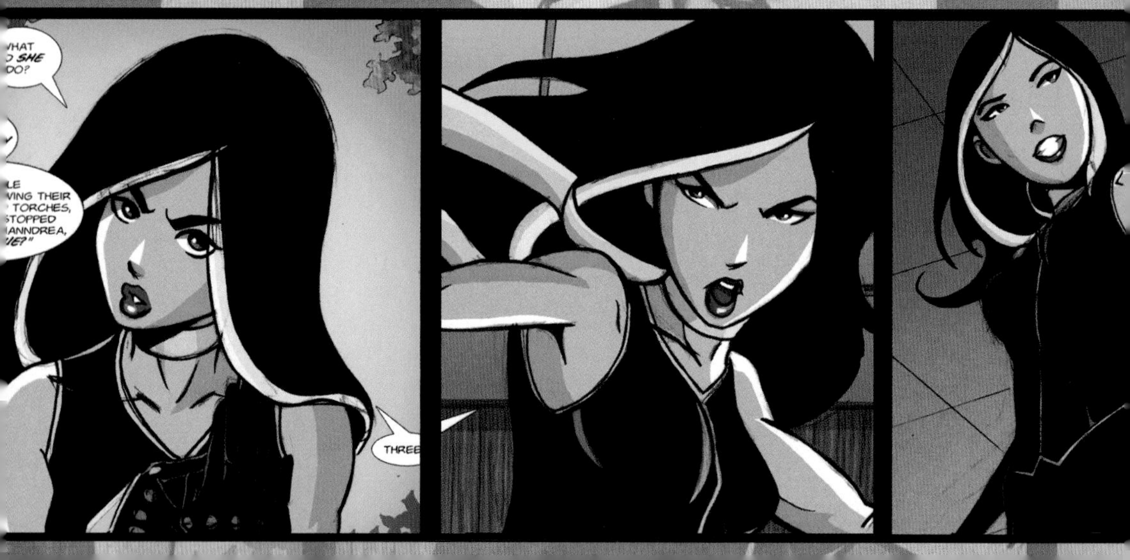
THREE

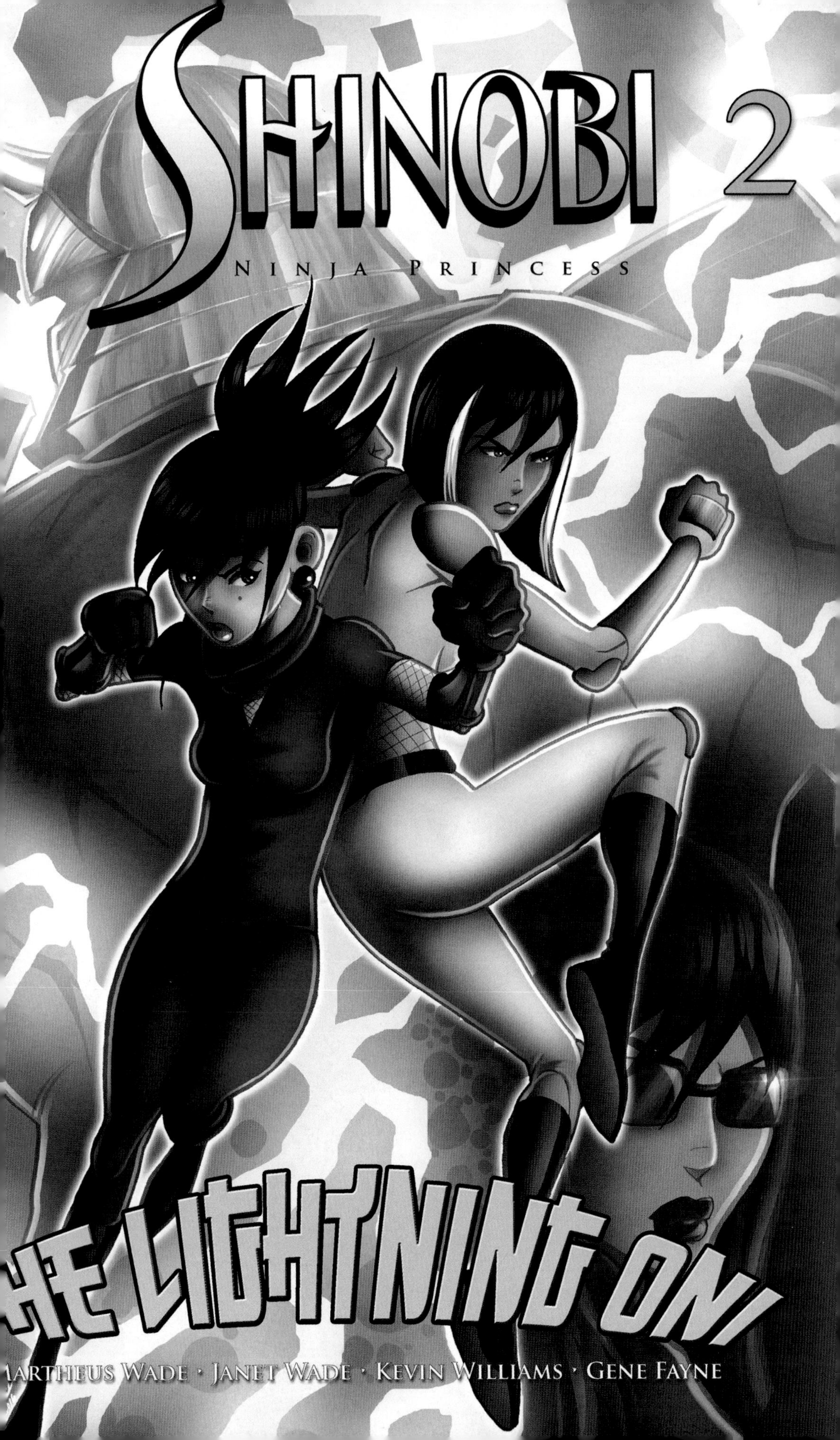
SHINOBI 2
NINJA PRINCESS
HE LIGHTNING ONI
ARTHEUS WADE · JANET WADE · KEVIN WILLIAMS · GENE FAYNE

ILLUSTRATIONS BY: MARTHEUS WADE
WRITTEN BY: MARTHEUS AND JANET WADE
INTERIOR COLORS BY: GENE FAYNE
COVER BY: MARTHEUS WADE & GENE FAYNE
©2017 MAW PRODUCTIONS

Bryan Seaton: Publisher/ CEO • Shawn Gabborin: Edito
Jason Martin: Publisher-Danger Zone • Nicole D'Andria: Marketing Dir
Jim Dietz: Social Media Manager • Danielle Davison: Executive Ad
Chad Cicconi: Noodle Oni • Shawn Pryor: President of Creato

SHINOBI: NINJA PRINCESS: THE LIGHTNING ONI #2,
2017. Copyright Martheus Antone Wade, 2017. Pub
Action Lab Entertainment. All rights reserved. All c
are fictional. Any likeness to anyone living or dead
coincidental. No part of this publication may be repro
transmitted without permission, except for review
Printed in Canada. Fir

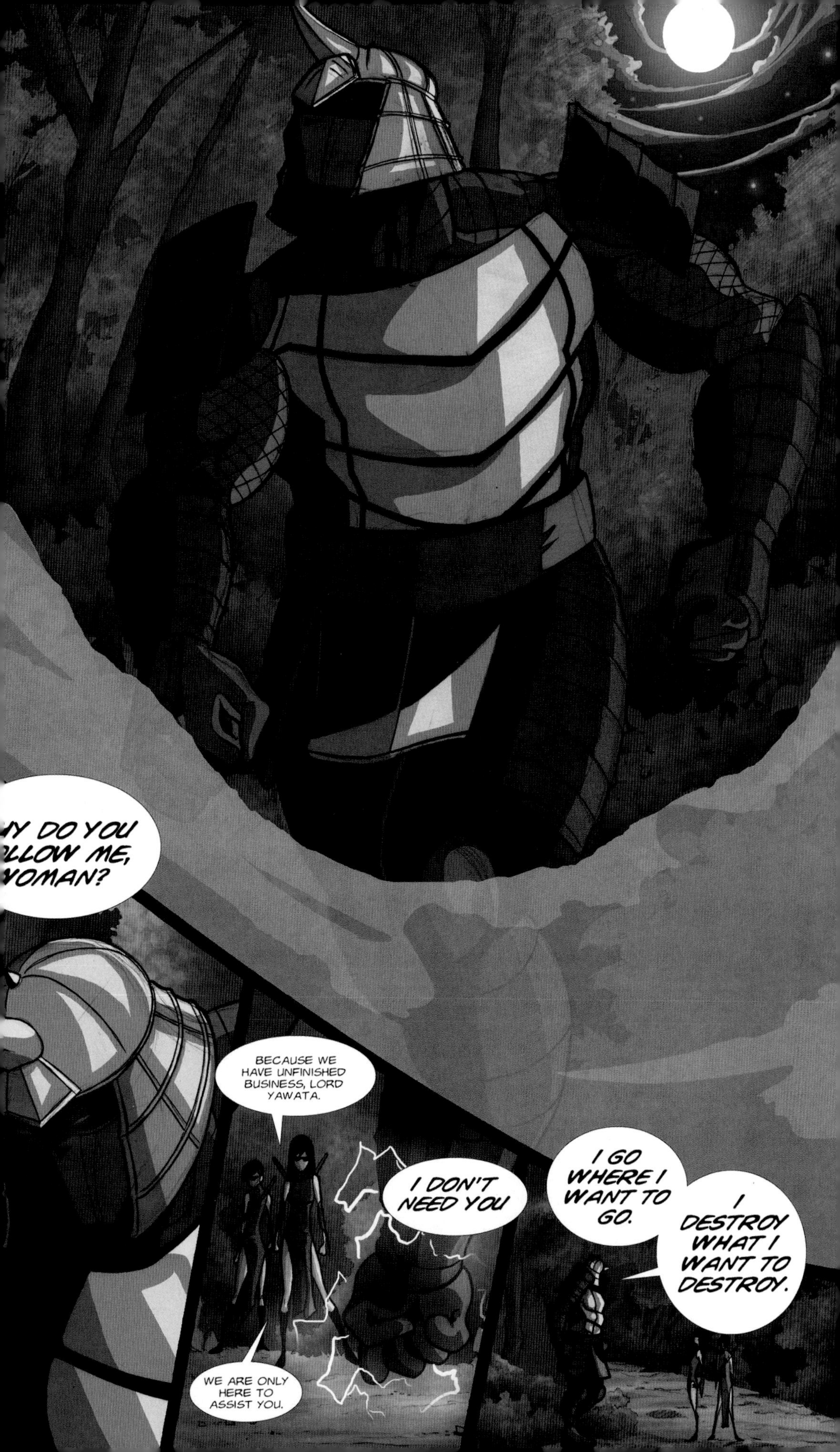

Y DO YOU OLLOW ME, OMAN?
BECAUSE WE HAVE UNFINISHED BUSINESS, LORD YAWATA.
I DON'T NEED YOU
WE ARE ONLY HERE TO ASSIST YOU.
I GO WHERE I WANT TO GO.
I DESTROY WHAT I WANT TO DESTROY.

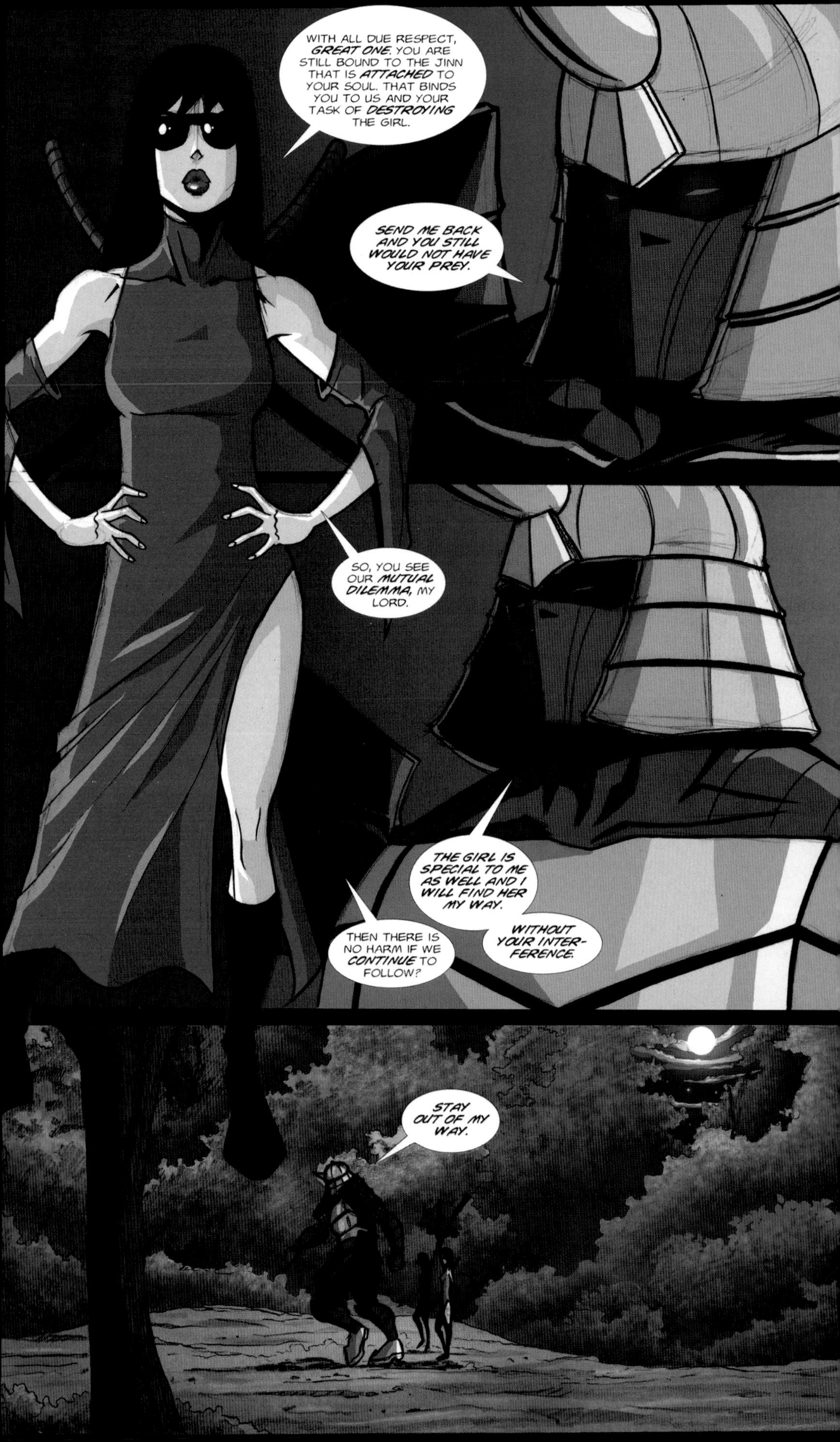
WITH ALL DUE RESPECT, GREAT ONE. YOU ARE STILL BOUND TO THE JINN THAT IS ATTACHED TO YOUR SOUL. THAT BINDS YOU TO US AND YOUR TASK OF DESTROYING THE GIRL.
SEND ME BACK AND YOU STILL WOULD NOT HAVE YOUR PREY.
SO, YOU SEE OUR MUTUAL DILEMMA, MY LORD.
THE GIRL IS SPECIAL TO ME AS WELL AND I WILL FIND HER MY WAY.
THEN THERE IS NO HARM IF WE CONTINUE TO FOLLOW?
WITHOUT YOUR INTER-FERENCE.
STAY OUT OF MY WAY.

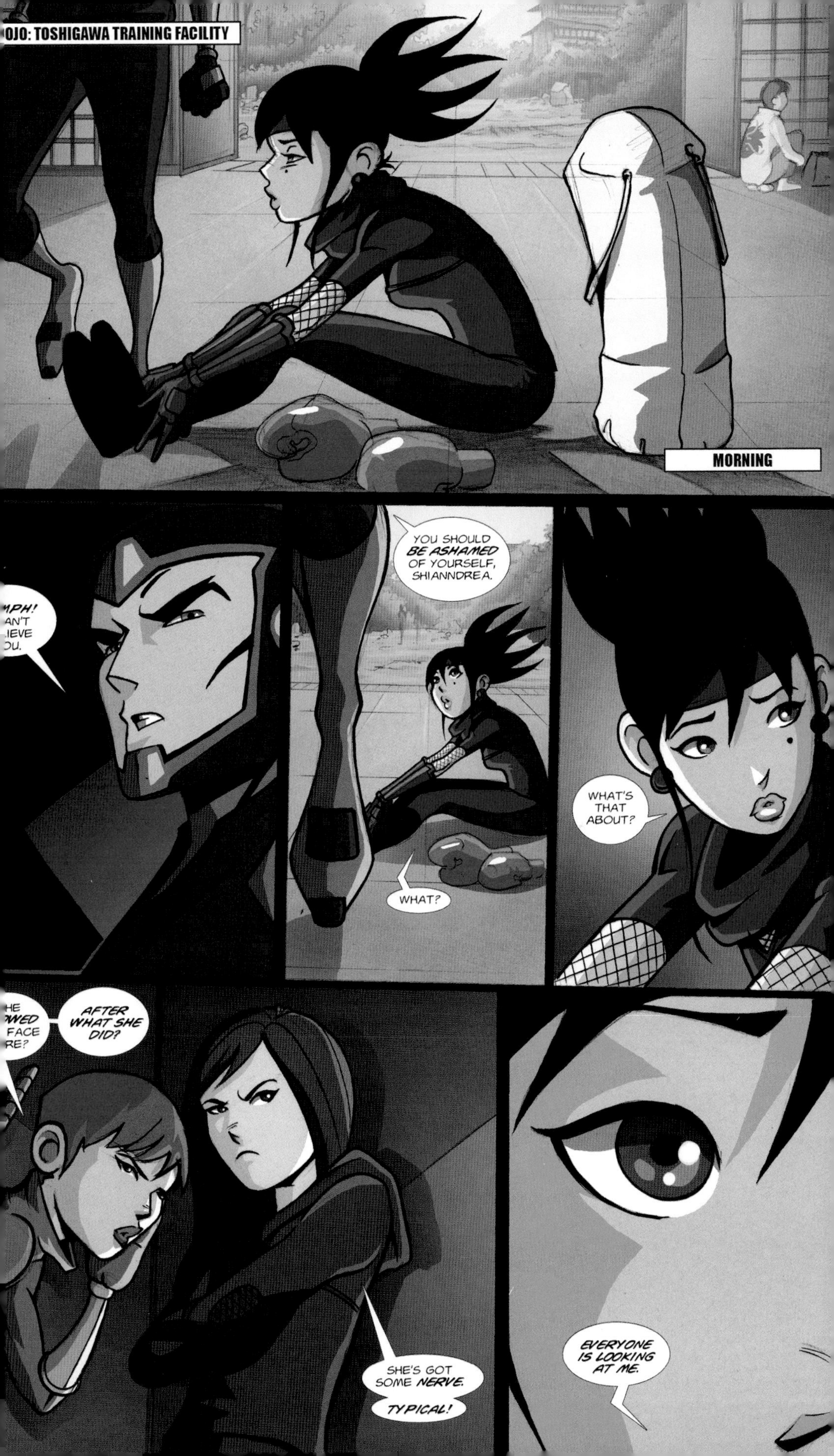
OJO: TOSHIGAWA TRAINING FACILITY
MORNING
YOU SHOULD BE ASHAMED OF YOURSELF, SHIANNDREA.
WHAT?
WHAT'S THAT ABOUT?
AFTER WHAT SHE DID?
SHE'S GOT SOME NERVE.
TYPICAL!
EVERYONE IS LOOKING AT ME.

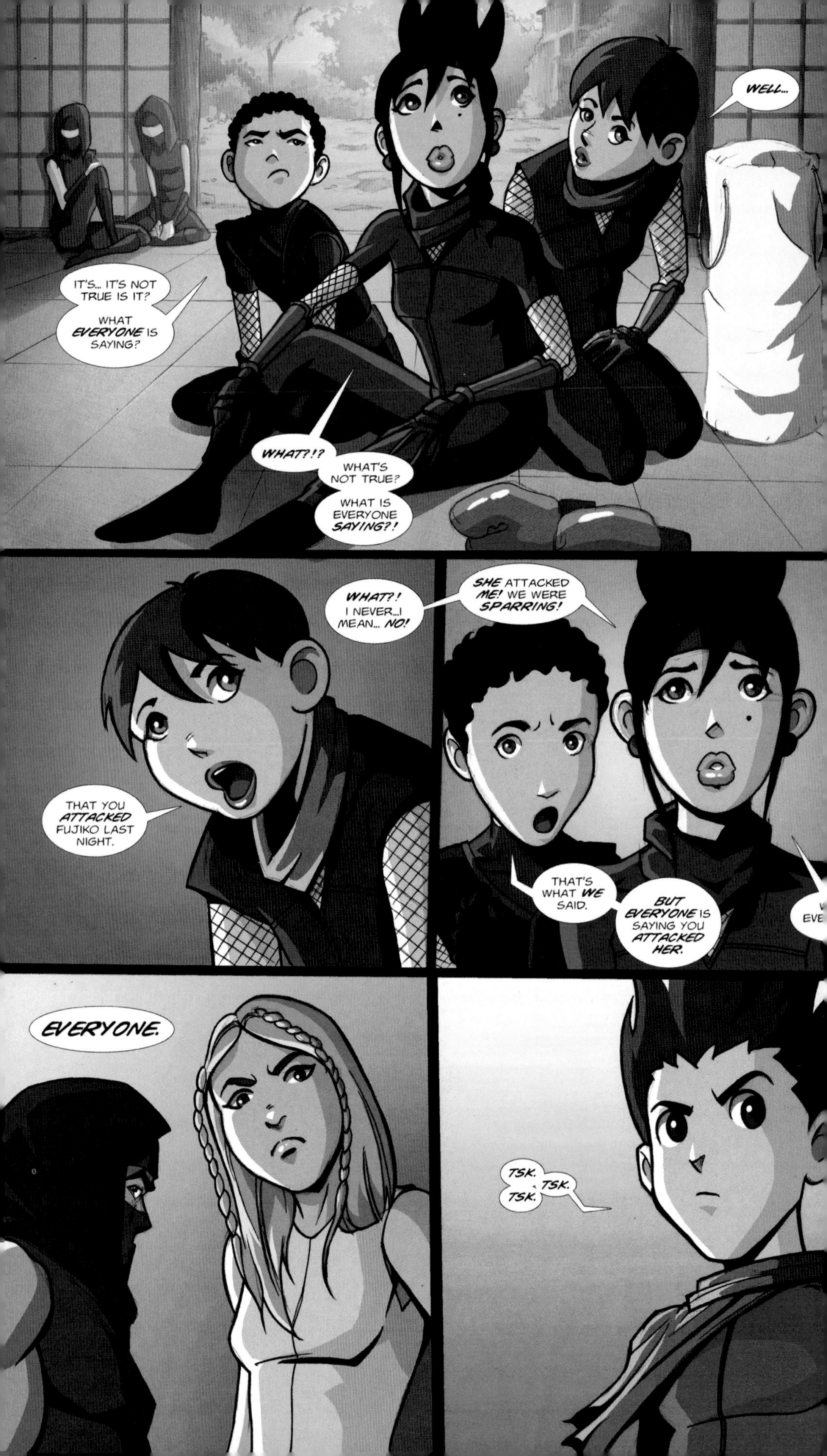
WELL...
IT'S... IT'S NOT TRUE IS IT?
WHAT EVERYONE IS SAYING?
WHAT?!?
WHAT'S NOT TRUE?
WHAT IS EVERYONE SAYING?!
THAT YOU ATTACKED FUJIKO LAST NIGHT.
WHAT?! I NEVER...I MEAN... NO!
SHE ATTACKED ME! WE WERE SPARRING!
THAT'S WHAT WE SAID.
BUT EVERYONE IS SAYING YOU ATTACKED HER.
EVERYONE.
TSK. TSK. TSK.

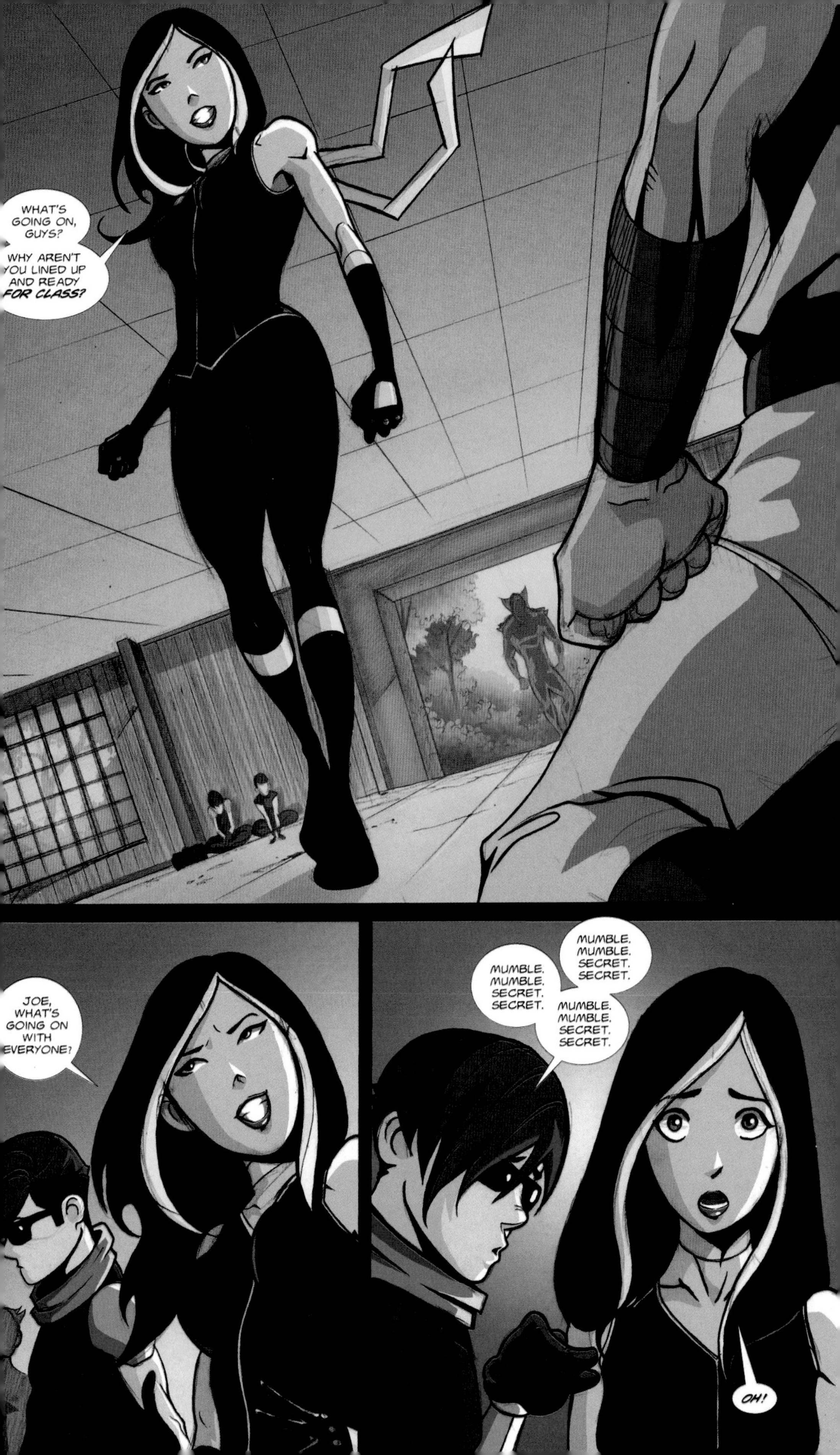
WHAT'S GOING ON, GUYS?
WHY AREN'T YOU LINED UP AND READY **FOR CLASS?**
JOE, WHAT'S GOING ON WITH EVERYONE?
MUMBLE. MUMBLE. SECRET. SECRET.
MUMBLE. MUMBLE. SECRET. SECRET.
MUMBLE. MUMBLE. SECRET. SECRET.
OH!

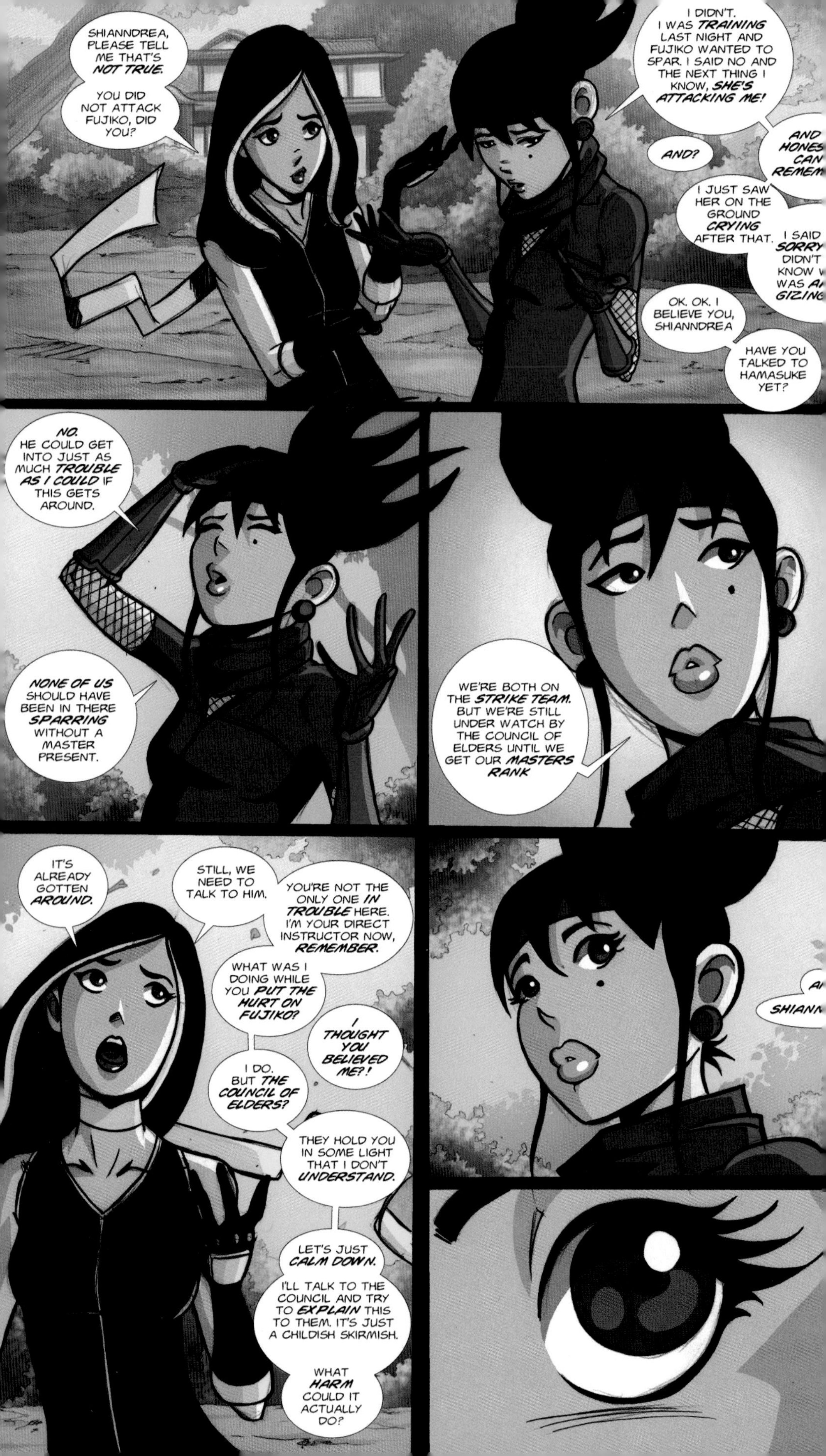

SHIANNDREA, PLEASE TELL ME THAT'S NOT TRUE.
YOU DID NOT ATTACK FUJIKO, DID YOU?
I DIDN'T. I WAS TRAINING LAST NIGHT AND FUJIKO WANTED TO SPAR. I SAID NO AND THE NEXT THING I KNOW, SHE'S ATTACKING ME!
AND?
AND HONES CAN REMEM
I JUST SAW HER ON THE GROUND CRYING AFTER THAT.
I SAID SORRY DIDN'T KNOW WAS A GIZING
OK. OK. I BELIEVE YOU, SHIANNDREA
HAVE YOU TALKED TO HAMASUKE YET?
NO. HE COULD GET INTO JUST AS MUCH TROUBLE AS I COULD IF THIS GETS AROUND.
NONE OF US SHOULD HAVE BEEN IN THERE SPARRING WITHOUT A MASTER PRESENT.
WE'RE BOTH ON THE STRIKE TEAM. BUT WE'RE STILL UNDER WATCH BY THE COUNCIL OF ELDERS UNTIL WE GET OUR MASTERS RANK
IT'S ALREADY GOTTEN AROUND.
STILL, WE NEED TO TALK TO HIM.
YOU'RE NOT THE ONLY ONE IN TROUBLE HERE. I'M YOUR DIRECT INSTRUCTOR NOW, REMEMBER.
WHAT WAS I DOING WHILE YOU PUT THE HURT ON FUJIKO?
I THOUGHT YOU BELIEVED ME?!
I DO. BUT THE COUNCIL OF ELDERS?
THEY HOLD YOU IN SOME LIGHT THAT I DON'T UNDERSTAND.
LET'S JUST CALM DOWN.
I'LL TALK TO THE COUNCIL AND TRY TO EXPLAIN THIS TO THEM. IT'S JUST A CHILDISH SKIRMISH.
WHAT HARM COULD IT ACTUALLY DO?
SHIANN

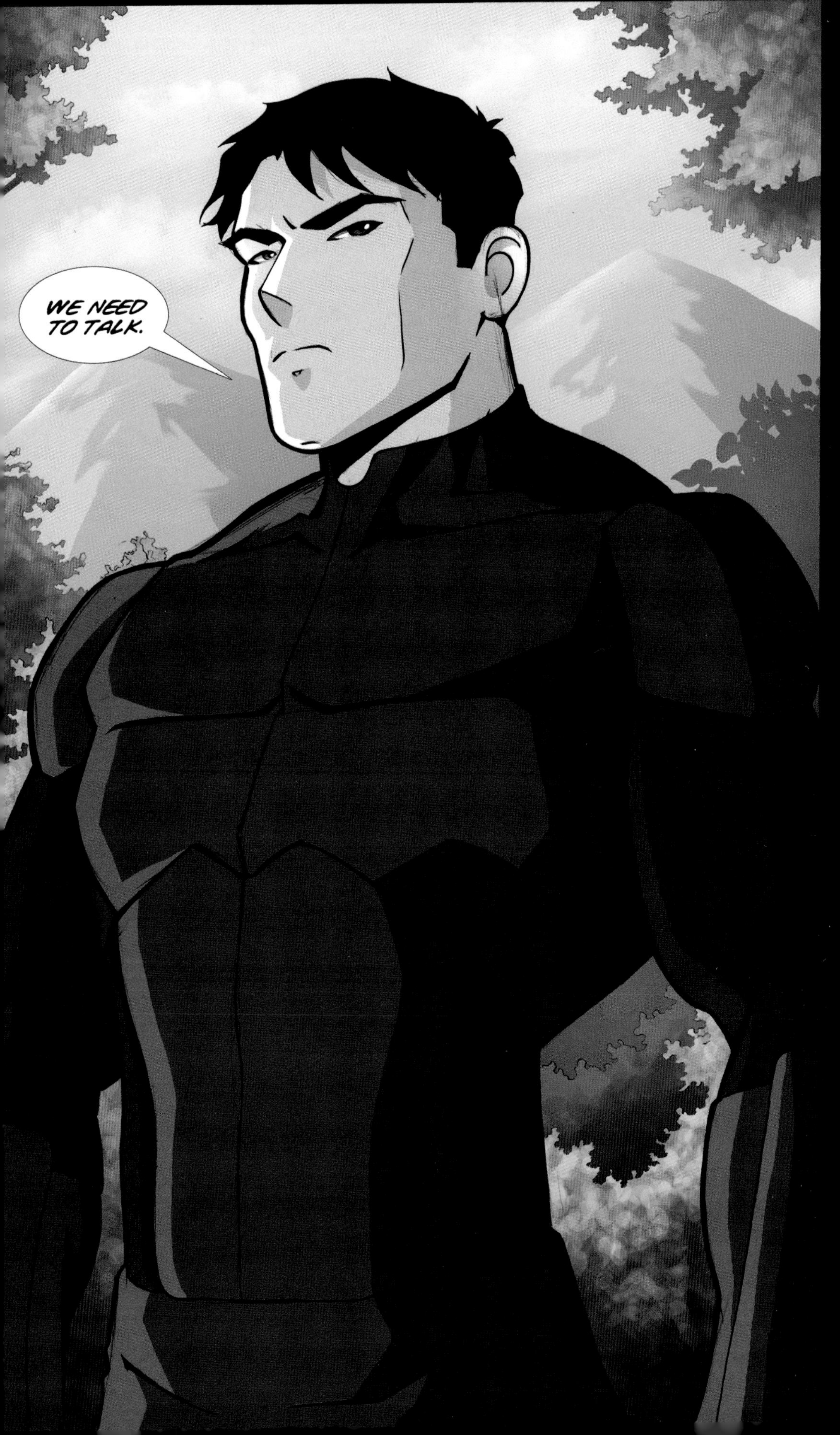
WE NEED TO TALK.

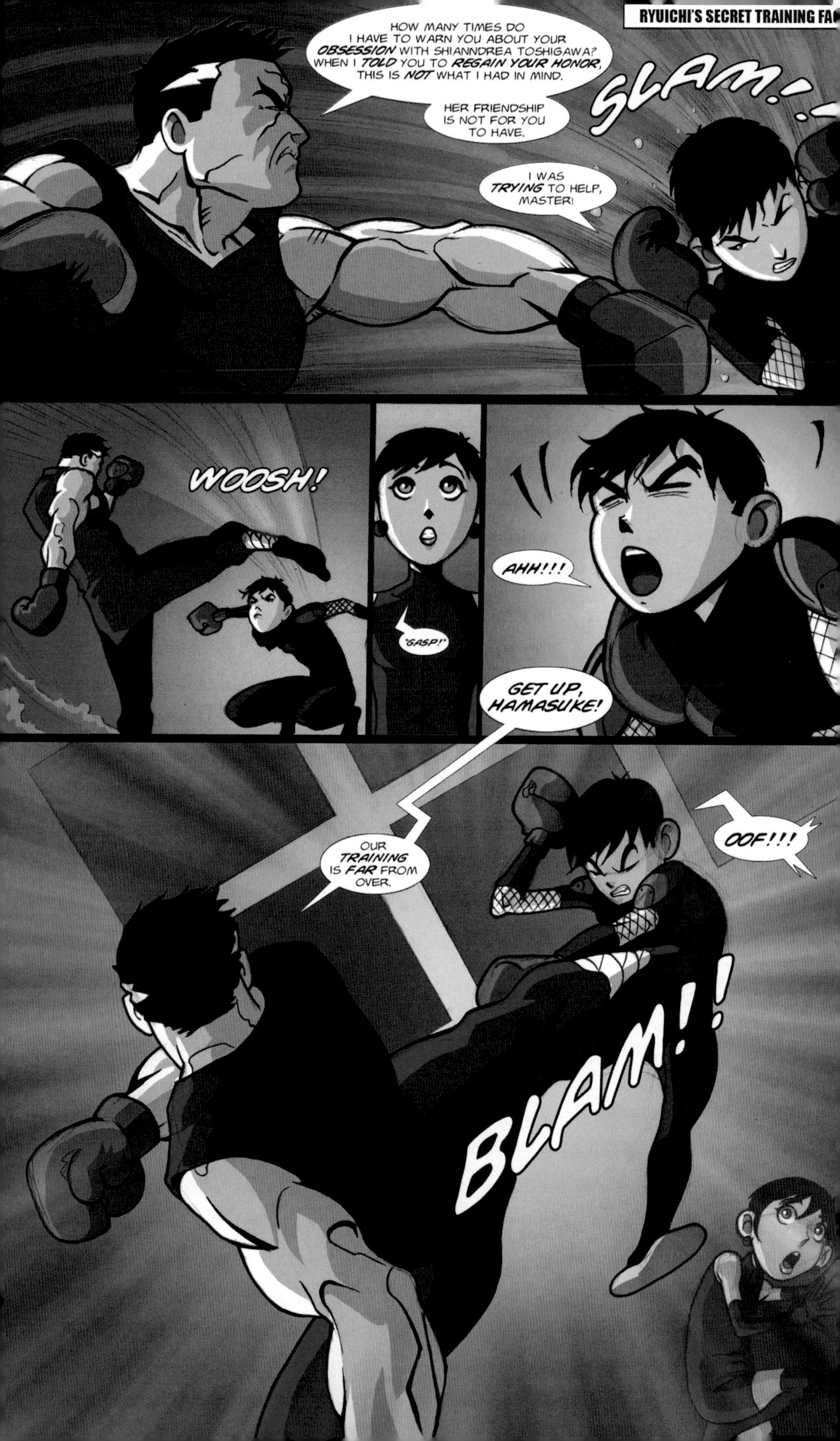
HOW MANY TIMES DO I HAVE TO WARN YOU ABOUT YOUR OBSESSION WITH SHIANNDREA TOSHIGAWA? WHEN I TOLD YOU TO REGAIN YOUR HONOR, THIS IS NOT WHAT I HAD IN MIND.
HER FRIENDSHIP IS NOT FOR YOU TO HAVE.
SLAM!!!
I WAS TRYING TO HELP, MASTER!
WOOSH!
"GASP!"
AHH!!!
GET UP, HAMASUKE!
OUR TRAINING IS FAR FROM OVER.
OOF!!!
BLAM!!

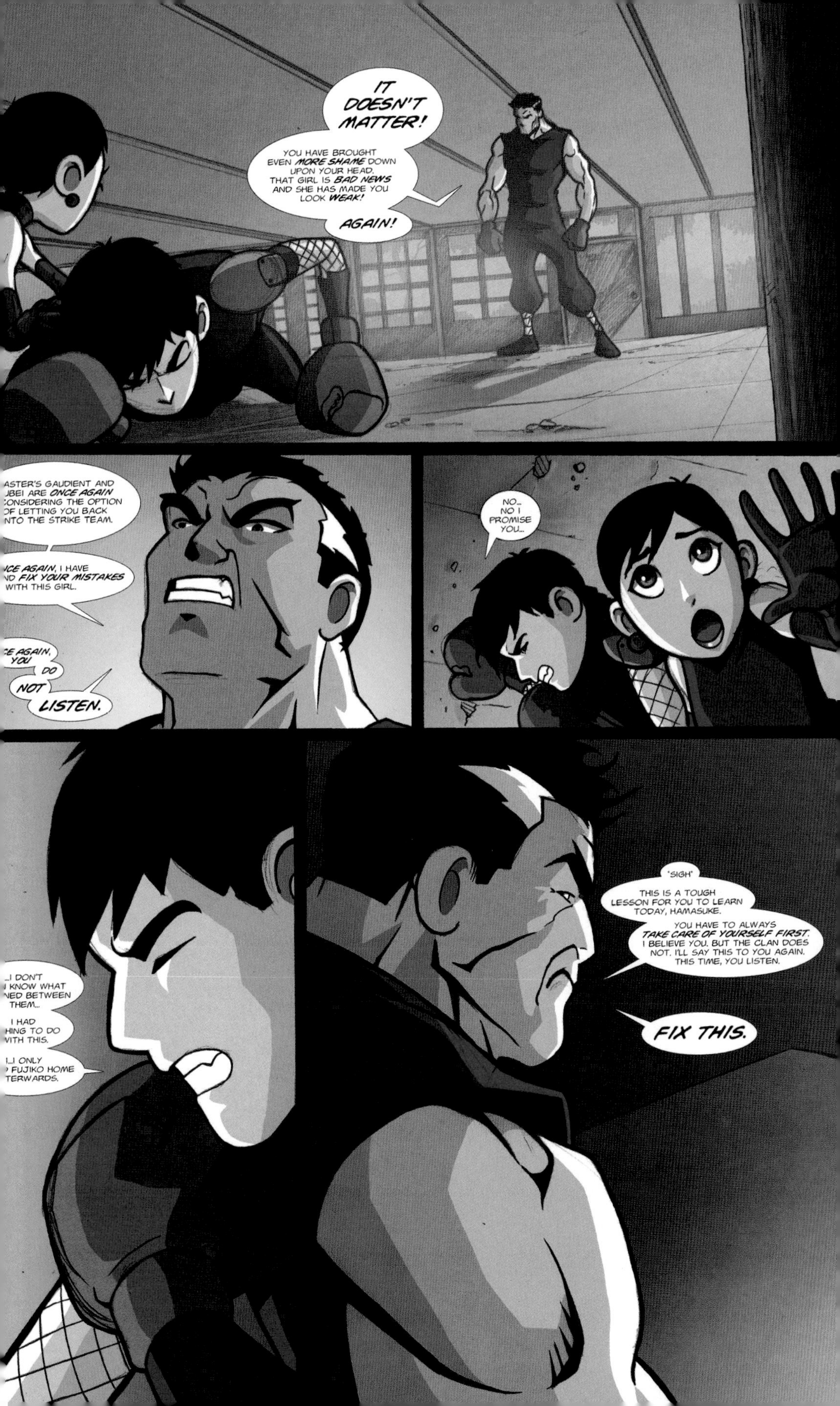
IT DOESN'T MATTER!
YOU HAVE BROUGHT EVEN MORE SHAME DOWN UPON YOUR HEAD. THAT GIRL IS BAD NEWS AND SHE HAS MADE YOU LOOK WEAK!
AGAIN!
ASTER'S GAUDIENT AND UBEI ARE ONCE AGAIN CONSIDERING THE OPTION OF LETTING YOU BACK INTO THE STRIKE TEAM.
ICE AGAIN, I HAVE ND FIX YOUR MISTAKES WITH THIS GIRL.
CE AGAIN, YOU DO NOT LISTEN.
NO... NO I PROMISE YOU...
...I DON'T I KNOW WHAT NED BETWEEN THEM...
I HAD HING TO DO WITH THIS.
I...I ONLY FUJIKO HOME TERWARDS.
SIGH
THIS IS A TOUGH LESSON FOR YOU TO LEARN TODAY, HAMASUKE.
YOU HAVE TO ALWAYS TAKE CARE OF YOURSELF FIRST. I BELIEVE YOU. BUT THE CLAN DOES NOT. I'LL SAY THIS TO YOU AGAIN. THIS TIME, YOU LISTEN.
FIX THIS.

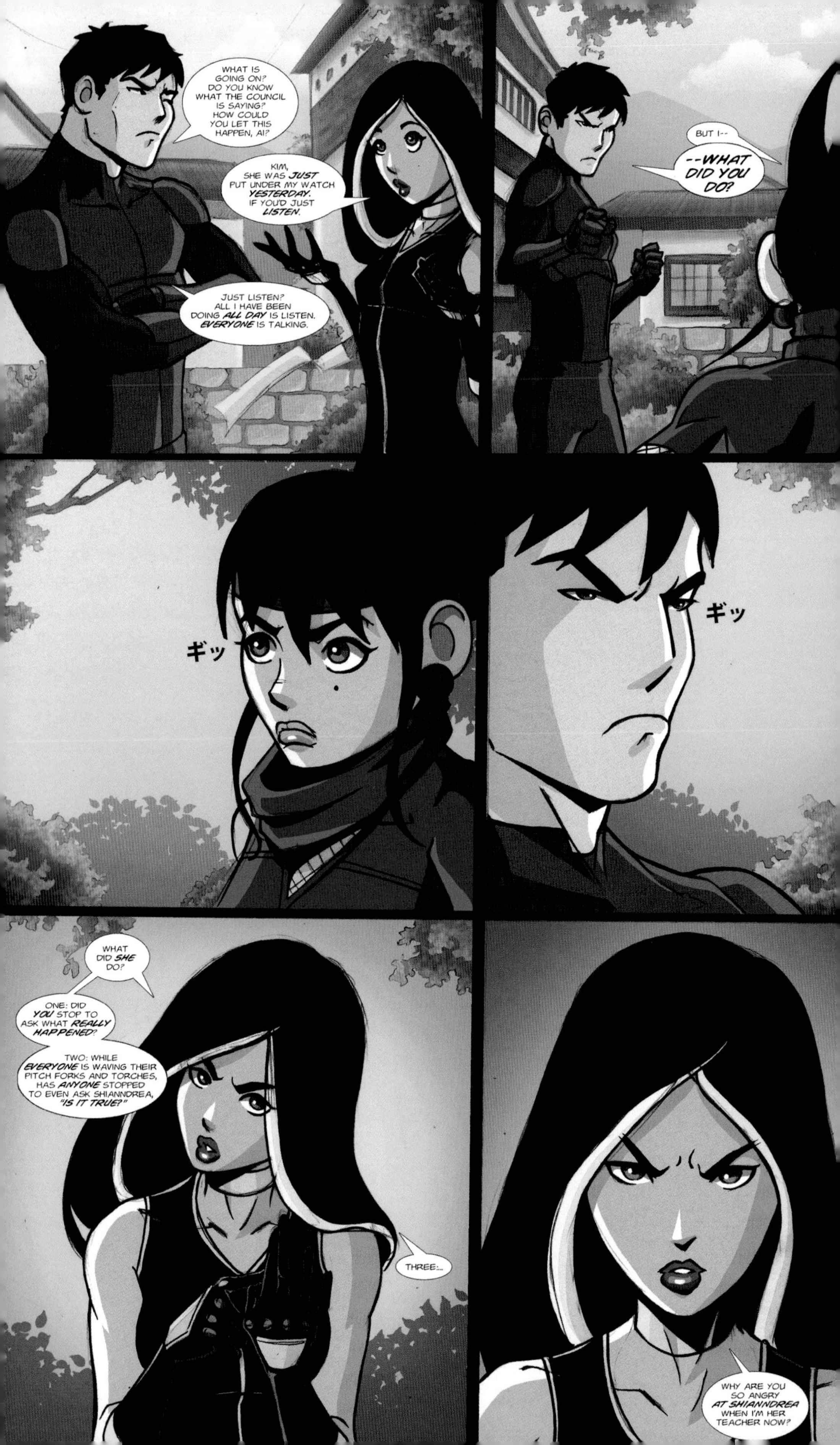
WHAT IS GOING ON? DO YOU KNOW WHAT THE COUNCIL IS SAYING? HOW COULD YOU LET THIS HAPPEN, AI?
KIM, SHE WAS JUST PUT UNDER MY WATCH YESTERDAY. IF YOU'D JUST LISTEN.
JUST LISTEN? ALL I HAVE BEEN DOING ALL DAY IS LISTEN. EVERYONE IS TALKING.
BUT I--
--WHAT DID YOU DO?
ギッ
ギッ
WHAT DID SHE DO?
ONE: DID YOU STOP TO ASK WHAT REALLY HAPPENED?
TWO: WHILE EVERYONE IS WAVING THEIR PITCH FORKS AND TORCHES, HAS ANYONE STOPPED TO EVEN ASK SHIANNDREA, "IS IT TRUE?"
THREE:...
WHY ARE YOU SO ANGRY AT SHIANNDREA WHEN I'M HER TEACHER NOW?

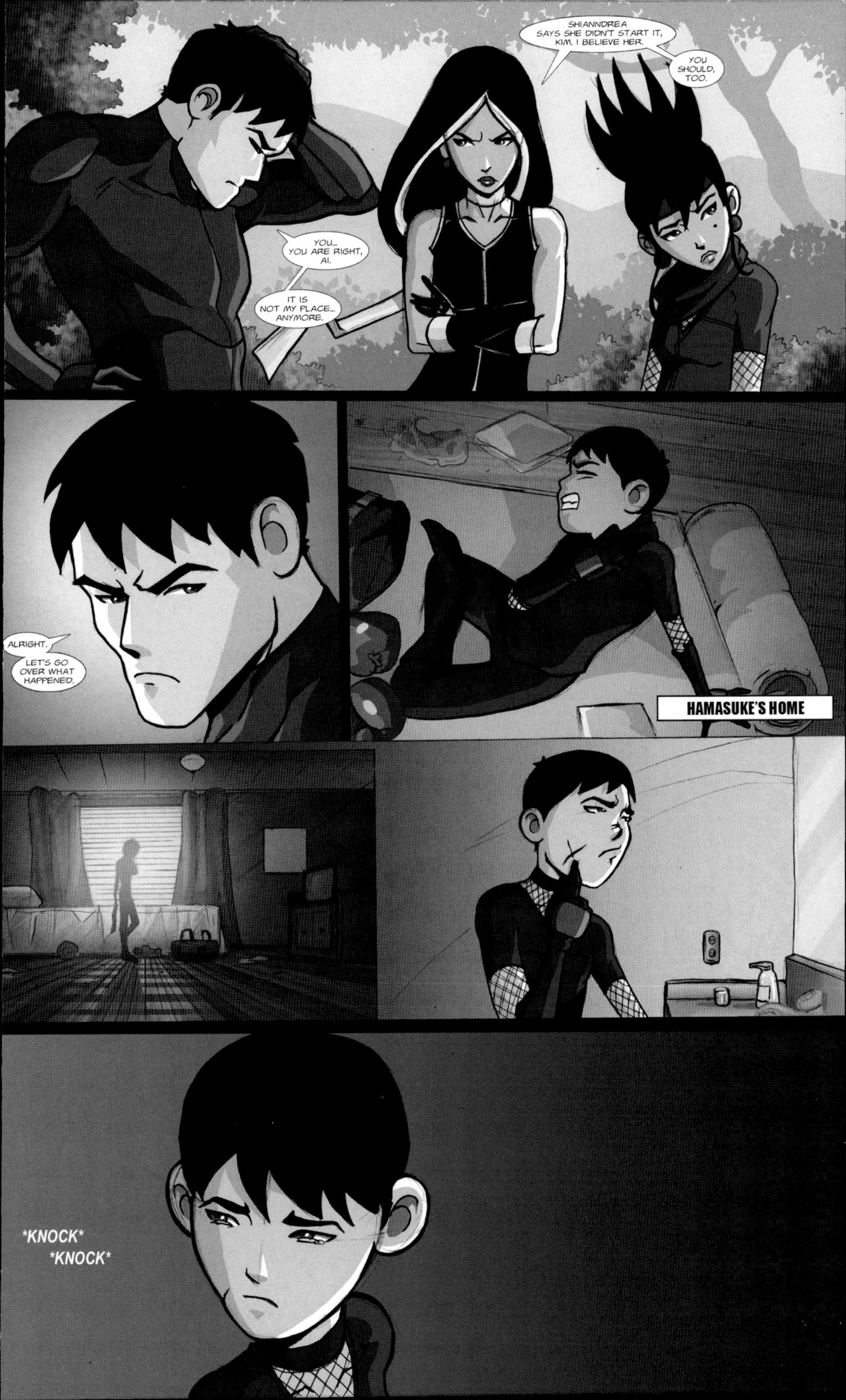

SHIANNDREA SAYS SHE DIDN'T START IT, KIM. I BELIEVE HER.
YOU SHOULD, TOO.
YOU... YOU ARE RIGHT, AI.
IT IS NOT MY PLACE... ANYMORE.
ALRIGHT.
LET'S GO OVER WHAT HAPPENED.
HAMASUKE'S HOME
KNOCK
KNOCK

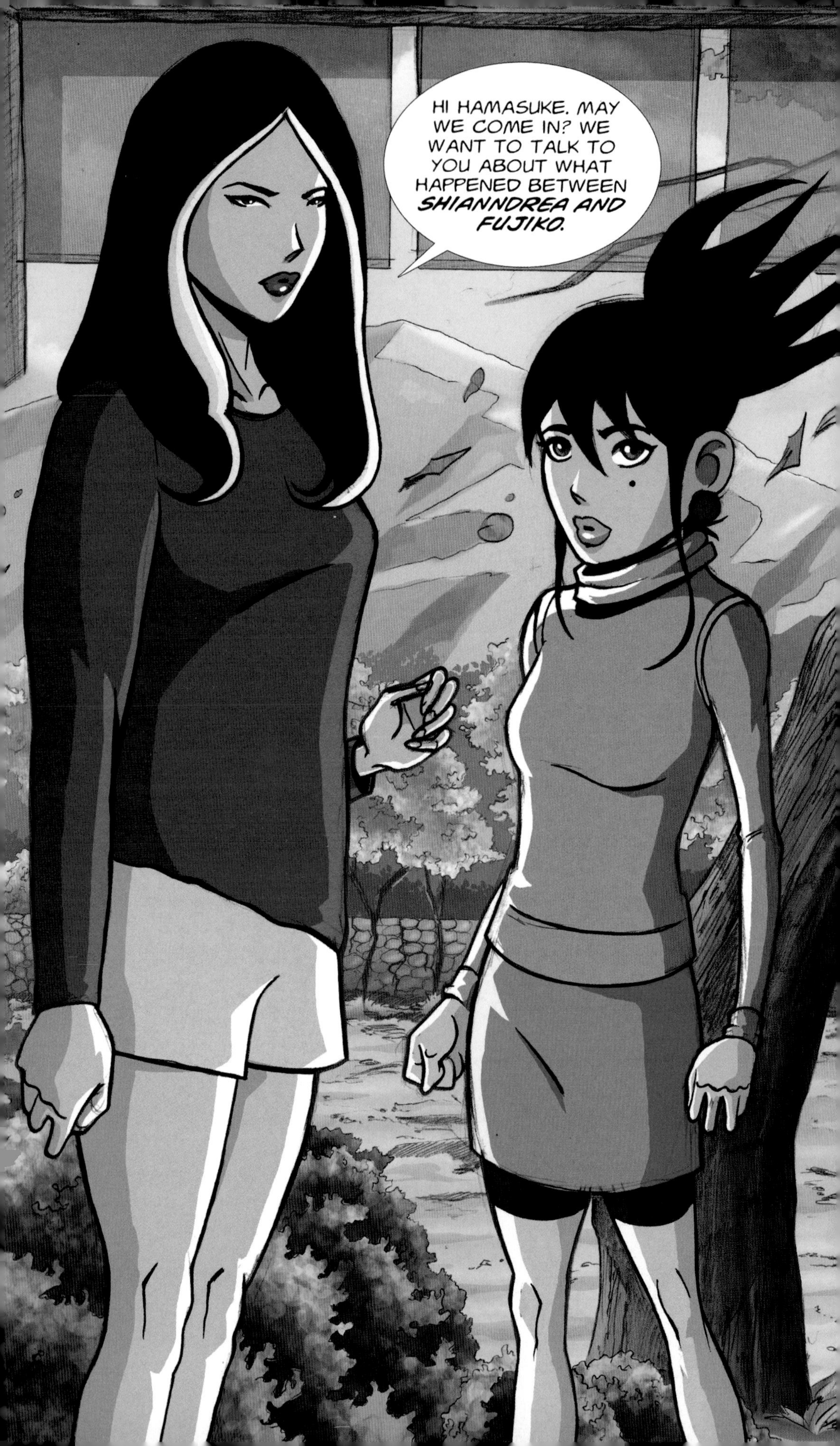
HI HAMASUKE. MAY WE COME IN? WE WANT TO TALK TO YOU ABOUT WHAT HAPPENED BETWEEN *SHIANNDREA AND FUJIKO.*

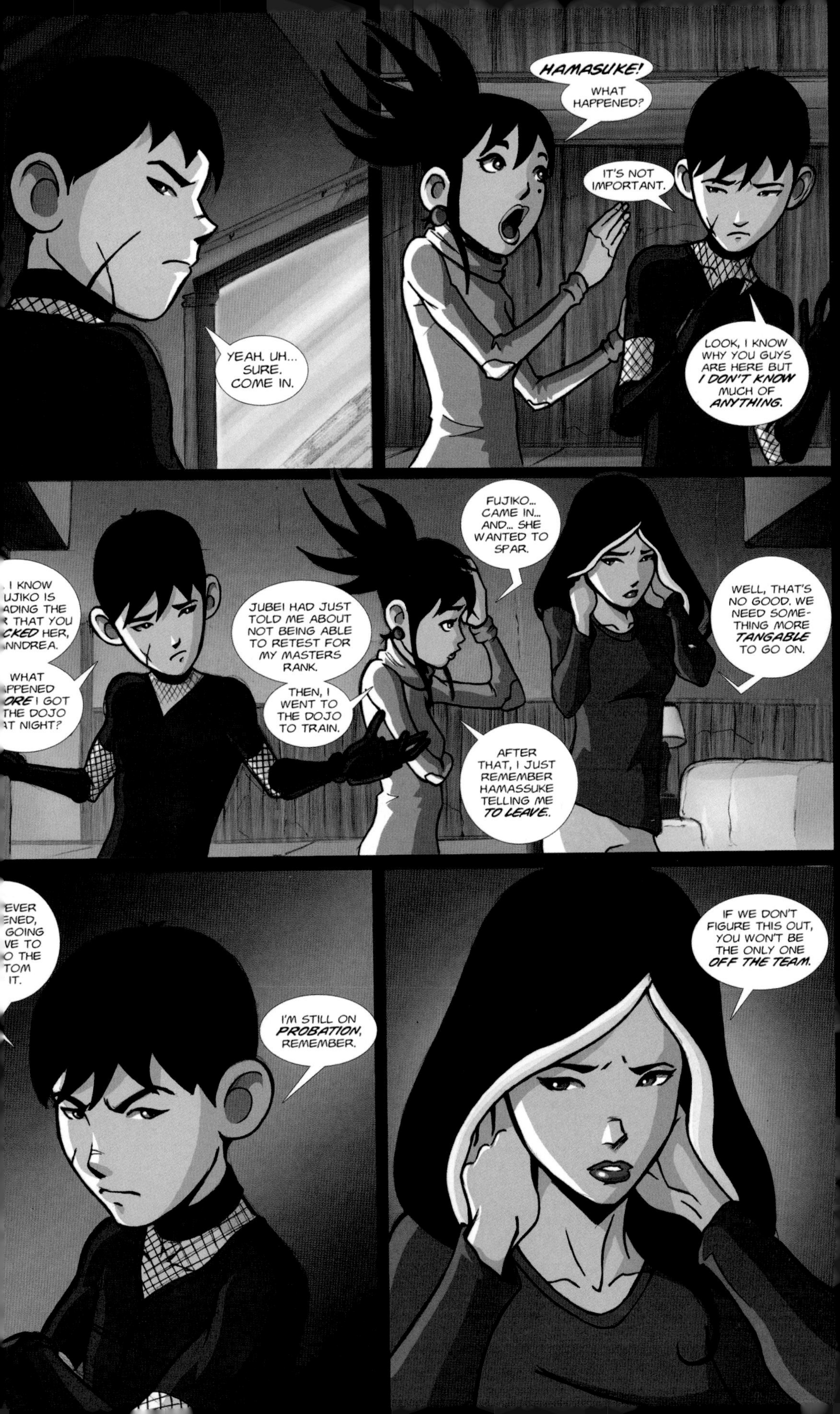
YEAH. UH... SURE. COME IN.
HAMASUKE!
WHAT HAPPENED?
IT'S NOT IMPORTANT.
LOOK, I KNOW WHY YOU GUYS ARE HERE BUT I DON'T KNOW MUCH OF ANYTHING.
I KNOW UJIKO IS ADING THE R THAT YOU CKED HER, NNDREA.
WHAT PPENED ORE I GOT THE DOJO AT NIGHT?
JUBEI HAD JUST TOLD ME ABOUT NOT BEING ABLE TO RETEST FOR MY MASTERS RANK.
THEN, I WENT TO THE DOJO TO TRAIN.
FUJIKO... CAME IN... AND... SHE WANTED TO SPAR.
AFTER THAT, I JUST REMEMBER HAMASSUKE TELLING ME TO LEAVE.
WELL, THAT'S NO GOOD. WE NEED SOMETHING MORE TANGABLE TO GO ON.
EVER ENED, GOING VE TO O THE TOM IT.
I'M STILL ON PROBATION, REMEMBER.
IF WE DON'T FIGURE THIS OUT, YOU WON'T BE THE ONLY ONE OFF THE TEAM.

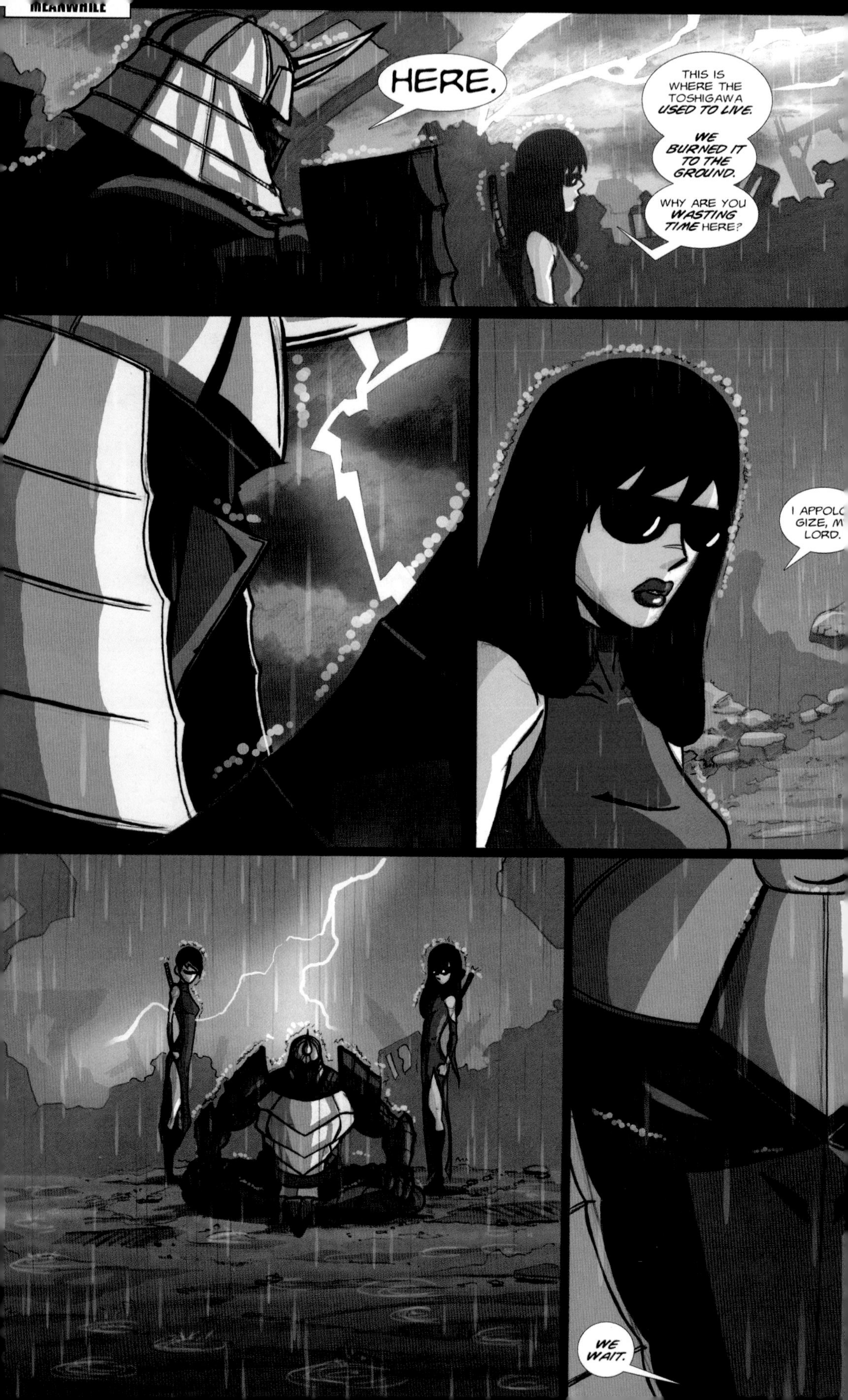
MEANWHILE
HERE.
THIS IS WHERE THE TOSHIGAWA USED TO LIVE.
WE BURNED IT TO THE GROUND.
WHY ARE YOU WASTING TIME HERE?
I APPOLO GIZE, M LORD.
WE WAIT.

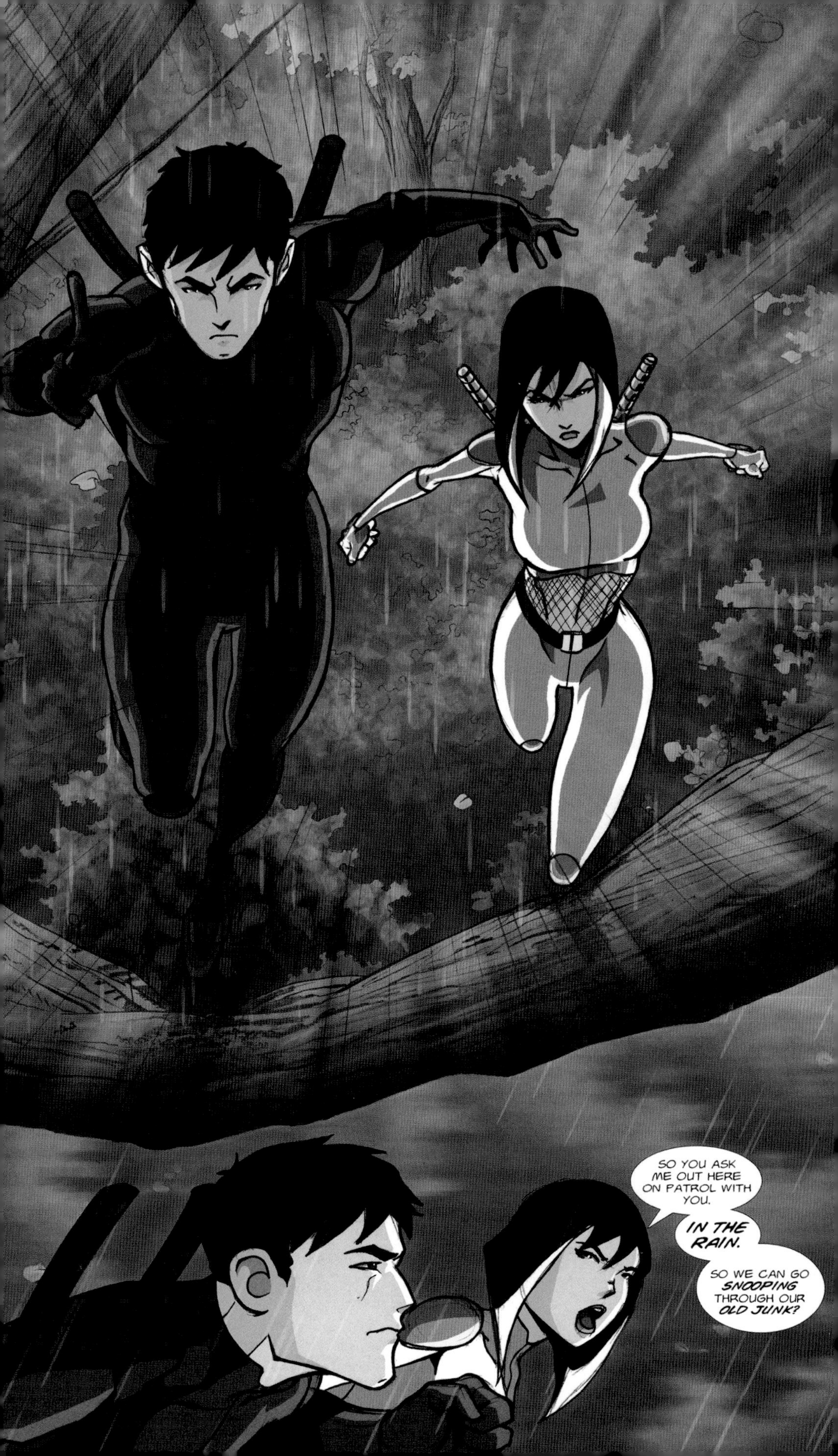
SO YOU ASK ME OUT HERE ON PATROL WITH YOU.
IN THE RAIN.
SO WE CAN GO SNOOPING THROUGH OUR OLD JUNK?

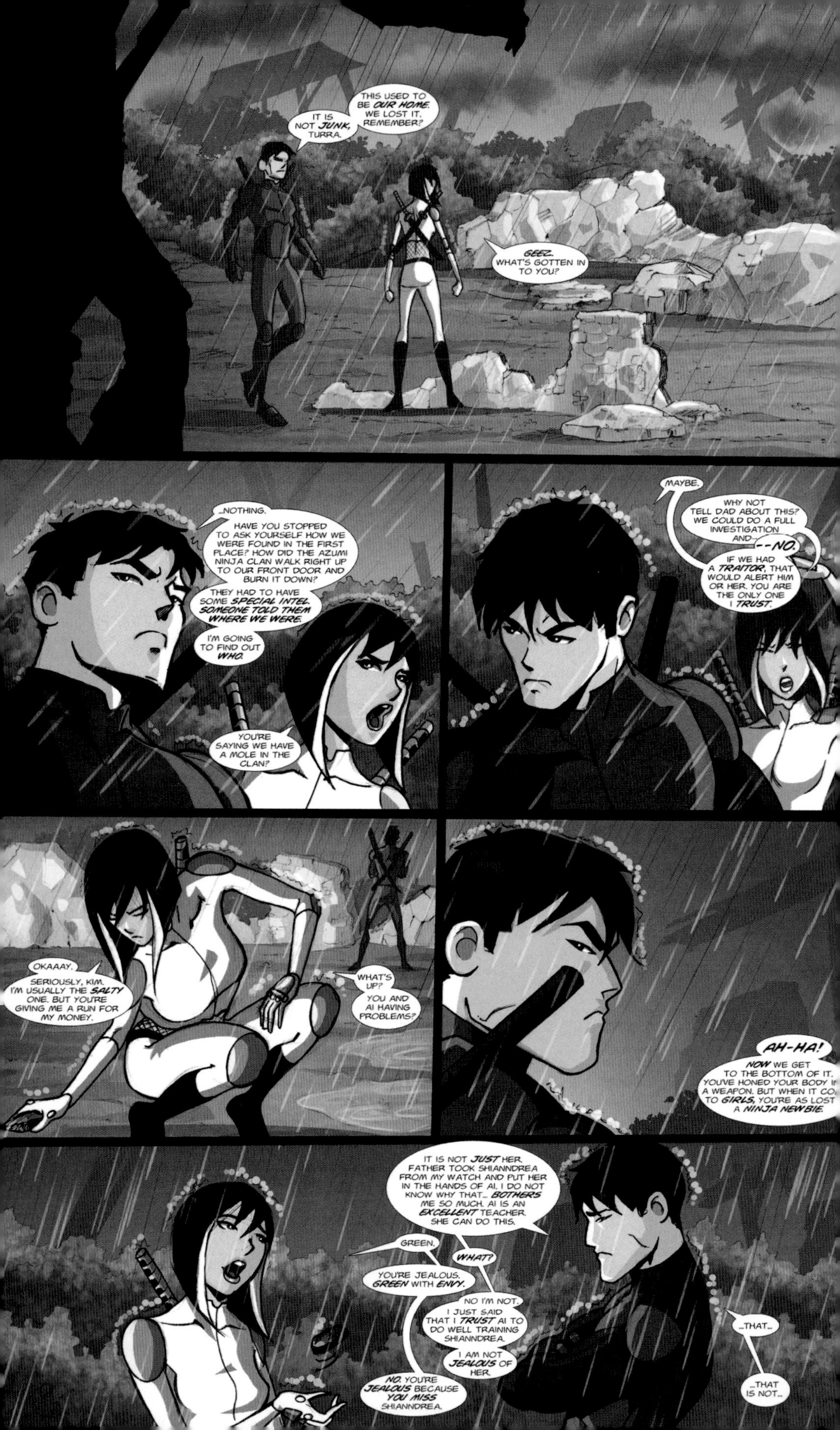
IT IS NOT JUNK, TURRA.
THIS USED TO BE OUR HOME. WE LOST IT. REMEMBER?
GEEZ. WHAT'S GOTTEN IN TO YOU?
...NOTHING.
HAVE YOU STOPPED TO ASK YOURSELF HOW WE WERE FOUND IN THE FIRST PLACE? HOW DID THE AZUMI NINJA CLAN WALK RIGHT UP TO OUR FRONT DOOR AND BURN IT DOWN?
THEY HAD TO HAVE SOME SPECIAL INTEL. SOMEONE TOLD THEM WHERE WE WERE.
I'M GOING TO FIND OUT WHO.
YOU'RE SAYING WE HAVE A MOLE IN THE CLAN?
MAYBE.
WHY NOT TELL DAD ABOUT THIS? WE COULD DO A FULL INVESTIGATION AND--
--NO.
IF WE HAD A TRAITOR, THAT WOULD ALERT HIM OR HER. YOU ARE THE ONLY ONE I TRUST.
OKAAAY. SERIOUSLY, KIM. I'M USUALLY THE SALTY ONE. BUT YOU'RE GIVING ME A RUN FOR MY MONEY.
WHAT'S UP? YOU AND AI HAVING PROBLEMS?
AH-HA!
NOW WE GET TO THE BOTTOM OF IT. YOU'VE HONED YOUR BODY I A WEAPON. BUT WHEN IT CO TO GIRLS, YOU'RE AS LOST A NINJA NEWBIE.
IT IS NOT JUST HER. FATHER TOOK SHIANNDREA FROM MY WATCH AND PUT HER IN THE HANDS OF AI. I DO NOT KNOW WHY THAT... BOTHERS ME SO MUCH. AI IS AN EXCELLENT TEACHER. SHE CAN DO THIS.
GREEN.
WHAT?
YOU'RE JEALOUS. GREEN WITH ENVY.
NO I'M NOT. I JUST SAID THAT I TRUST AI TO DO WELL TRAINING SHIANNDREA.
I AM NOT JEALOUS OF HER.
NO, YOU'RE JEALOUS BECAUSE YOU MISS SHIANNDREA.
...THAT...
...THAT IS NOT...

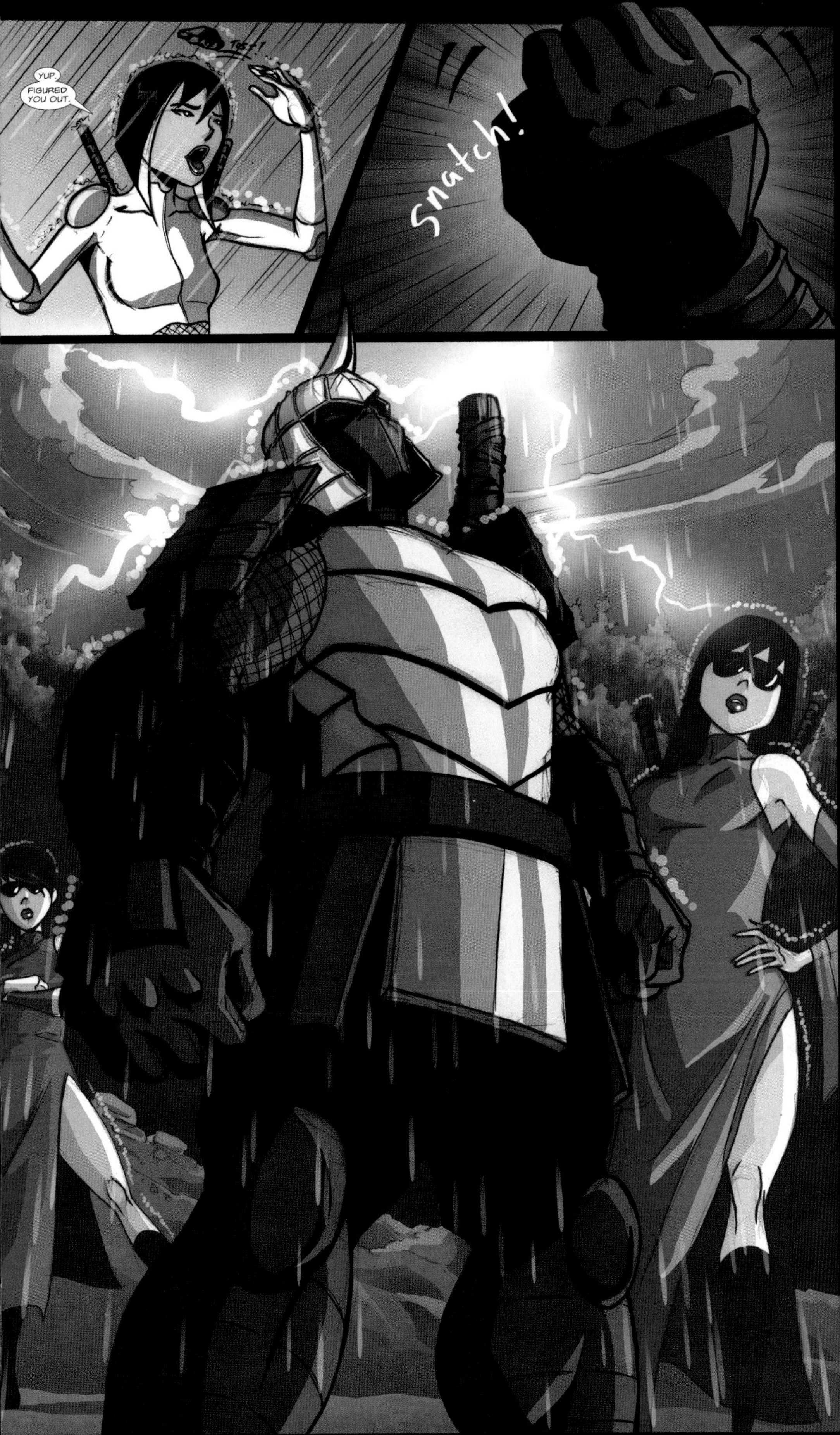
Toss!
YUP. FIGURED YOU OUT.
snatch!

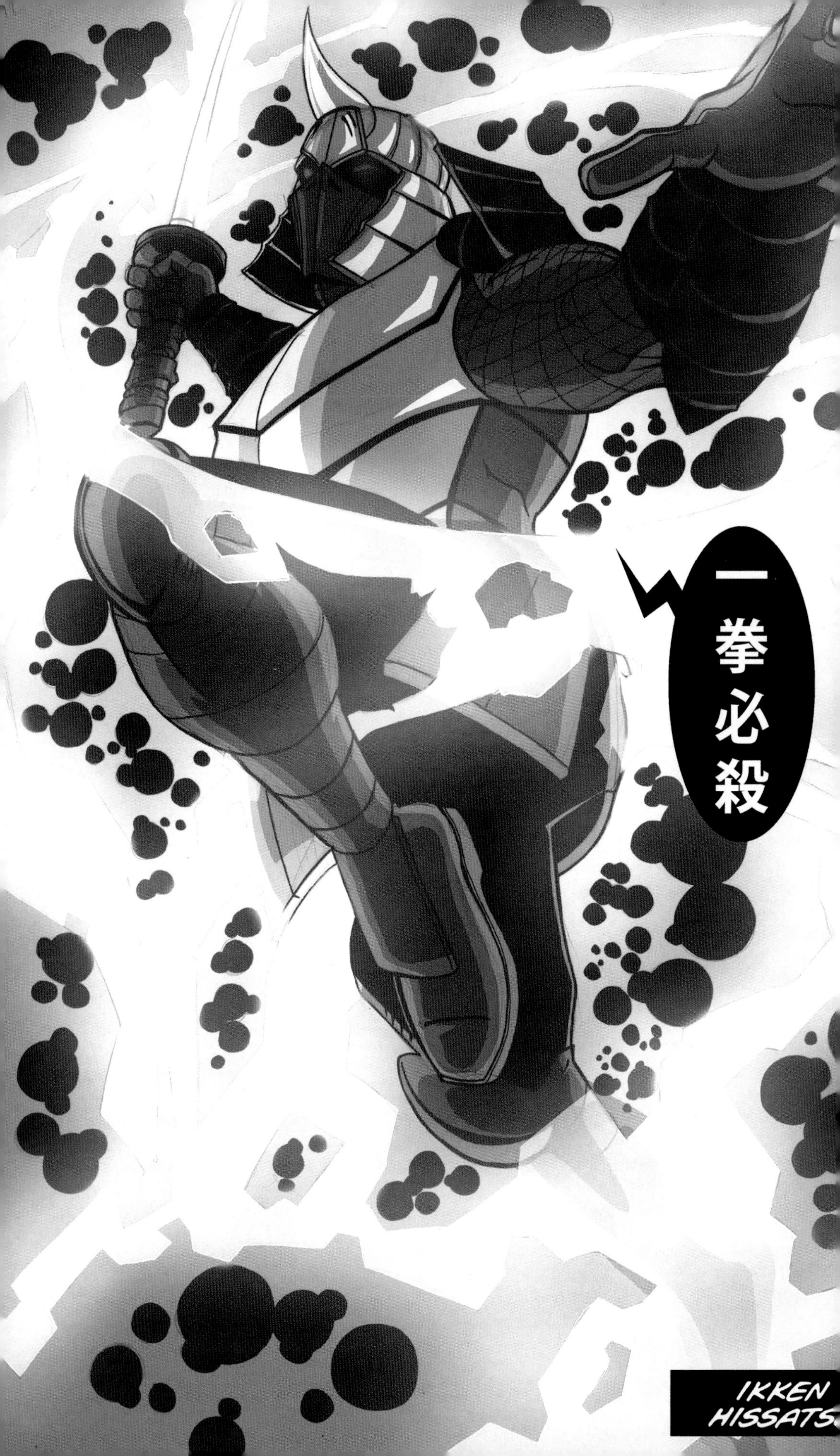
一拳必殺
IKKEN
HISSATS

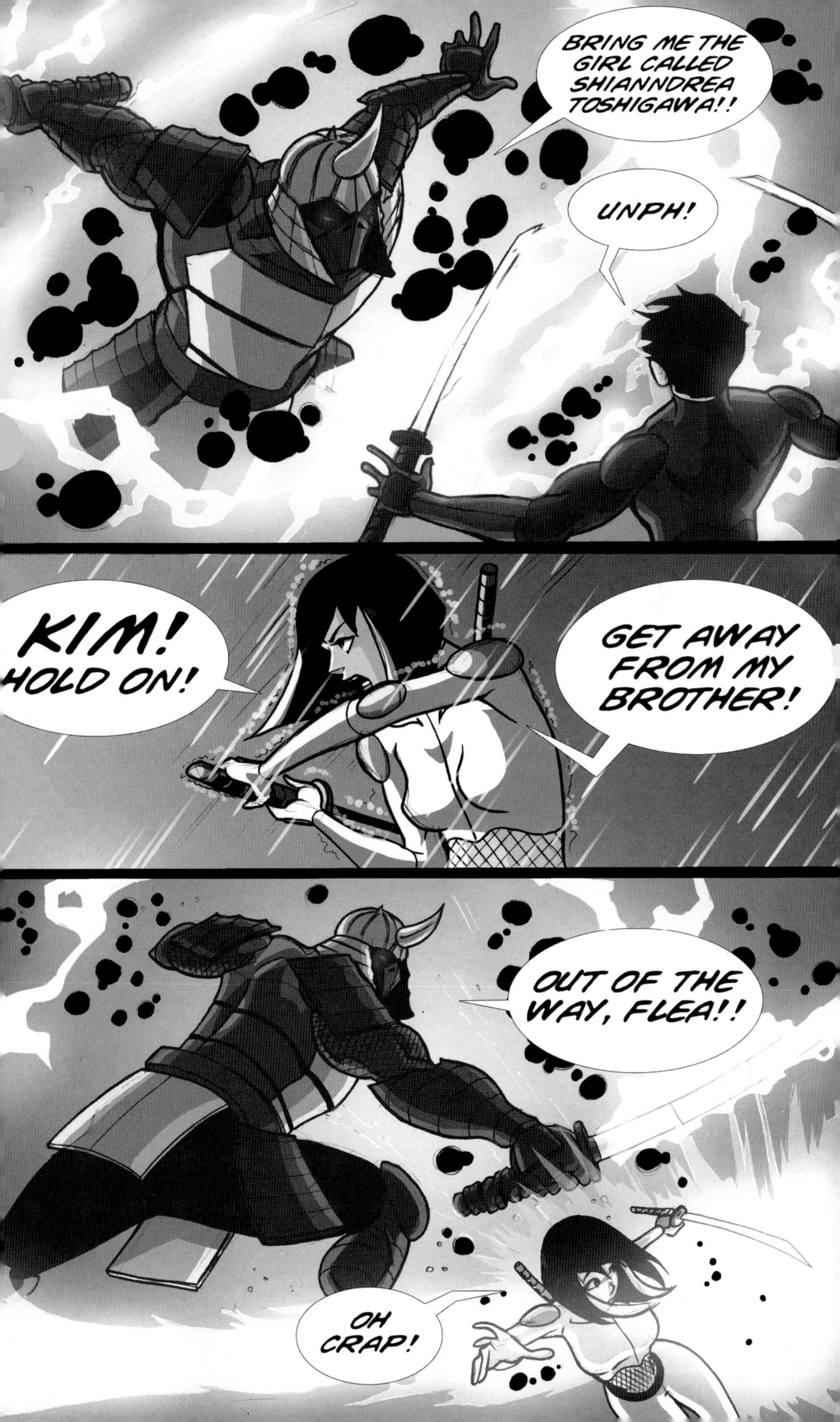
BRING ME THE GIRL CALLED SHIANNDREA TOSHIGAWA!!
UNPH!
KIM! HOLD ON!
GET AWAY FROM MY BROTHER!
OUT OF THE WAY, FLEA!!
OH CRAP!

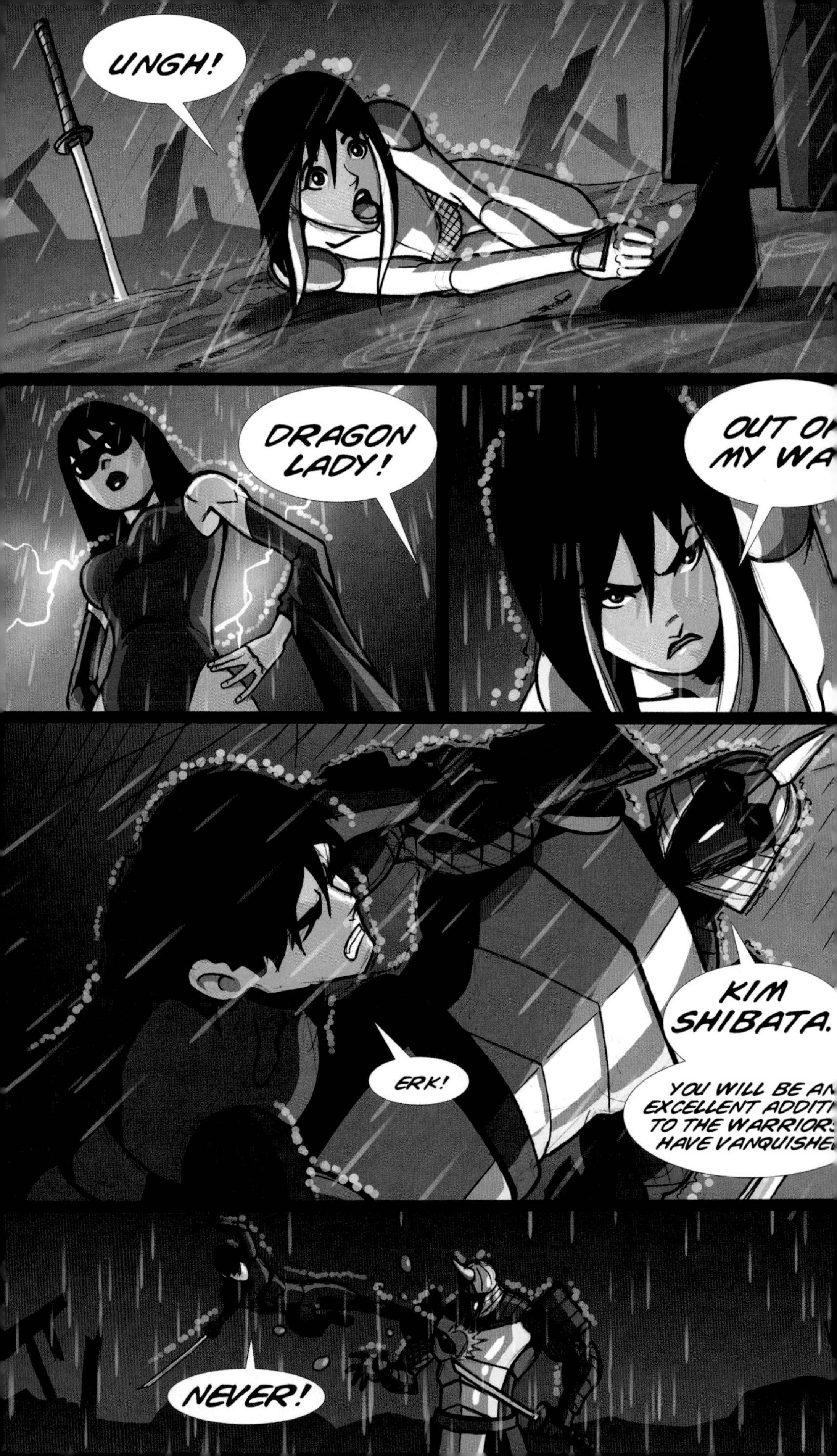
UNGH!
DRAGON LADY!
OUT OF MY WA
KIM SHIBATA.
ERK!
YOU WILL BE AN EXCELLENT ADDITI TO THE WARRIORS HAVE VANQUISHE
NEVER!

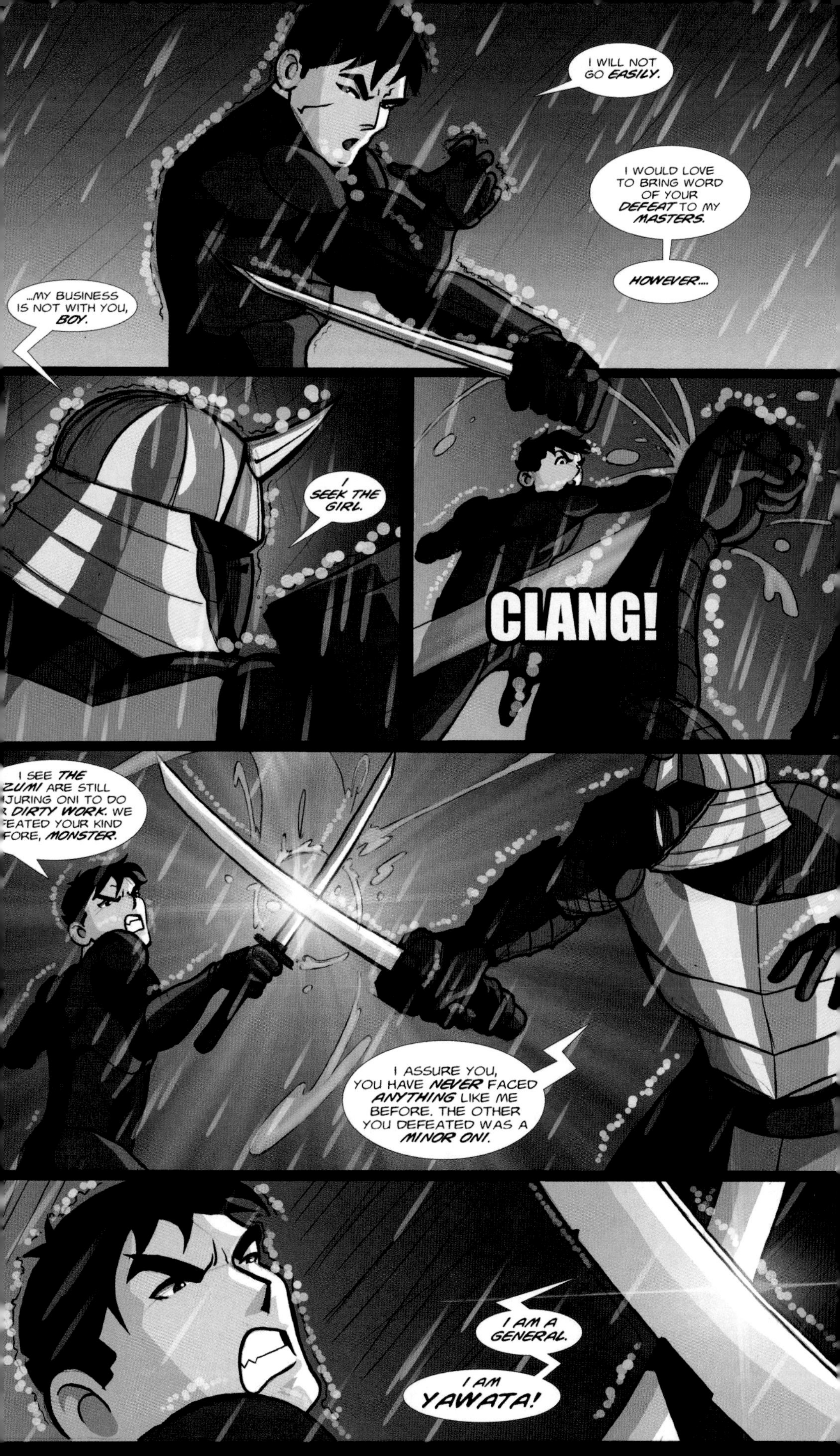
I WILL NOT GO EASILY.
I WOULD LOVE TO BRING WORD OF YOUR DEFEAT TO MY MASTERS.
HOWEVER....
...MY BUSINESS IS NOT WITH YOU, BOY.
I SEEK THE GIRL.
CLANG!
I SEE THE ZUMI ARE STILL JURING ONI TO DO R DIRTY WORK. WE FEATED YOUR KIND FORE, MONSTER.
I ASSURE YOU, YOU HAVE NEVER FACED ANYTHING LIKE ME BEFORE. THE OTHER YOU DEFEATED WAS A MINOR ONI.
I AM A GENERAL.
I AM YAWATA!

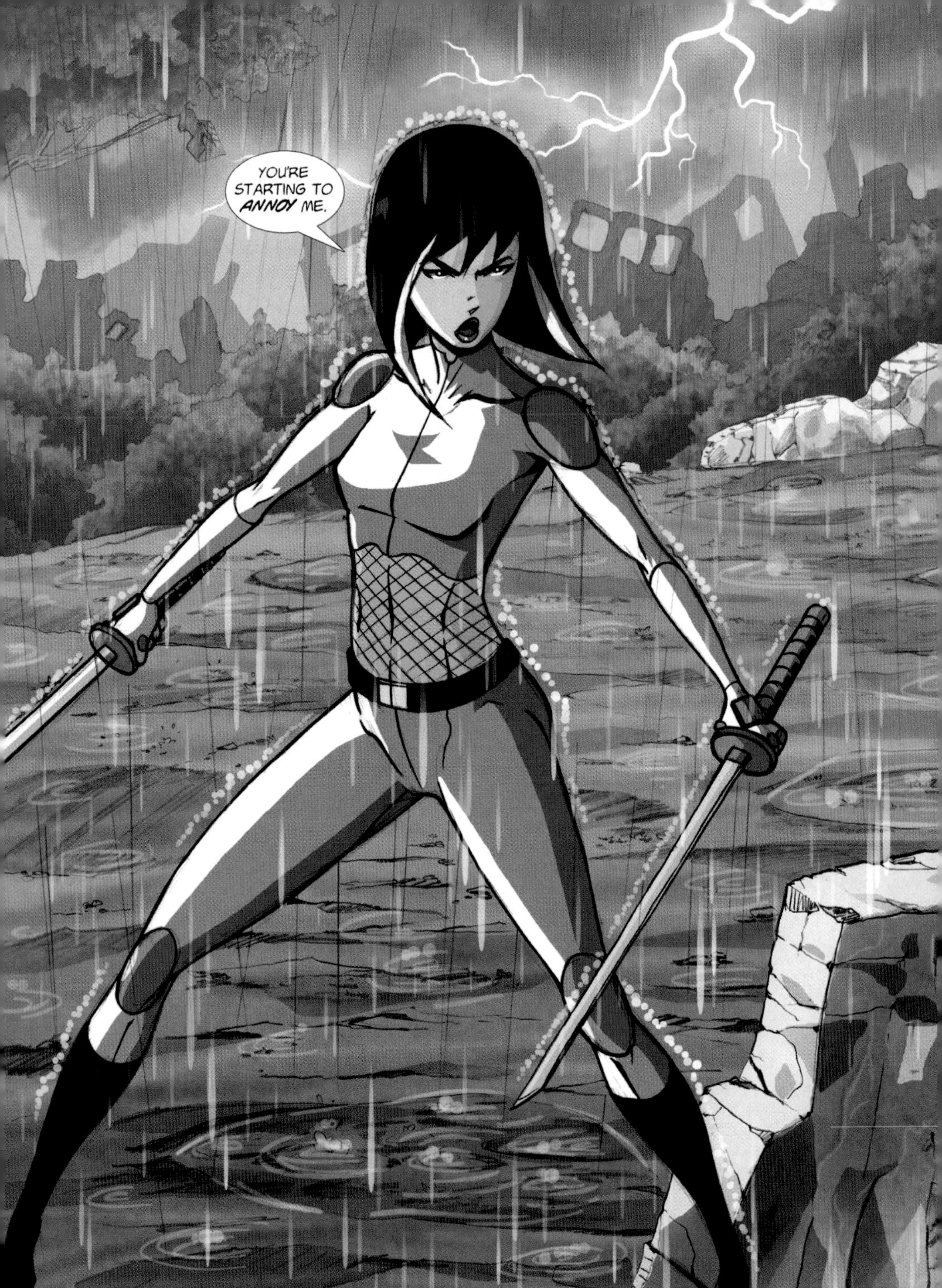
YOU'RE STARTING TO ANNOY ME.
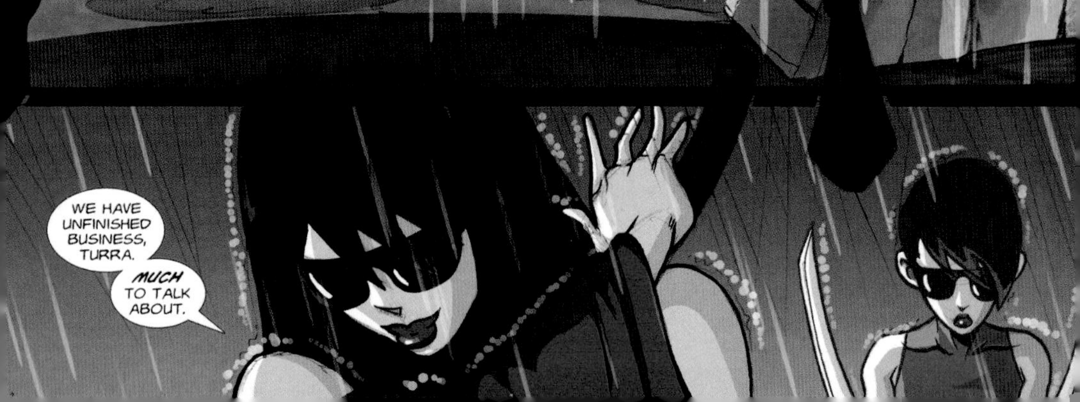
WE HAVE UNFINISHED BUSINESS, TURRA. MUCH TO TALK ABOUT.

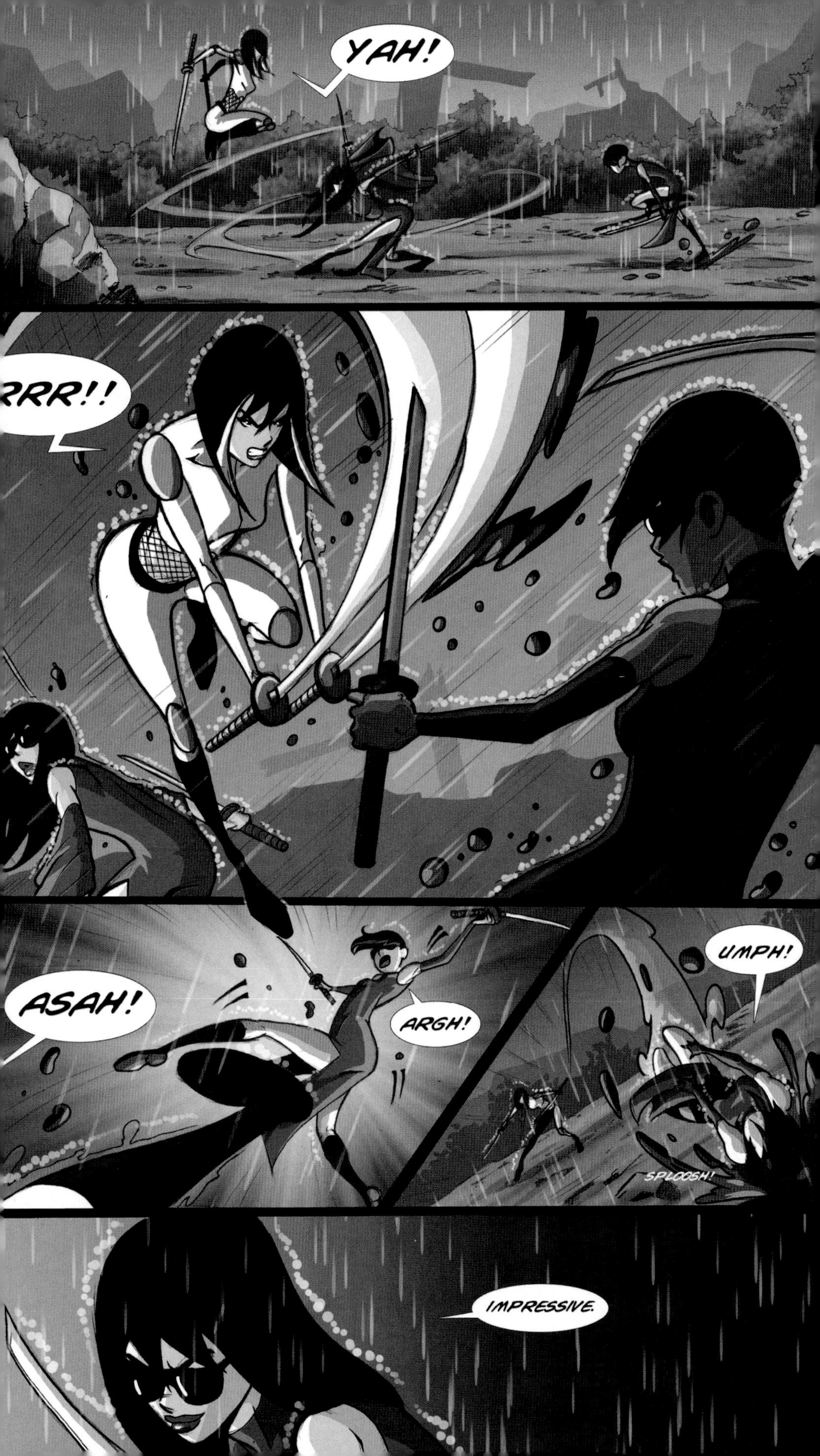
YAH!
RRR!!
ASAH!
ARGH!
UMPH!
SPLOOSH!
IMPRESSIVE.

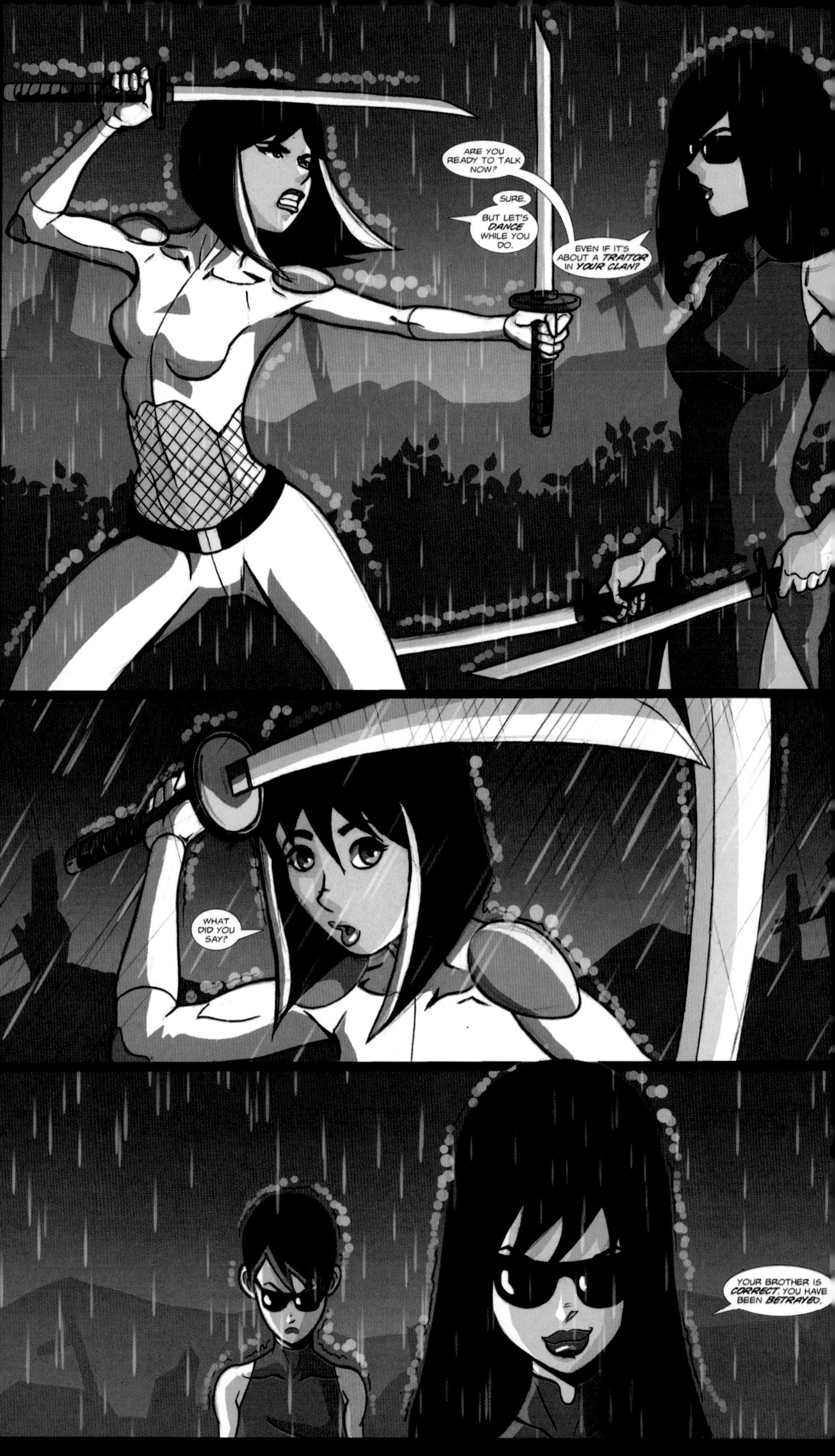
ARE YOU READY TO TALK NOW?
SURE, BUT LET'S *DANCE* WHILE YOU DO.
EVEN IF IT'S ABOUT A *TRAITOR* IN *YOUR CLAN?*
WHAT DID YOU SAY?
YOUR BROTHER IS *CORRECT*. YOU HAVE BEEN *BETRAYED*.

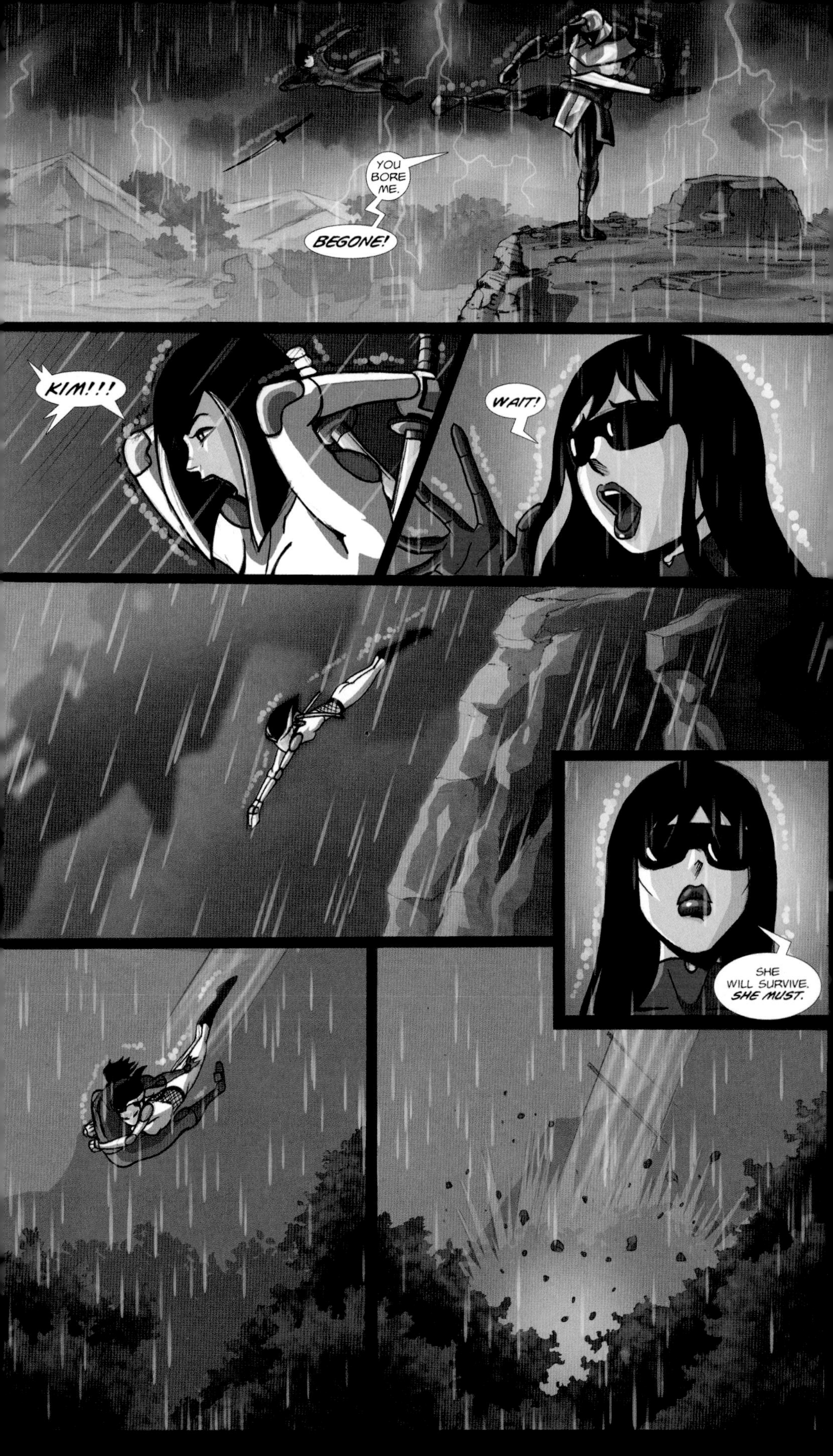
YOU BORE ME.
BEGONE!
KIM!!!
WAIT!
SHE WILL SURVIVE. SHE MUST.

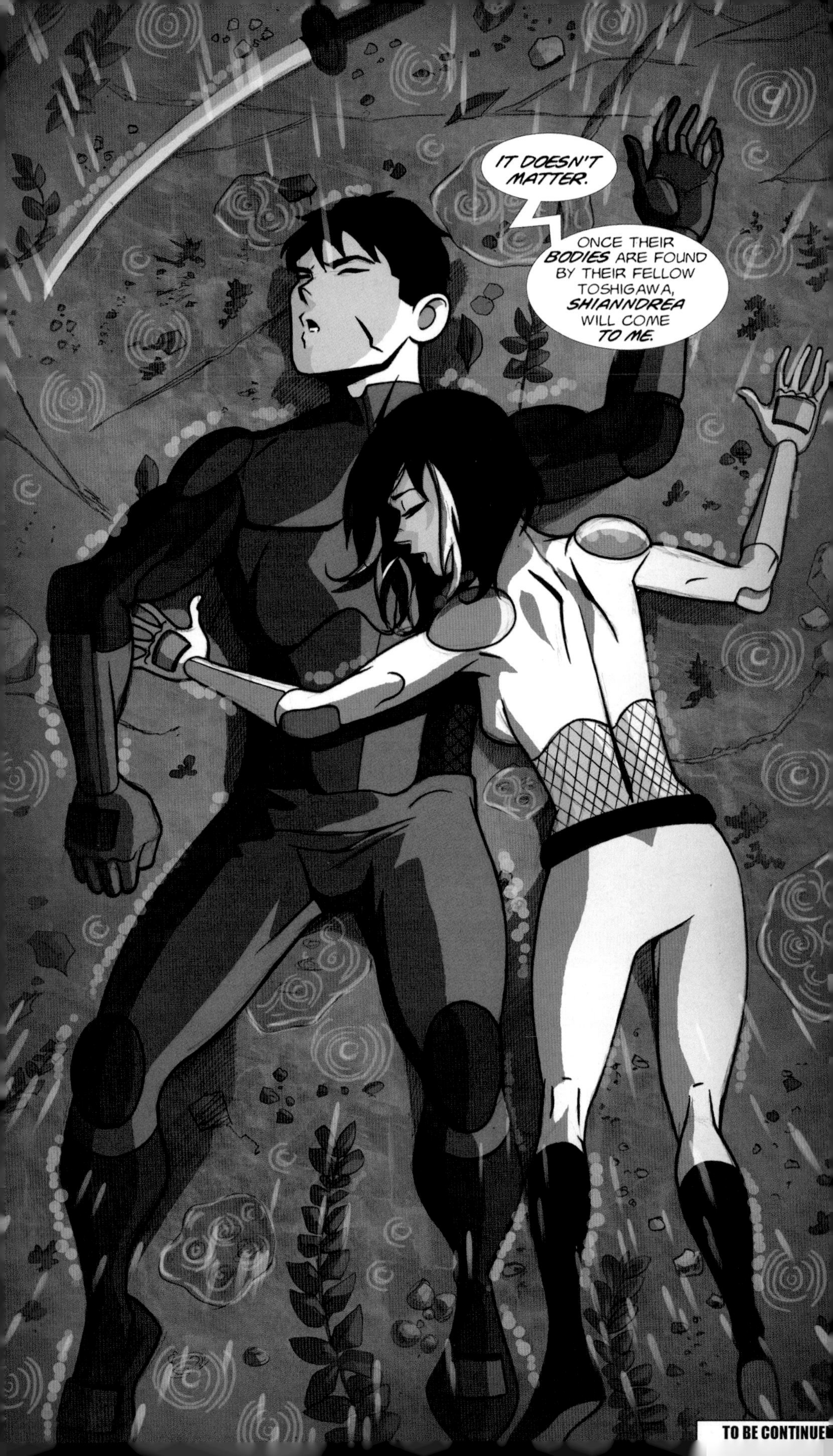
IT DOESN'T MATTER.
ONCE THEIR BODIES ARE FOUND BY THEIR FELLOW TOSHIGAWA, SHIANNDREA WILL COME TO ME.
TO BE CONTINUED

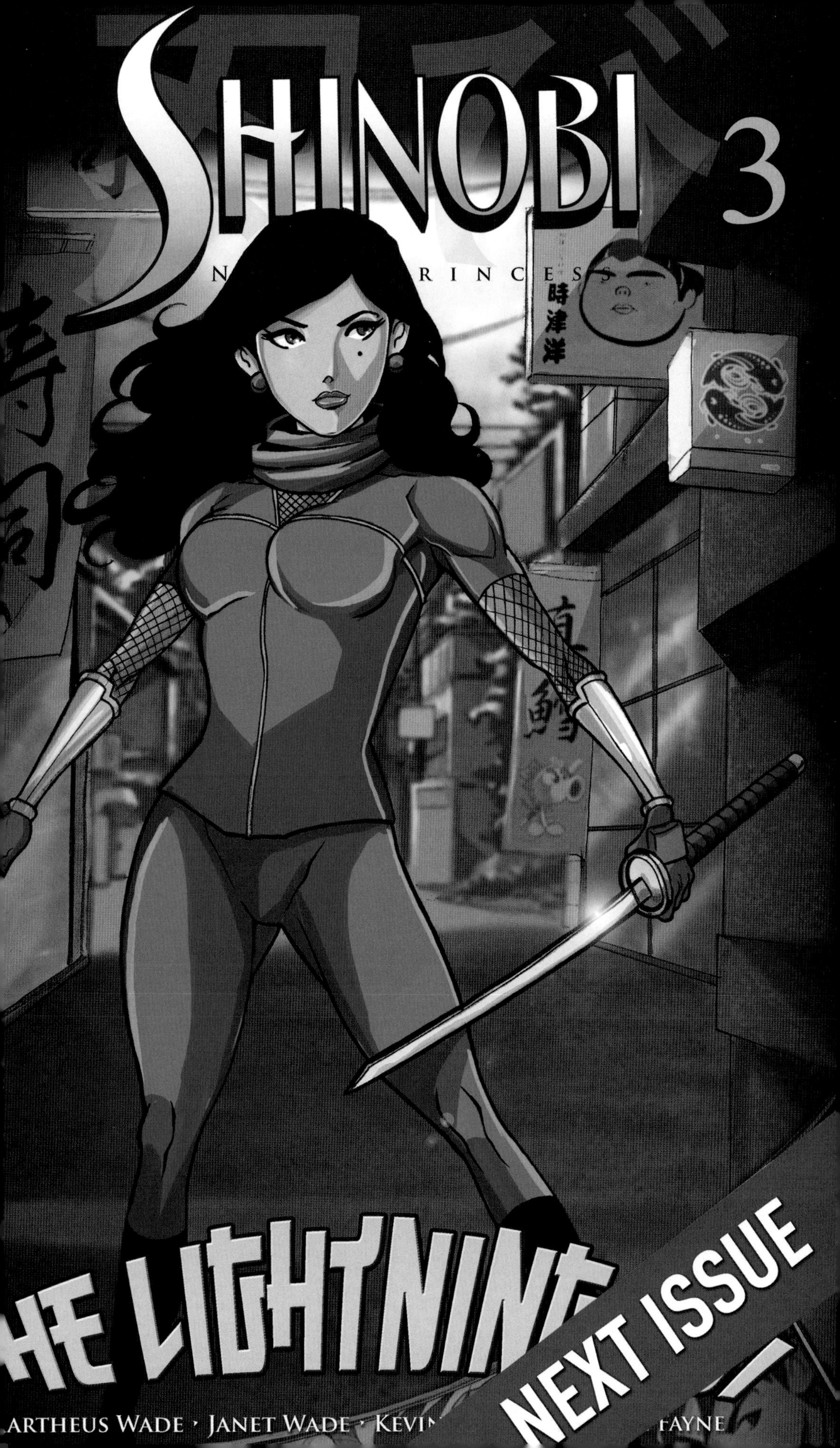
SHINOBI
3
N RINCESS
時津洋
HE LIGHTNIN
NEXT ISSUE
ARTHEUS WADE · JANET WADE · KEVIN
FAYNE

MEGUMI GOYA

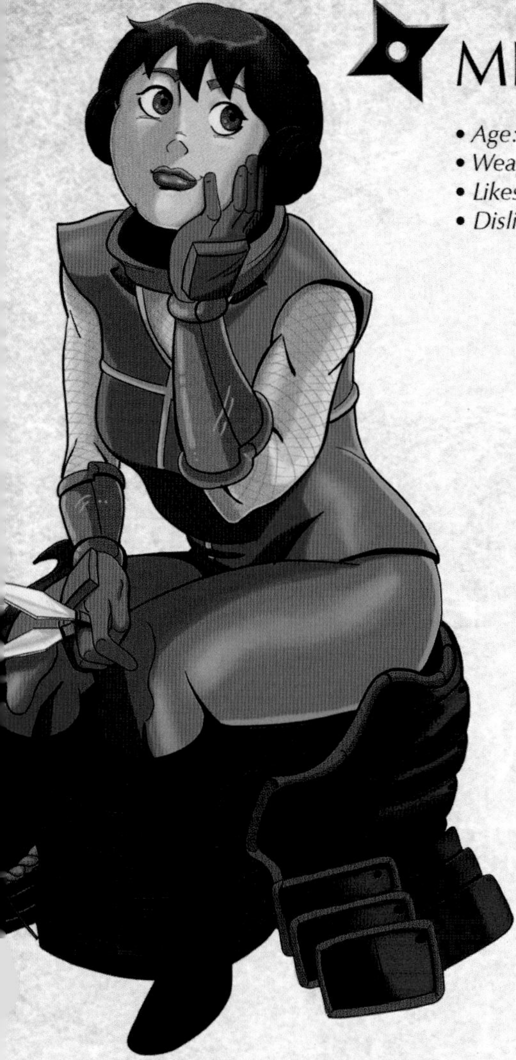

- *Age: 14*
- *Weapon: Exploding kunai*
- *Likes: Music, green tea mochi, the latest techno-gadgets*
- *Dislikes: Smack talkers*

If Shianndrea has a best friend, it's Megumi Goya. She is a loyal and good friend. Meek and very shy, Megumi and Shianndrea feed off of each others' confidence and can be seen whispering to each other in the corner about the guys that pass by. Although she is mostly shy, she is quick tempered when it comes to defending her friends, especially Shianndrea.

Megumi comes from a long line of Toshigawa supporters and has followed her lineage into the Toshigawa ninja ranks. However, her abilities are not what they should be. Although her ninja skill needs much work, her skills with throwing stars are almost unmatched. She often wishes she could leave the life of the ninja behind and pursue a life outside the clan. But she couldn't do so without her best friend.

Megumi hides a secret that only the Toshigawa Council of Elders know. She is very wealthy and is heir to Goya Industries which is currently (jointly) controlled by her brother, Sumaru Goya and the Emperor of Japan, Terminus.

w. He said you were perfect. That's the
st praise I've seen Kim give anyone.
egumi

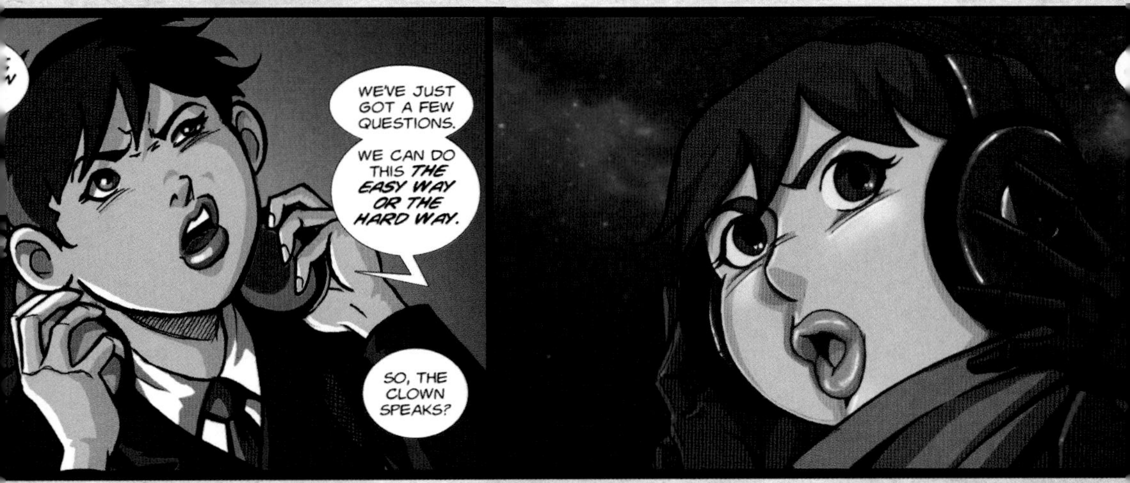
WE'VE JUST GOT A FEW QUESTIONS.
WE CAN DO THIS THE EASY WAY OR THE HARD WAY.
SO, THE CLOWN SPEAKS?

GAUDIENT SHIBAT

- *Age: 45*
- *Weapon: He IS a weapon*
- *Likes: Kim, Turra (sometimes), duty*
- *Dislikes: Everything*

Gaudient is a curmudgeon. If it's fun, he hates it. If it training, he loves it. He is the youngest member of the igawa Council of Elders, the commander of the ninja teams, and Turra and Kim's father. Strict and very Gaudient is a man of many secrets which have strain relationship with his daughter and has further harder heart. His main sense of pride comes from his duty son. In Kim, he sees the perfect ninja. However, Kim flaw is his secret compassion for a certain young ninj a poofy black ponytail. Gaudient wishes that was ar tion his son could purge.

This is war, Kim. Nothing is fair.
-Gaudient

FUJIKO ASUNA

- *Age: 15*
- *Weapon: Pink Katana*
- *Likes: Hamasuke, her crew, underlings*
- *Dislikes: Shianndrea, Shianndrea, Shianndrea!!*

If there were ever a poster girl for "The Mean Girl", it would be Fujiko. She takes great pride in being the "Alpha" in her crew of mean girls that follow her around and answer to her every whim. Her only weakness is Hamasuke, who she believes is the best (and cutest) ninja warrior around. However, because he was injured in a battle where he tried defending Shianndrea, Fujiko has focused her attention on bringing the "Ninja Princess" down a peg. Cold, calculating, and conniving, Fujiko is always looking for a way to discredit Shianndrea. However, don't think she is a pushover when it comes to hand-to-hand combat. Fujiko can battle with the best of them, making this blonde ninja a force to be reckoned with.

I HATE SHIANNDREA TOSHIGAWA! I'd
like nothing more than to take that poofy
black ponytail and stick it in some mud!
-Fujiko

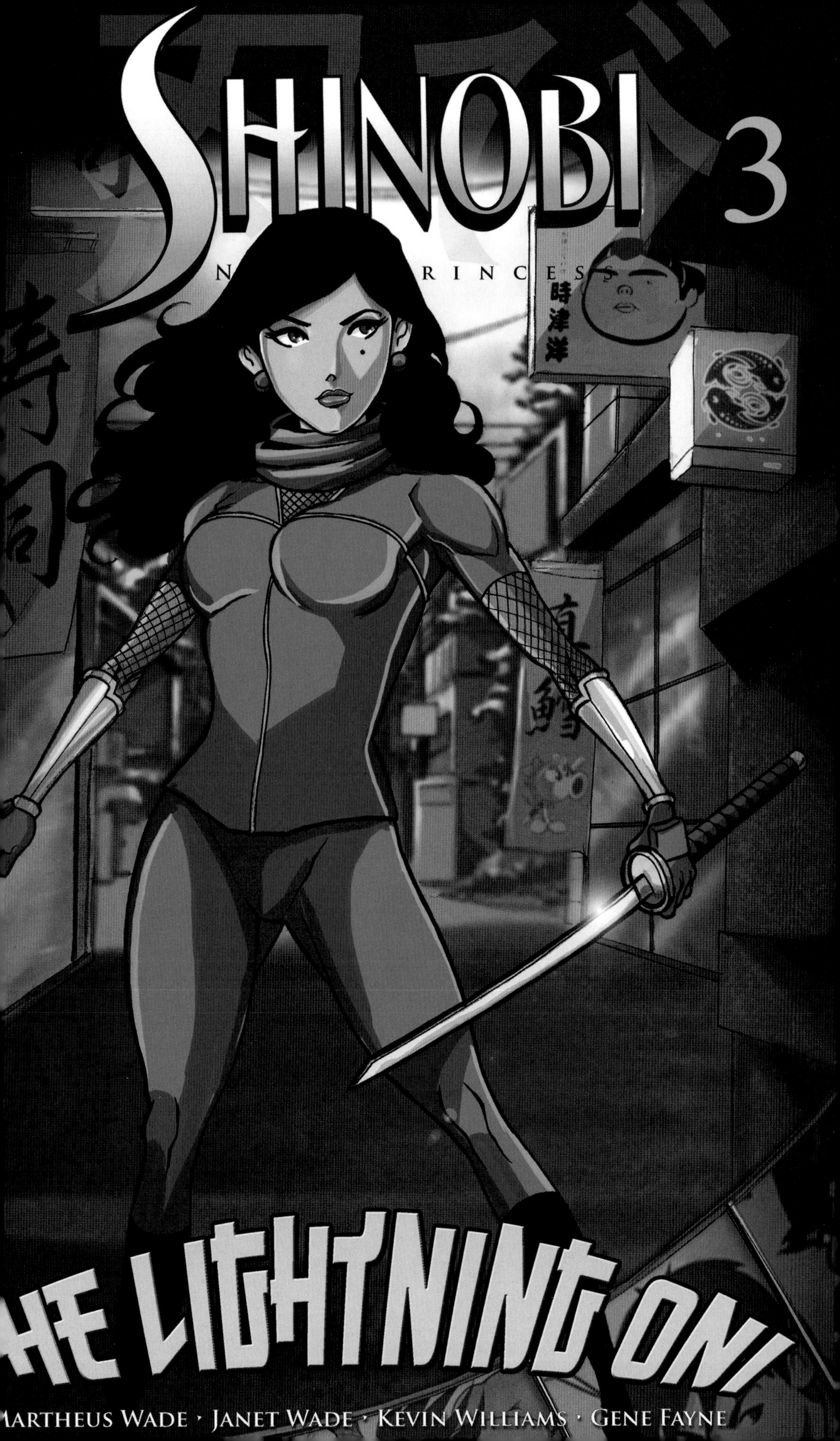
SHINOBI
3
時津洋
HE LIGHTNING ONI
ARTHEUS WADE · JANET WADE · KEVIN WILLIAMS · GENE FAYNE

ILLUSTRATIONS BY: MARTHEUS WADE
WRITEN BY: MARTHEUS AND JANET WADE
INTERIOR COLORS BY: GENE FAYNE
COVER BY: MARTHEUS WADE
©2017 MAW PRODUCTIONS

Bryan Seaton: Publisher/ CEO • Shawn Gabborin: Editor
Jason Martin: Publisher-Danger Zone • Nicole D'Andria: Marketing Dire
Danielle Davison: Executive Administrator • Chad Cicconi: Noodle On
Pryor: President of Creato

SHINOBI: NINJA PRINCESS: THE LIGHTNING ONI #3, N
2017. Copyright Martheus Antone Wade, 2017. Pub
Action Lab Entertainment. All rights reserved. All ch
are fictional. Any likeness to anyone living or dead
coincidental. No part of this publication may be repro
transmitted without permission, except for review p
Printed in Canada. First

YEARS AGO

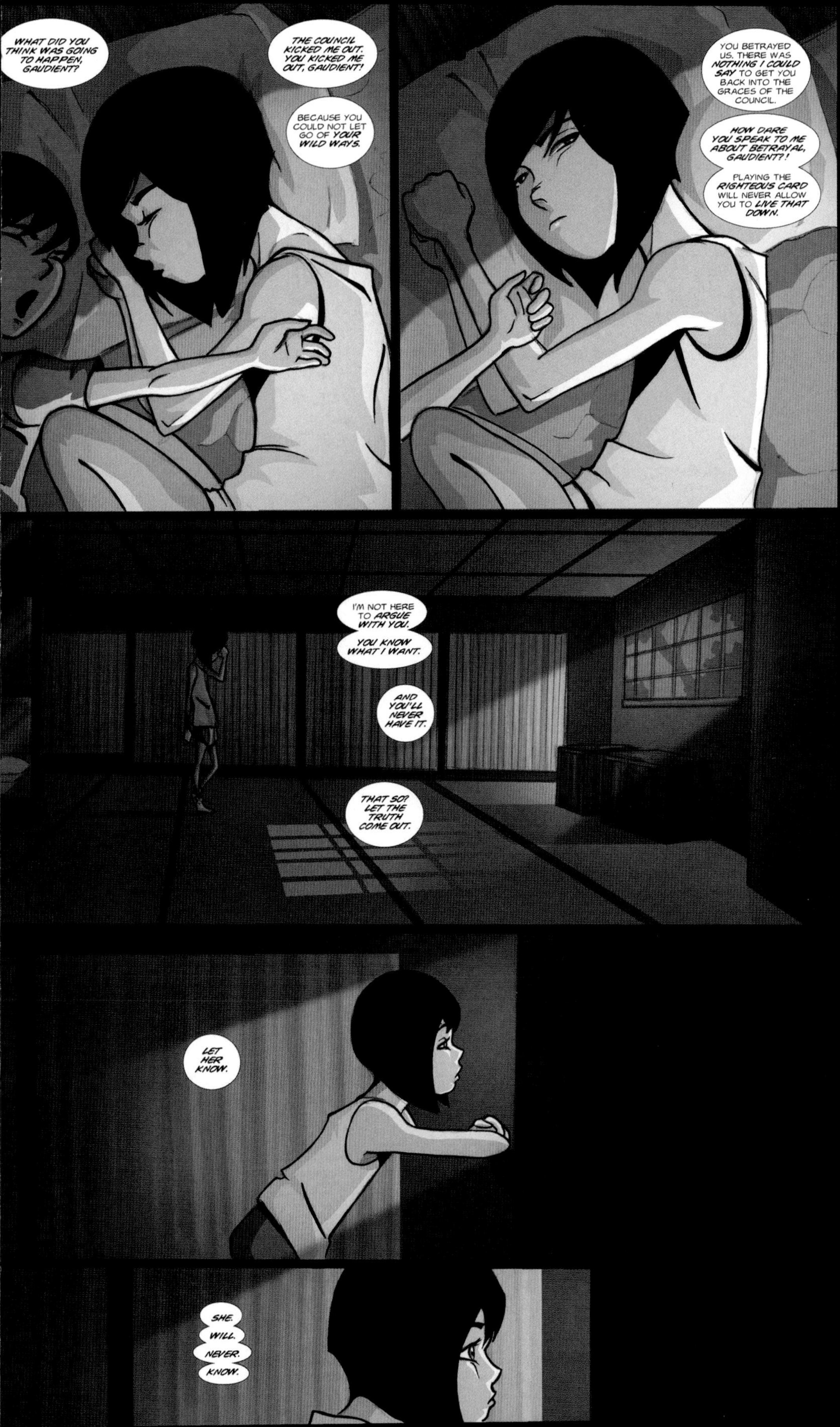
WHAT DID YOU THINK WAS GOING TO HAPPEN, GAUDIENT?
THE COUNCIL KICKED ME OUT. YOU KICKED ME OUT, GAUDIENT!
BECAUSE YOU COULD NOT LET GO OF YOUR WILD WAYS.
YOU BETRAYED US. THERE WAS NOTHING I COULD SAY TO GET YOU BACK INTO THE GRACES OF THE COUNCIL.
HOW DARE YOU SPEAK TO ME ABOUT BETRAYAL, GAUDIENT?!
PLAYING THE RIGHTEOUS CARD WILL NEVER ALLOW YOU TO LIVE THAT DOWN.
I'M NOT HERE TO ARGUE WITH YOU.
YOU KNOW WHAT I WANT.
AND YOU'LL NEVER HAVE IT.
THAT SO? LET THE TRUTH COME OUT.
LET HER KNOW.
SHE.
WILL.
NEVER.
KNOW.

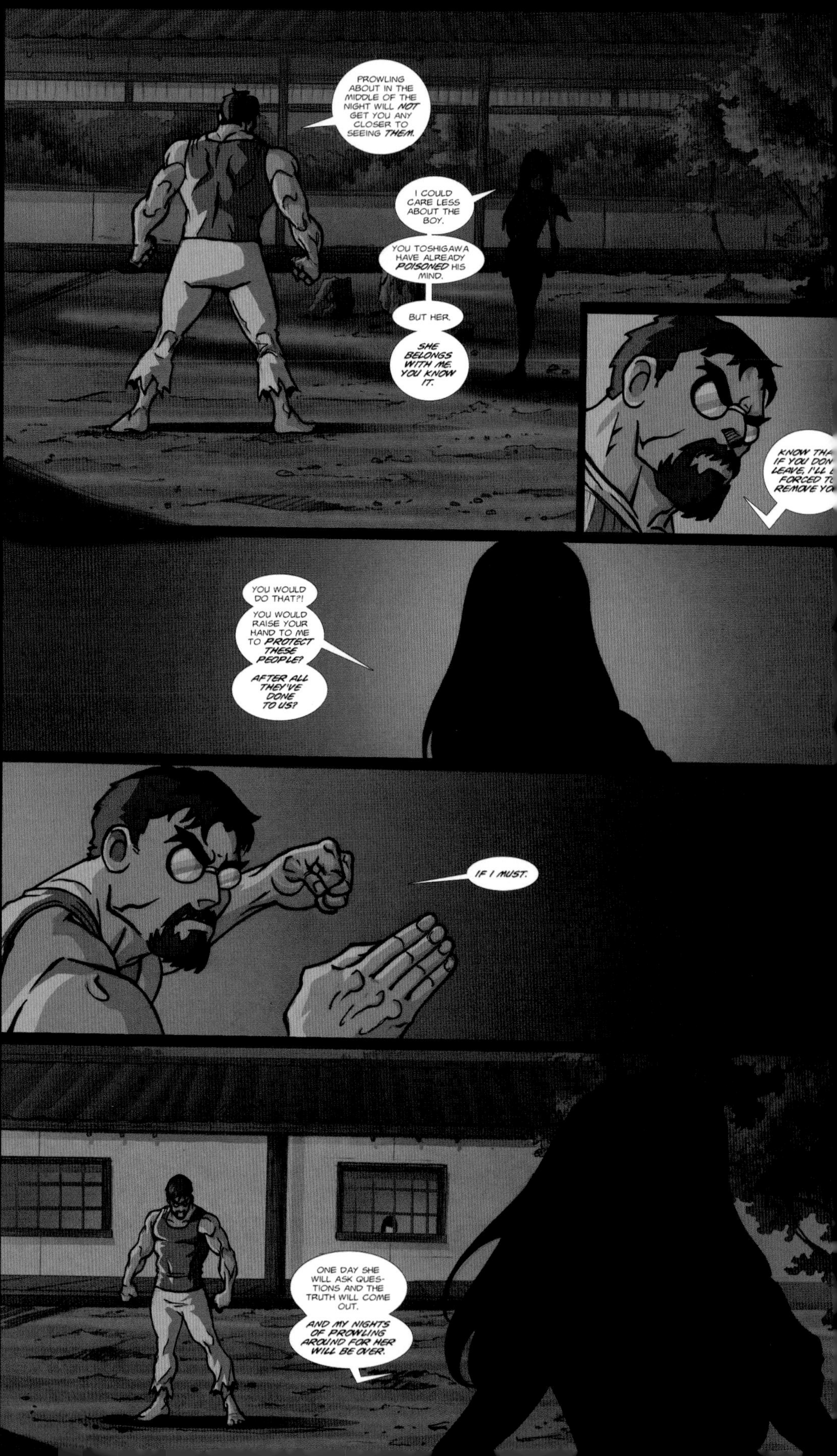
PROWLING ABOUT IN THE MIDDLE OF THE NIGHT WILL *NOT* GET YOU ANY CLOSER TO SEEING *THEM*.
I COULD CARE LESS ABOUT THE BOY.
YOU TOSHIGAWA HAVE ALREADY *POISONED* HIS MIND.
BUT HER.
SHE BELONGS WITH ME. YOU KNOW IT.
KNOW THA IF YOU DON LEAVE, I'LL FORCED T REMOVE YO
YOU WOULD DO THAT?!
YOU WOULD RAISE YOUR HAND TO ME TO *PROTECT THESE PEOPLE?*
AFTER ALL THEY'VE DONE TO US?
IF I MUST.
ONE DAY SHE WILL ASK QUES-TIONS AND THE TRUTH WILL COME OUT.
AND MY NIGHTS OF PROWLING AROUND FOR HER WILL BE OVER.

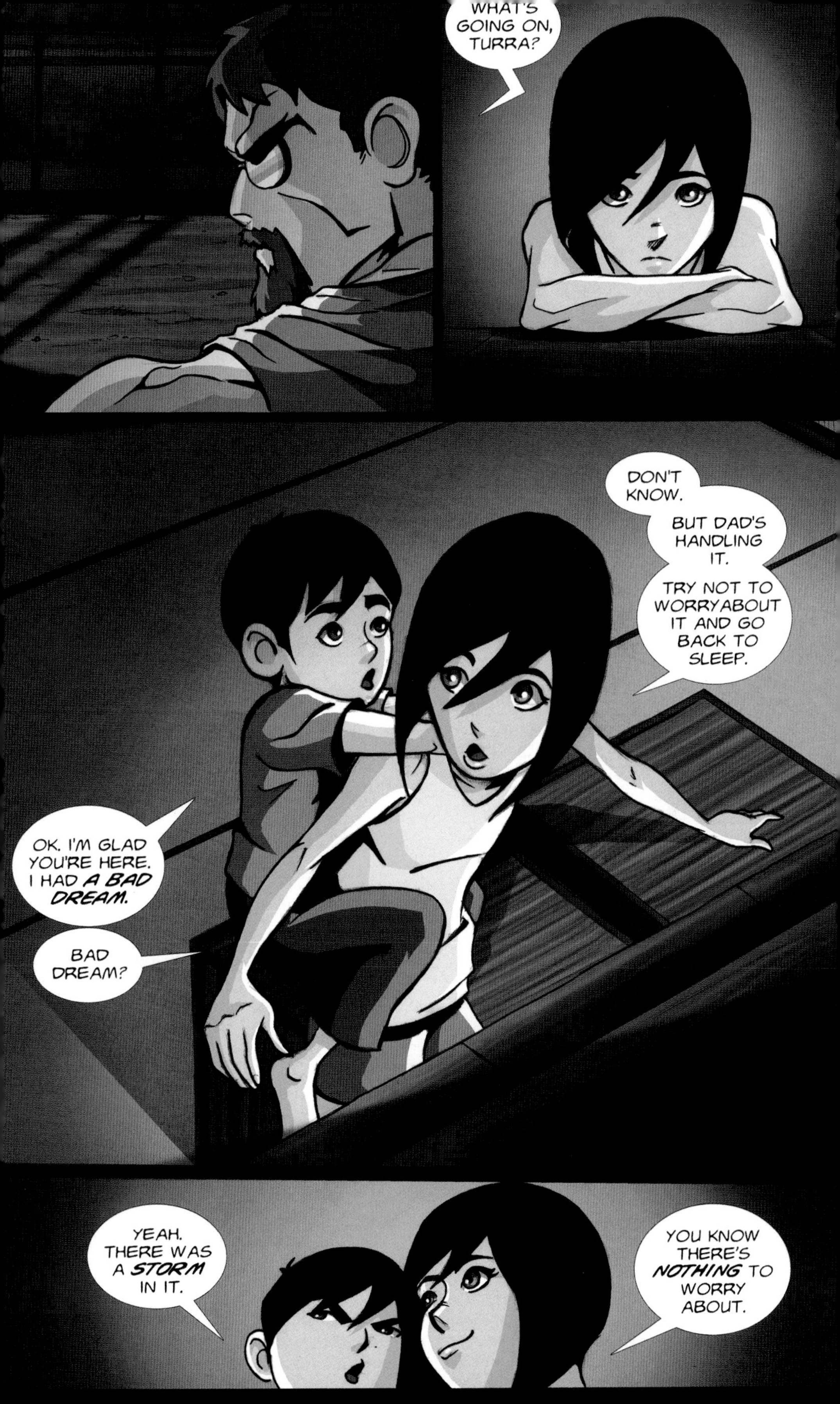
WHAT'S GOING ON, TURRA?
DON'T KNOW.
BUT DAD'S HANDLING IT.
TRY NOT TO WORRYABOUT IT AND GO BACK TO SLEEP.
OK. I'M GLAD YOU'RE HERE. I HAD *A BAD DREAM.*
BAD DREAM?
YEAH. THERE WAS A *STORM* IN IT.
YOU KNOW THERE'S *NOTHING* TO WORRY ABOUT.

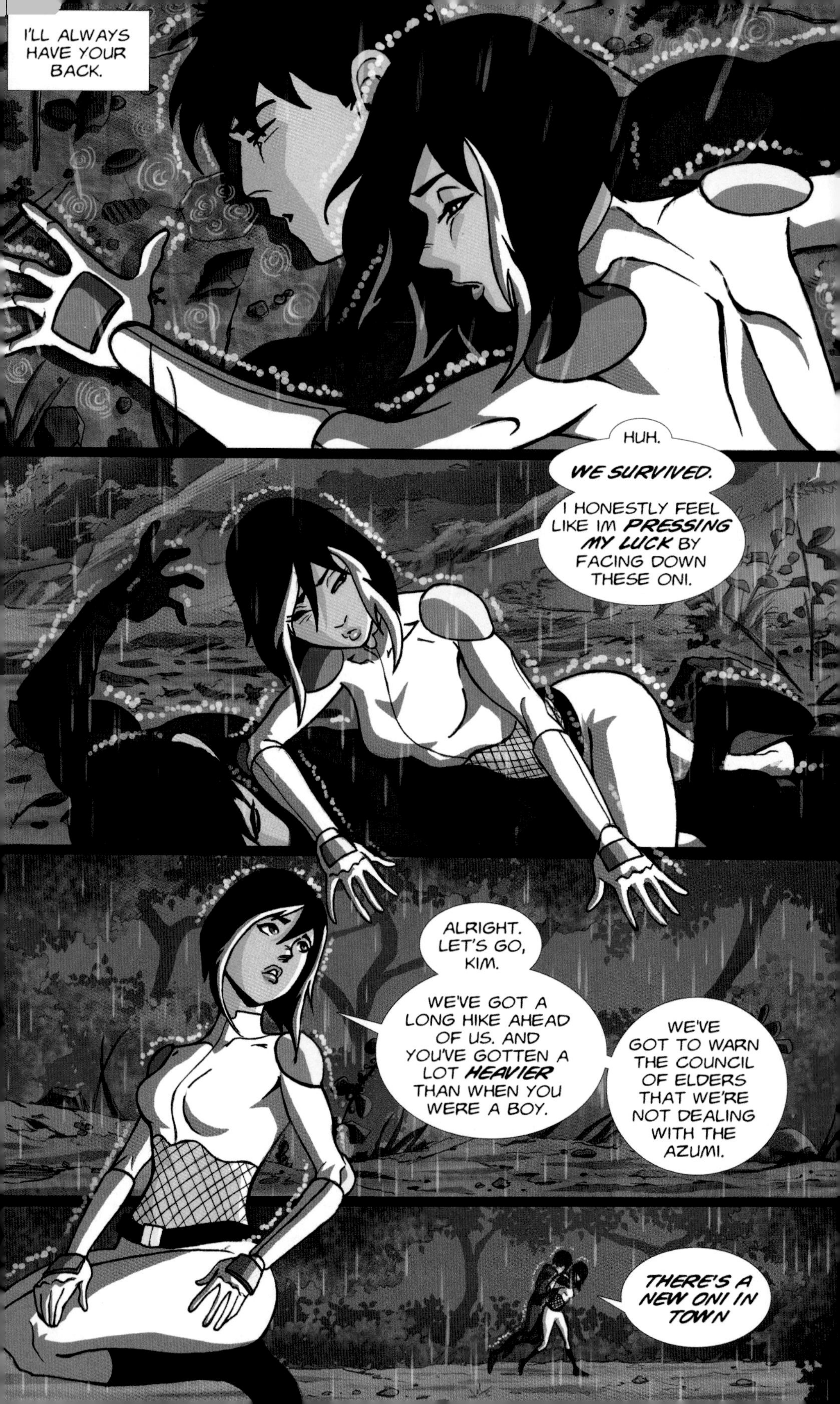
I'LL ALWAYS HAVE YOUR BACK.
HUH.
WE SURVIVED.
I HONESTLY FEEL LIKE IM PRESSING MY LUCK BY FACING DOWN THESE ONI.
ALRIGHT. LET'S GO, KIM.
WE'VE GOT A LONG HIKE AHEAD OF US. AND YOU'VE GOTTEN A LOT HEAVIER THAN WHEN YOU WERE A BOY.
WE'VE GOT TO WARN THE COUNCIL OF ELDERS THAT WE'RE NOT DEALING WITH THE AZUMI.
THERE'S A NEW ONI IN TOWN

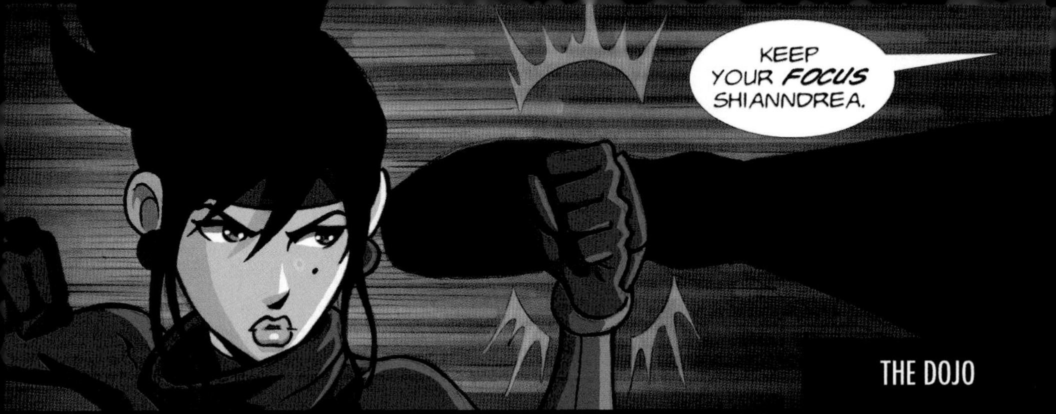
KEEP YOUR FOCUS SHIANNDREA.
THE DOJO

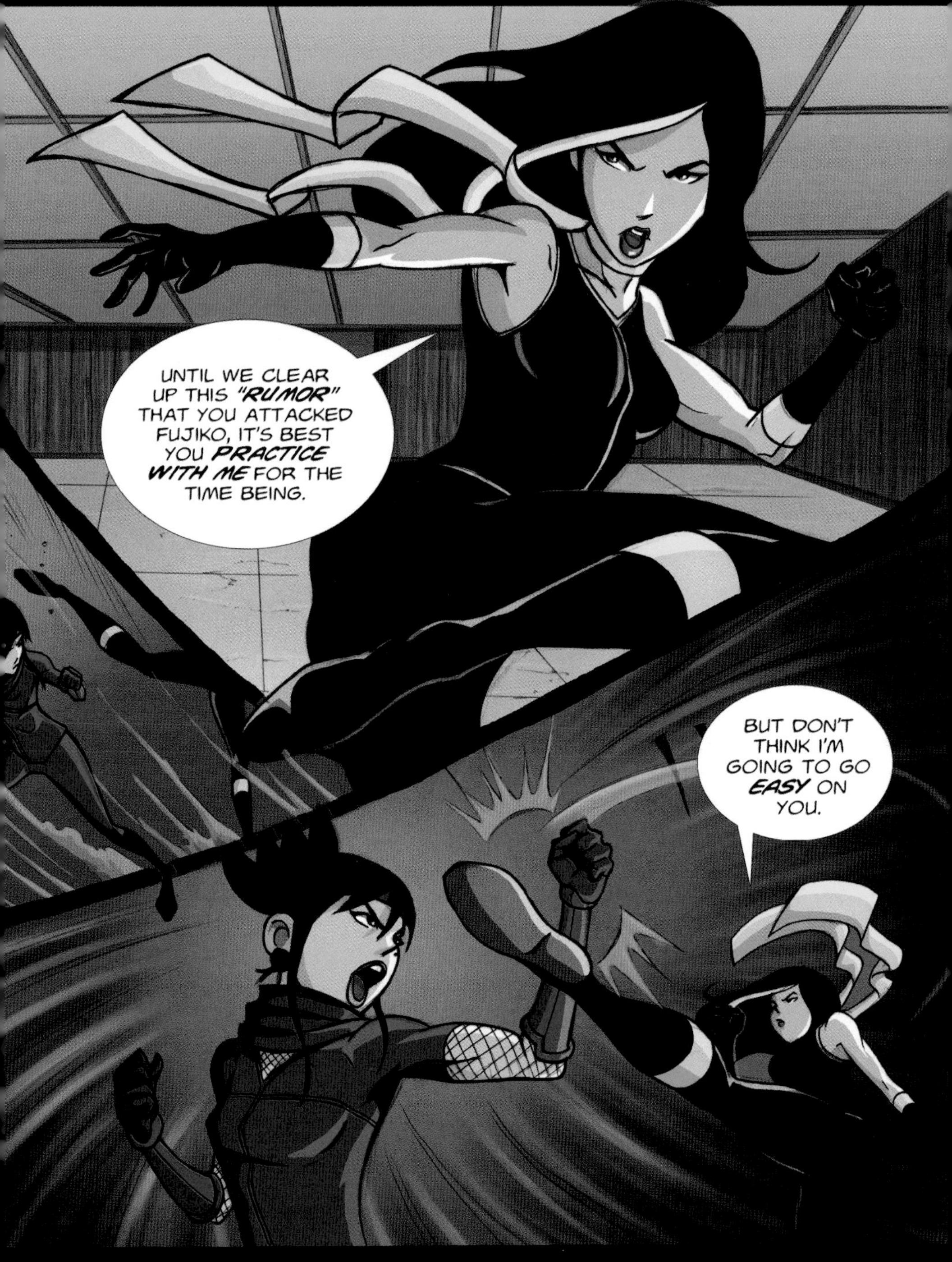
UNTIL WE CLEAR UP THIS "RUMOR" THAT YOU ATTACKED FUJIKO, IT'S BEST YOU PRACTICE WITH ME FOR THE TIME BEING.
BUT DON'T THINK I'M GOING TO GO EASY ON YOU.

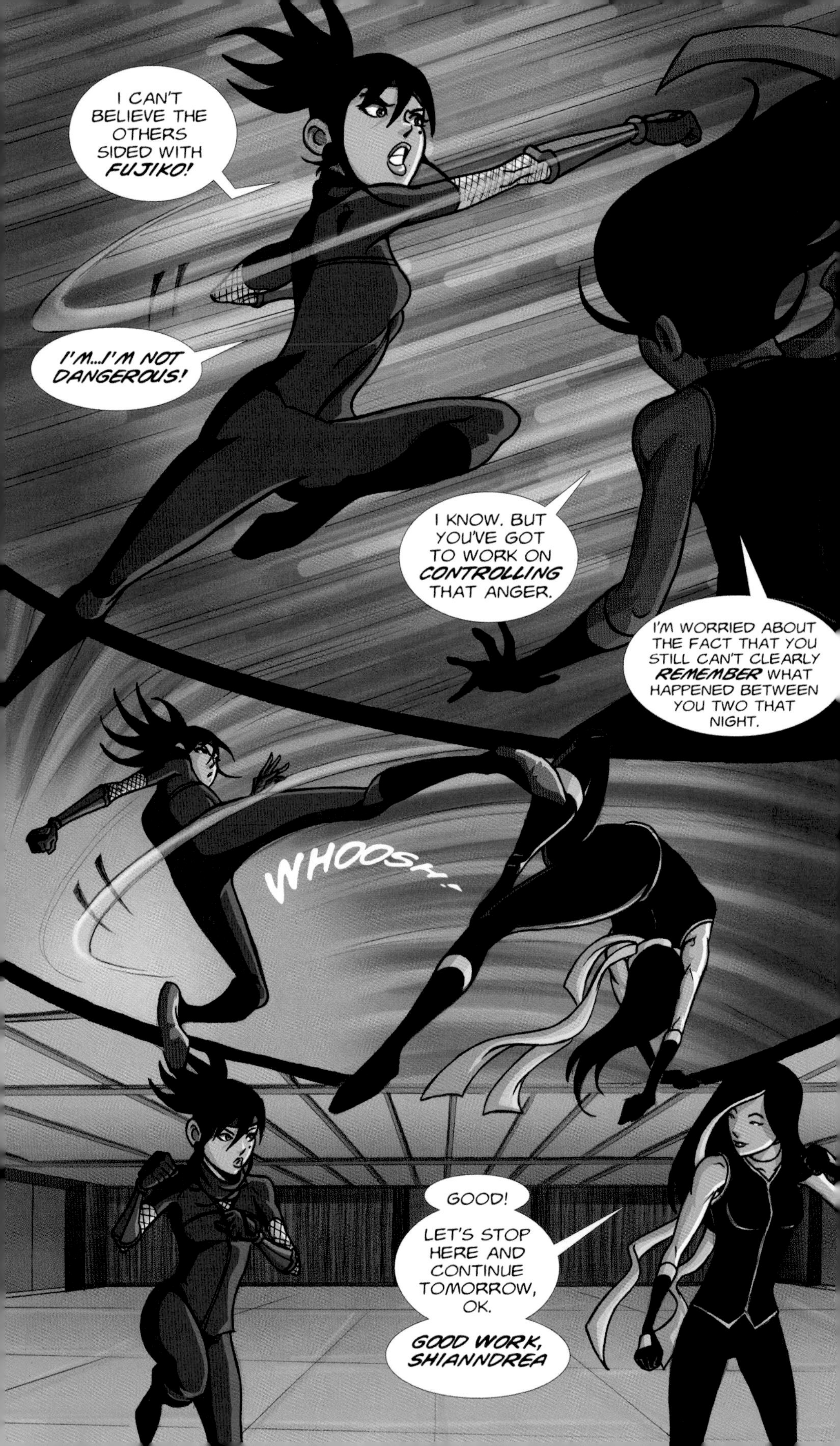
I CAN'T BELIEVE THE OTHERS SIDED WITH FUJIKO!
I'M...I'M NOT DANGEROUS!
I KNOW. BUT YOU'VE GOT TO WORK ON CONTROLLING THAT ANGER.
I'M WORRIED ABOUT THE FACT THAT YOU STILL CAN'T CLEARLY REMEMBER WHAT HAPPENED BETWEEN YOU TWO THAT NIGHT.
WHOOSH!
GOOD!
LET'S STOP HERE AND CONTINUE TOMORROW, OK.
GOOD WORK, SHIANNDREA

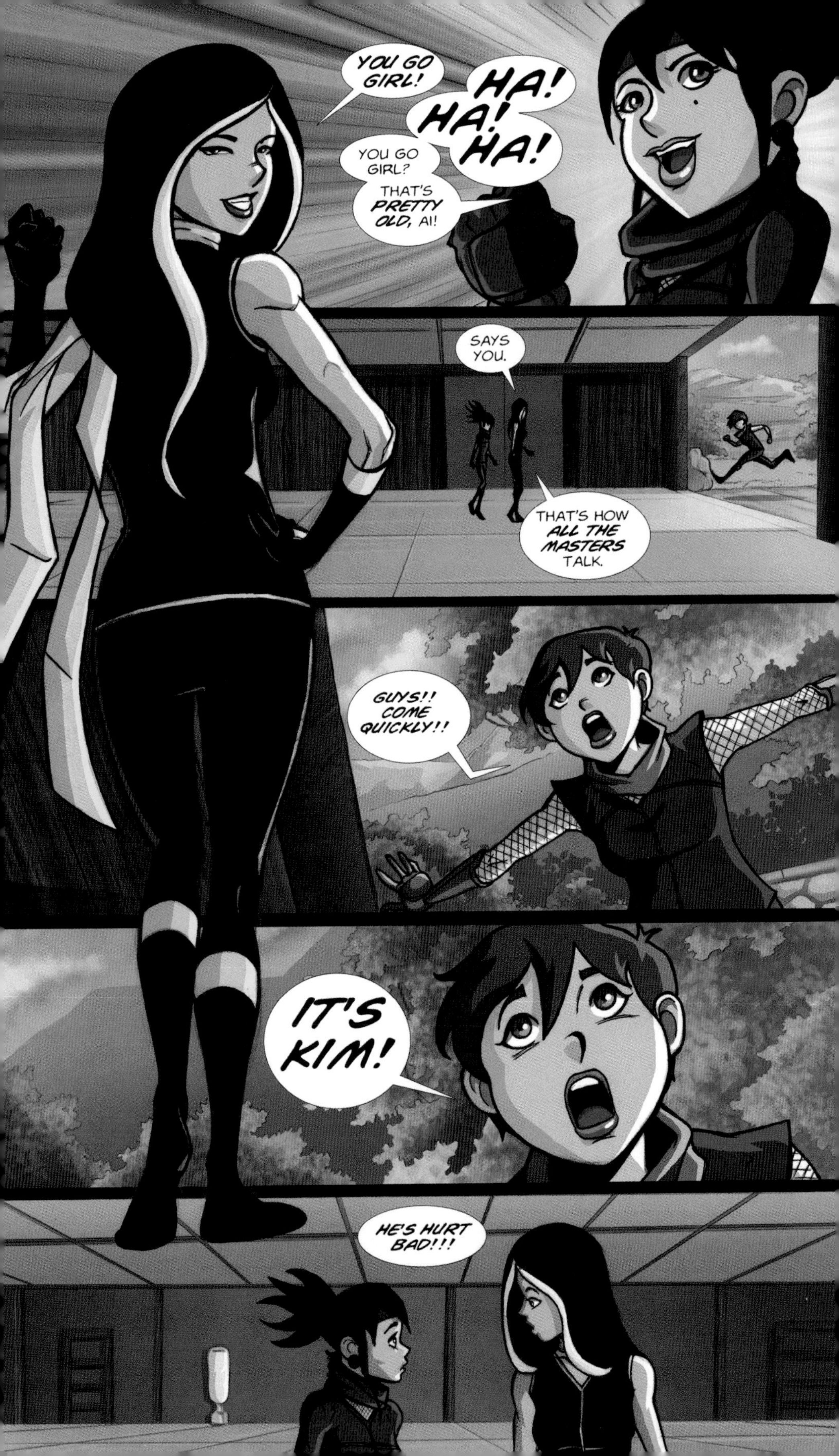
YOU GO GIRL!
HA! HA! HA!
YOU GO GIRL?
THAT'S PRETTY OLD, AI!
SAYS YOU.
THAT'S HOW ALL THE MASTERS TALK.
GUYS!! COME QUICKLY!!
IT'S KIM!
HE'S HURT BAD!!!

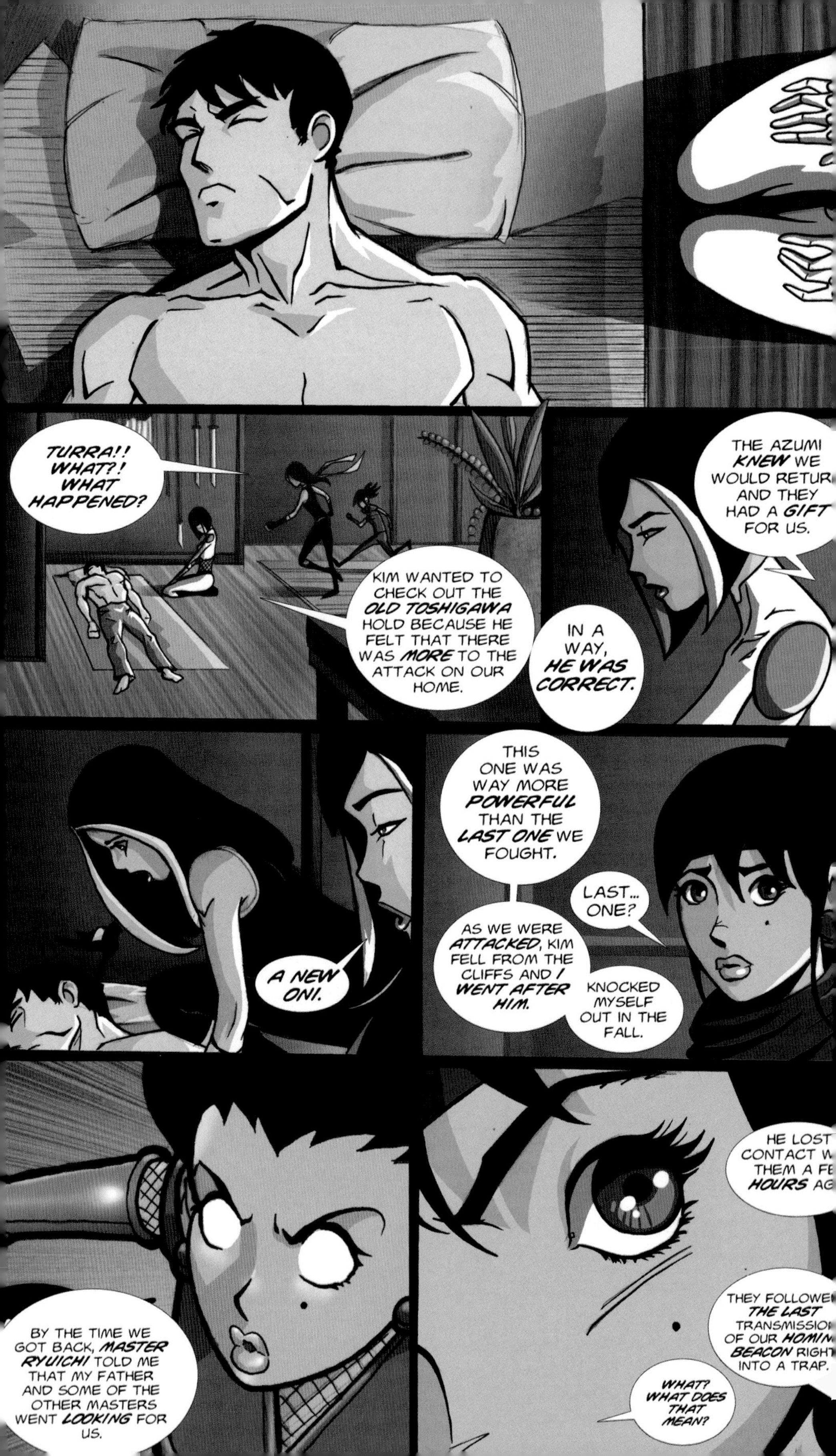
TURRA!! WHAT?! WHAT HAPPENED?
KIM WANTED TO CHECK OUT THE OLD TOSHIGAWA HOLD BECAUSE HE FELT THAT THERE WAS MORE TO THE ATTACK ON OUR HOME.
IN A WAY, HE WAS CORRECT.
THE AZUMI KNEW WE WOULD RETUR
AND THEY HAD A GIFT FOR US.
A NEW ONI.
THIS ONE WAS WAY MORE POWERFUL THAN THE LAST ONE WE FOUGHT.
LAST... ONE?
AS WE WERE ATTACKED, KIM FELL FROM THE CLIFFS AND I WENT AFTER HIM.
KNOCKED MYSELF OUT IN THE FALL.
BY THE TIME WE GOT BACK, MASTER RYUICHI TOLD ME THAT MY FATHER AND SOME OF THE OTHER MASTERS WENT LOOKING FOR US.
HE LOST CONTACT W THEM A FE HOURS AG
THEY FOLLOWE THE LAST TRANSMISSIO OF OUR HOMIN BEACON RIGHT INTO A TRAP.
WHAT? WHAT DOES THAT MEAN?

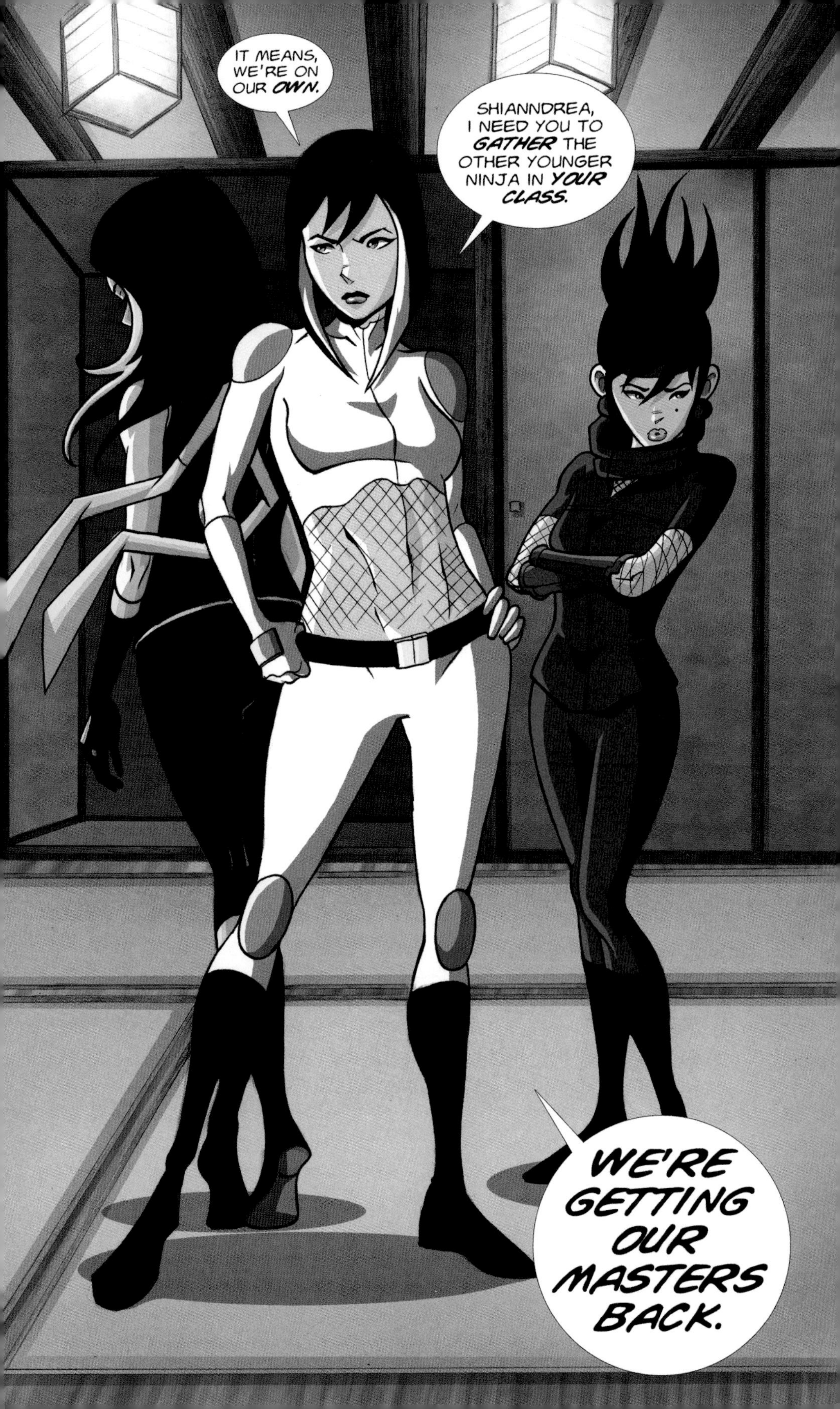
IT MEANS, WE'RE ON OUR OWN.
SHIANNDREA, I NEED YOU TO GATHER THE OTHER YOUNGER NINJA IN YOUR CLASS.
WE'RE GETTING OUR MASTERS BACK.

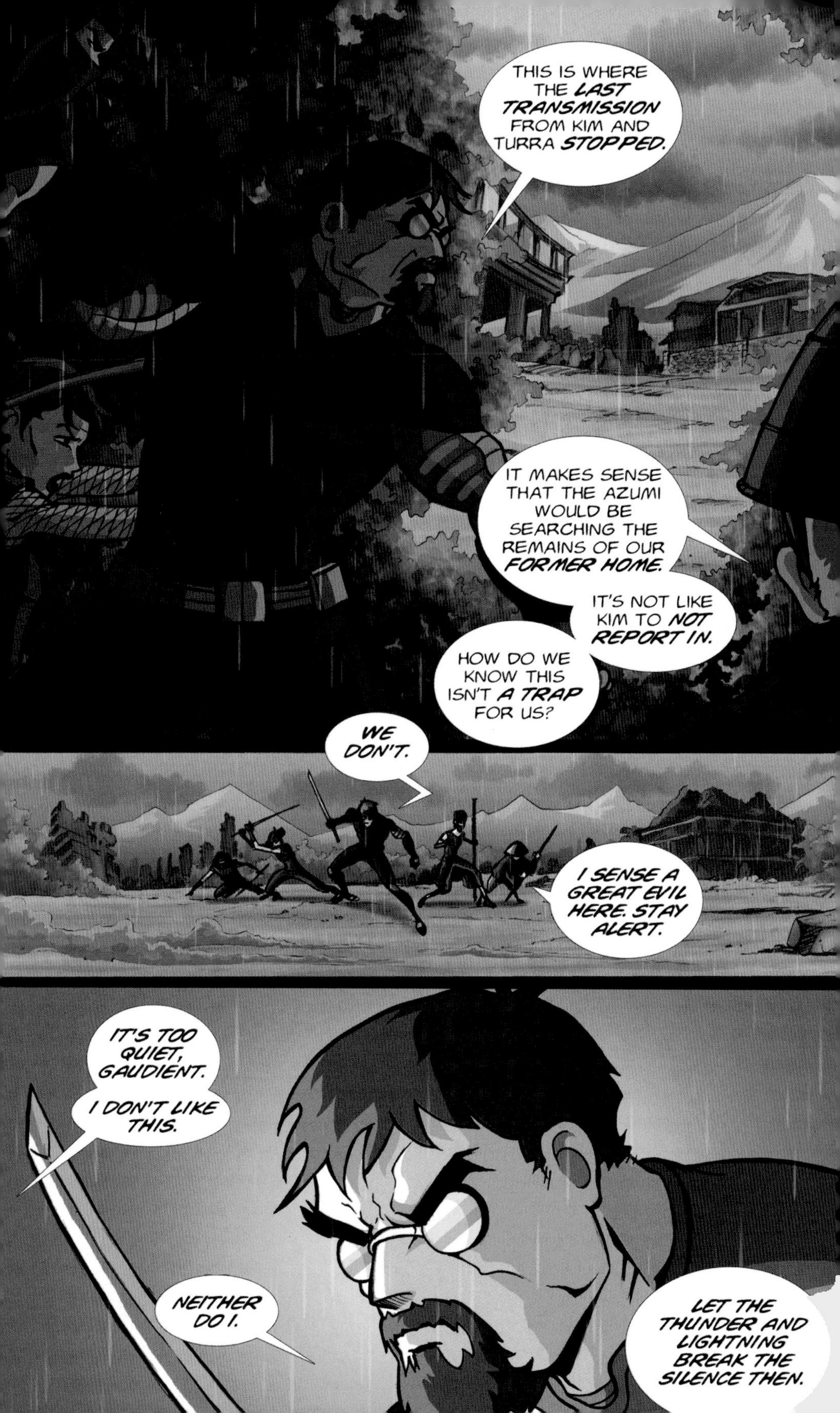
THIS IS WHERE THE *LAST TRANSMISSION* FROM KIM AND TURRA *STOPPED.*
IT MAKES SENSE THAT THE AZUMI WOULD BE SEARCHING THE REMAINS OF OUR *FORMER HOME.*
IT'S NOT LIKE KIM TO *NOT REPORT IN.*
HOW DO WE KNOW THIS ISN'T *A TRAP* FOR US?
WE DON'T.
I SENSE A GREAT EVIL HERE. STAY ALERT.
IT'S TOO QUIET, GAUDIENT.
I DON'T LIKE THIS.
NEITHER DO I.
LET THE THUNDER AND LIGHTNING BREAK THE SILENCE THEN.

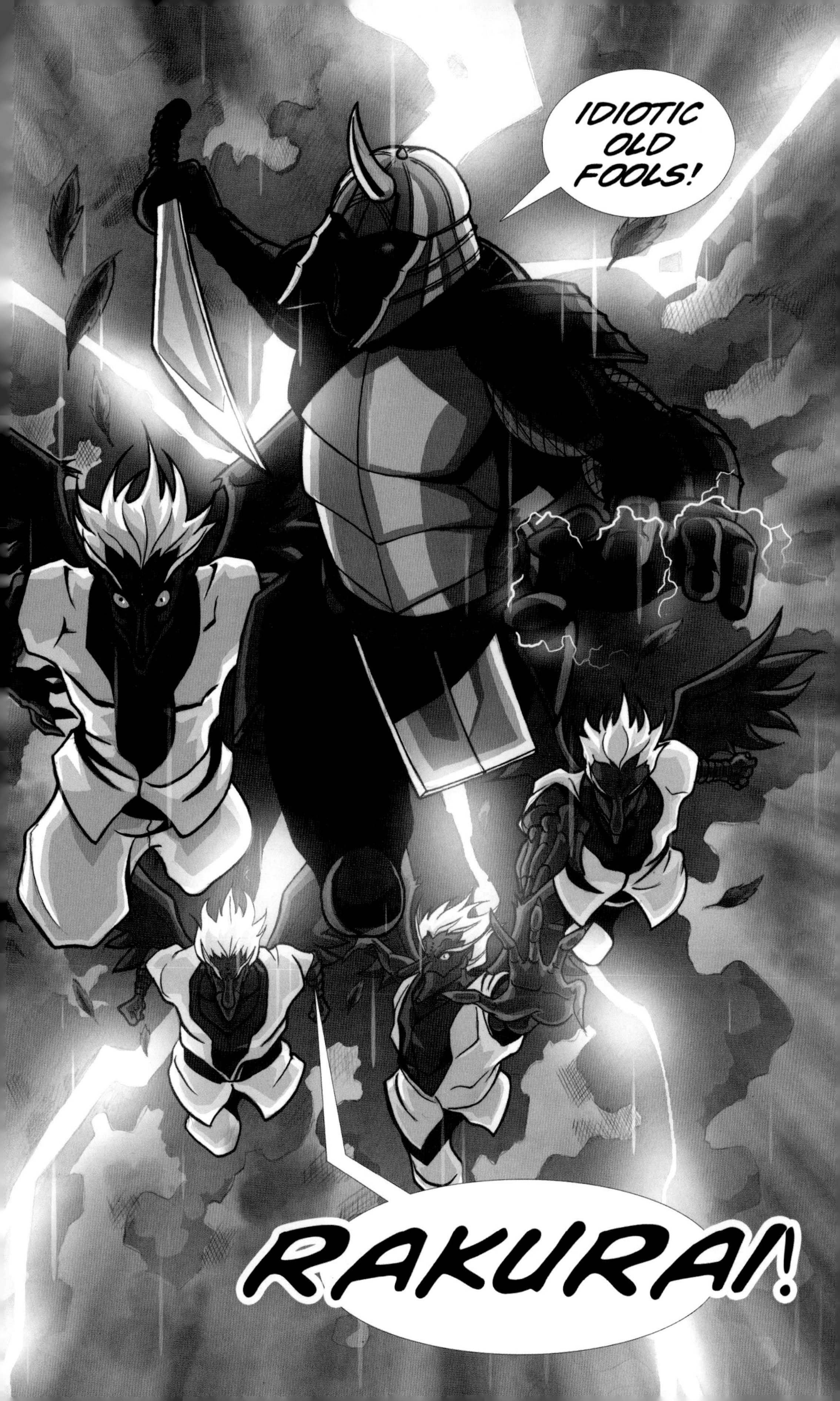
IDIOTIC OLD FOOLS!
RAKURAI!

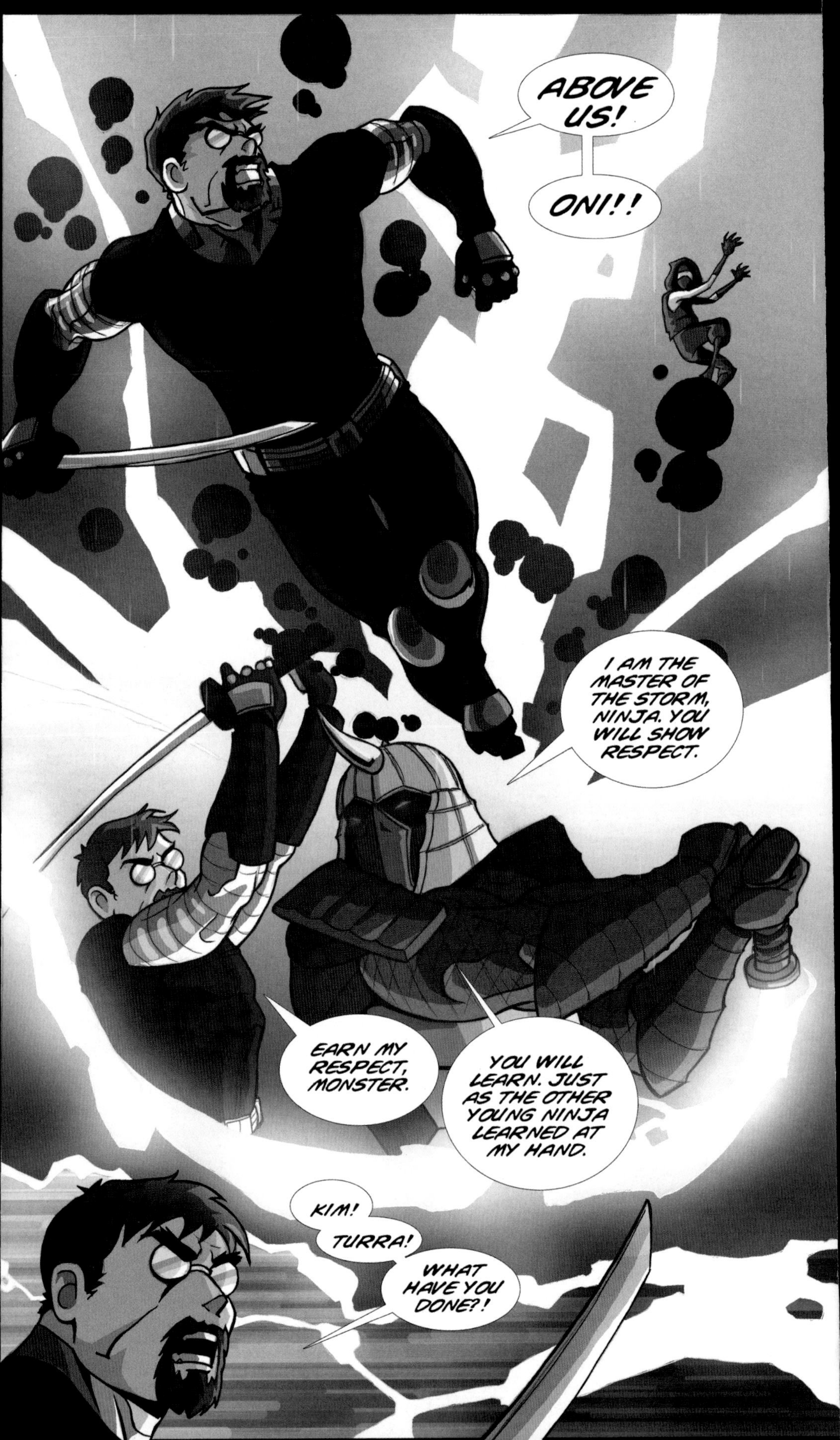
ABOVE US!
ONI!!
I AM THE MASTER OF THE STORM, NINJA. YOU WILL SHOW RESPECT.
EARN MY RESPECT, MONSTER.
YOU WILL LEARN. JUST AS THE OTHER YOUNG NINJA LEARNED AT MY HAND.
KIM!
TURRA!
WHAT HAVE YOU DONE?!

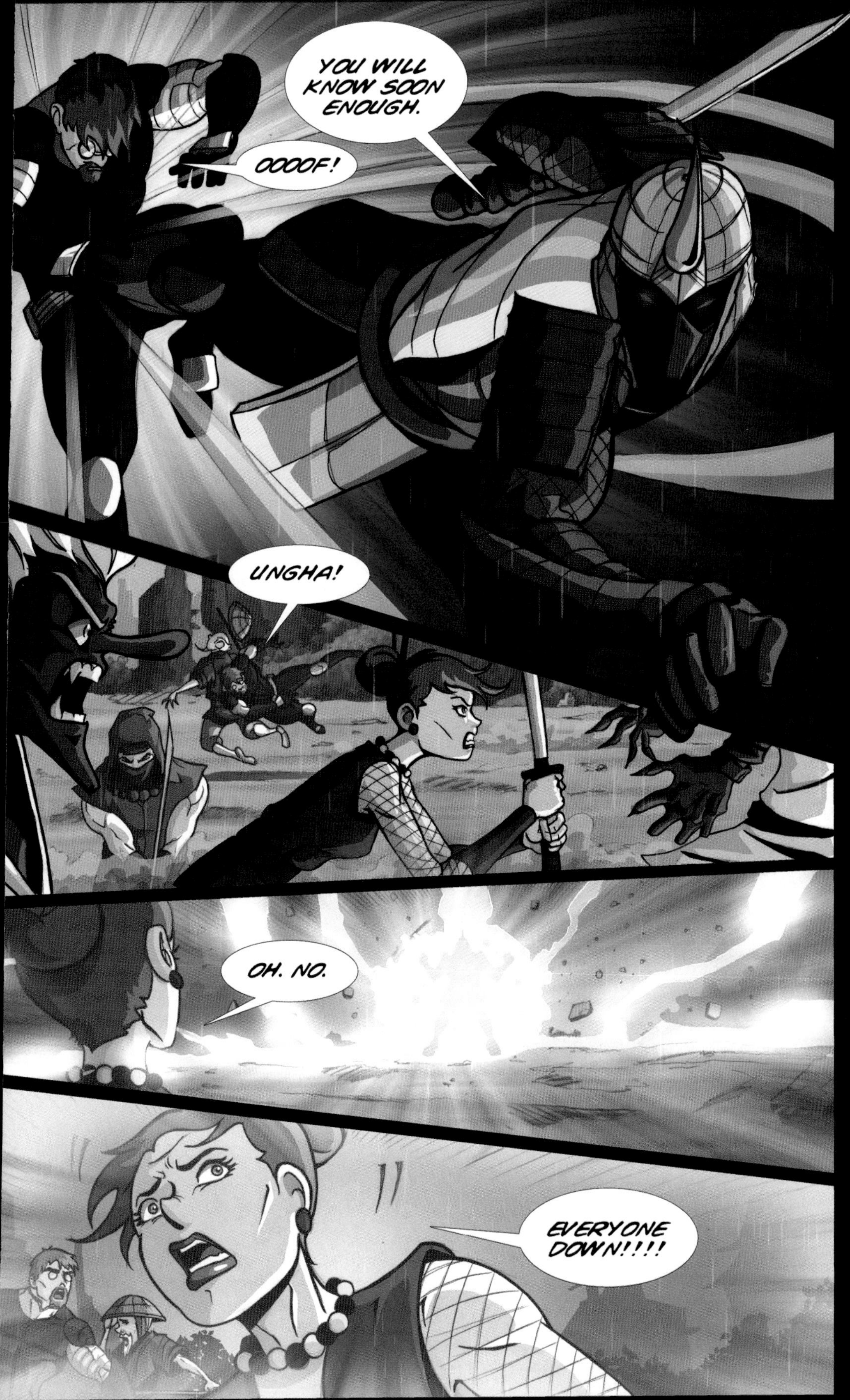
OOOOF!
YOU WILL KNOW SOON ENOUGH.
UNGHA!
OH. NO.
EVERYONE DOWN!!!!!

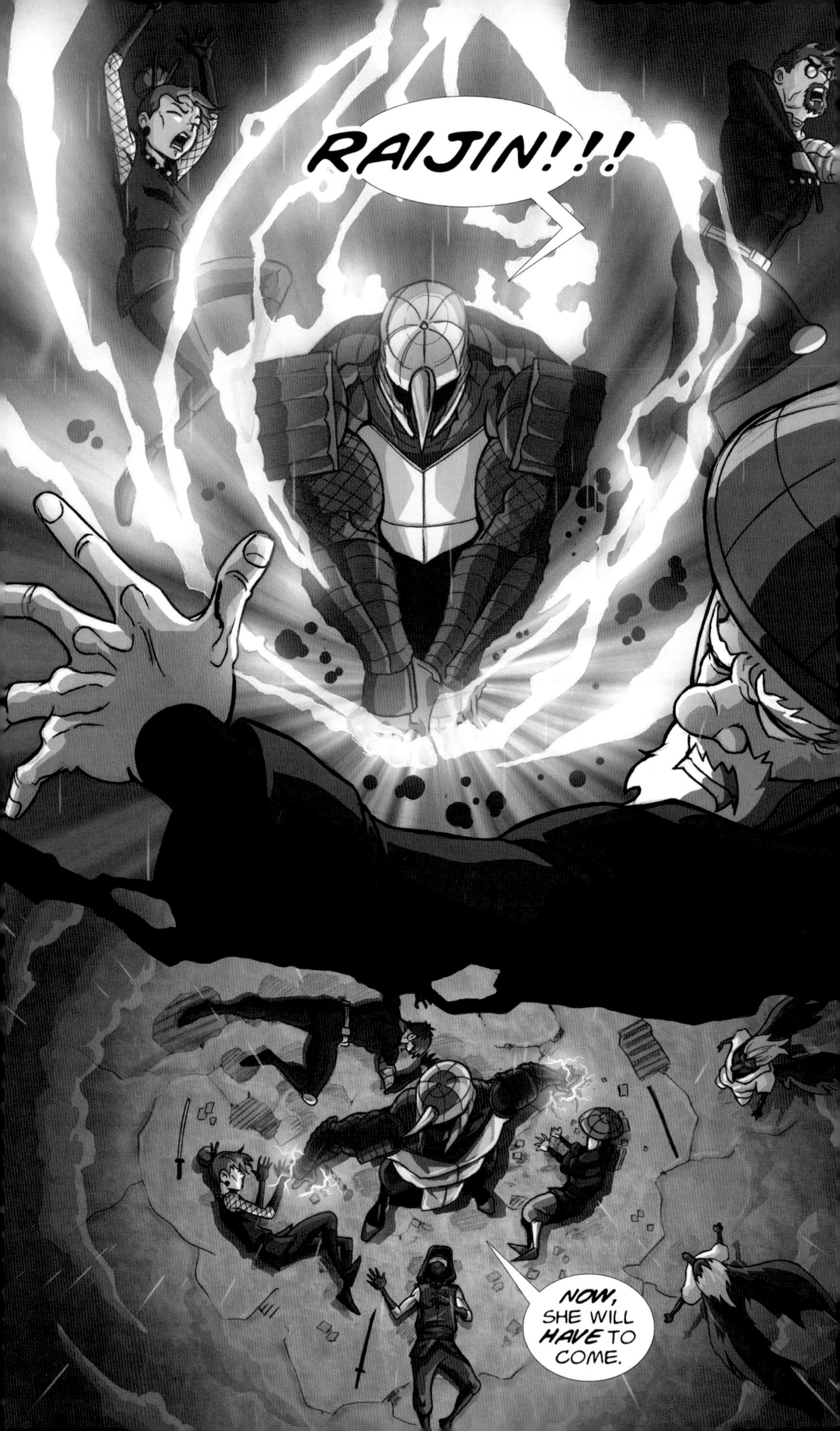
RAIJIN!!!
NOW, SHE WILL HAVE TO COME.

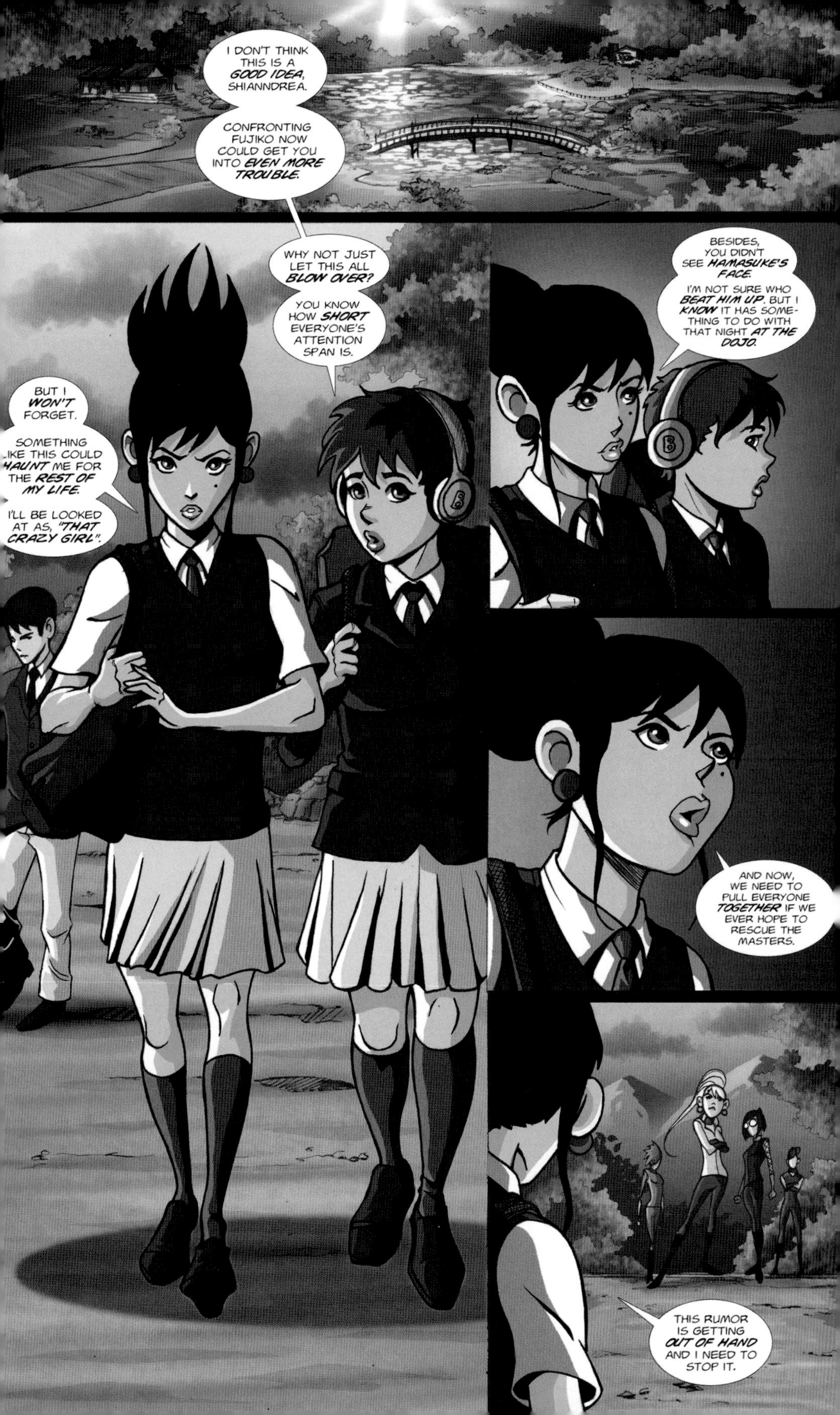

I DON'T THINK THIS IS A GOOD IDEA, SHIANNDREA.
CONFRONTING FUJIKO NOW COULD GET YOU INTO EVEN MORE TROUBLE.
WHY NOT JUST LET THIS ALL BLOW OVER?
YOU KNOW HOW SHORT EVERYONE'S ATTENTION SPAN IS.
BUT I WON'T FORGET.
SOMETHING LIKE THIS COULD HAUNT ME FOR THE REST OF MY LIFE.
I'LL BE LOOKED AT AS, "THAT CRAZY GIRL".
BESIDES, YOU DIDN'T SEE HAMASUKE'S FACE.
I'M NOT SURE WHO BEAT HIM UP. BUT I KNOW IT HAS SOMETHING TO DO WITH THAT NIGHT AT THE DOJO.
AND NOW, WE NEED TO PULL EVERYONE TOGETHER IF WE EVER HOPE TO RESCUE THE MASTERS.
THIS RUMOR IS GETTING OUT OF HAND AND I NEED TO STOP IT.

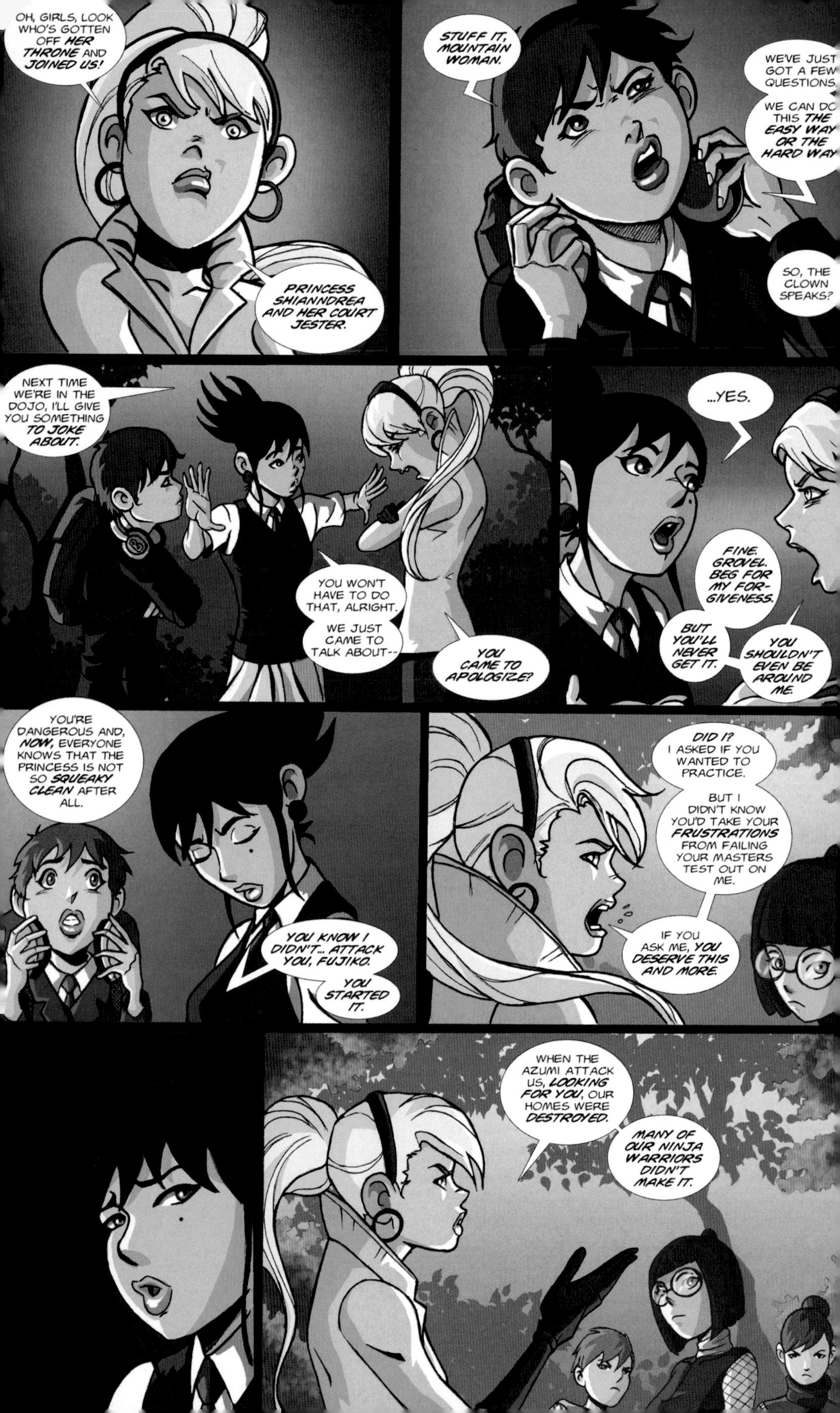
OH, GIRLS, LOOK WHO'S GOTTEN OFF HER THRONE AND JOINED US!
PRINCESS SHIANNDREA AND HER COURT JESTER.
STUFF IT, MOUNTAIN WOMAN.
WE'VE JUST GOT A FEW QUESTIONS.
WE CAN DO THIS THE EASY WAY OR THE HARD WAY
SO, THE CLOWN SPEAKS?
NEXT TIME WE'RE IN THE DOJO, I'LL GIVE YOU SOMETHING TO JOKE ABOUT.
YOU WON'T HAVE TO DO THAT, ALRIGHT.
WE JUST CAME TO TALK ABOUT--
YOU CAME TO APOLOGIZE?
...YES.
FINE. GROVEL. BEG FOR MY FOR-GIVENESS.
BUT YOU'LL NEVER GET IT.
YOU SHOULDN'T EVEN BE AROUND ME.
YOU'RE DANGEROUS AND, NOW, EVERYONE KNOWS THAT THE PRINCESS IS NOT SO SQUEAKY CLEAN AFTER ALL.
YOU KNOW I DIDN'T... ATTACK YOU, FUJIKO.
YOU STARTED IT.
DID I? I ASKED IF YOU WANTED TO PRACTICE.
BUT I DIDN'T KNOW YOU'D TAKE YOUR FRUSTRATIONS FROM FAILING YOUR MASTERS TEST OUT ON ME.
IF YOU ASK ME, YOU DESERVE THIS AND MORE.
WHEN THE AZUMI ATTACK US, LOOKING FOR YOU, OUR HOMES WERE DESTROYED.
MANY OF OUR NINJA WARRIORS DIDN'T MAKE IT.

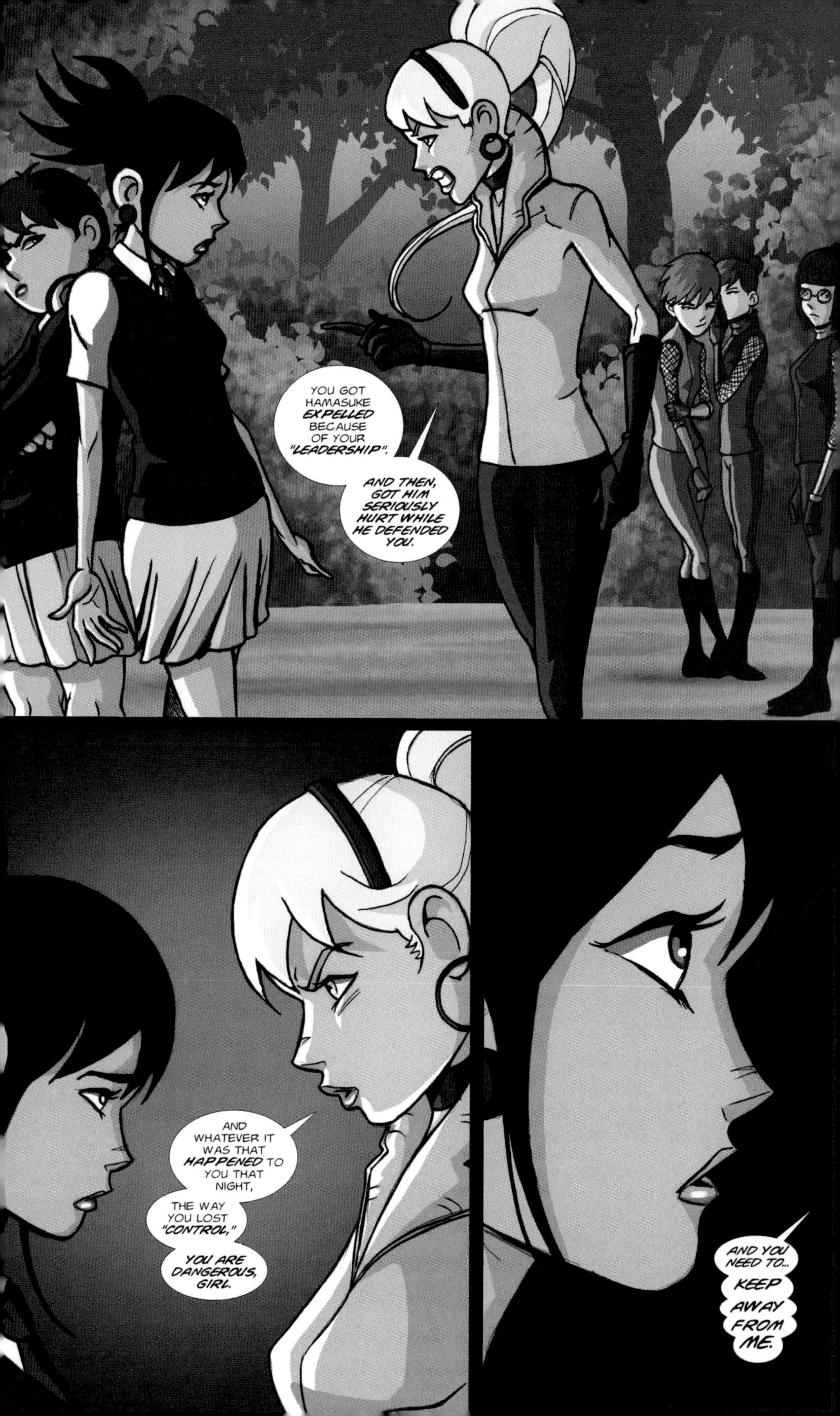
YOU GOT HAMASUKE **EXPELLED** BECAUSE OF YOUR **"LEADERSHIP"**.
AND THEN, GOT HIM SERIOUSLY HURT WHILE HE DEFENDED YOU.
AND WHATEVER IT WAS THAT **HAPPENED** TO YOU THAT NIGHT,
THE WAY YOU LOST **"CONTROL,"**
YOU ARE DANGEROUS, GIRL.
AND YOU NEED TO... KEEP AWAY FROM ME.

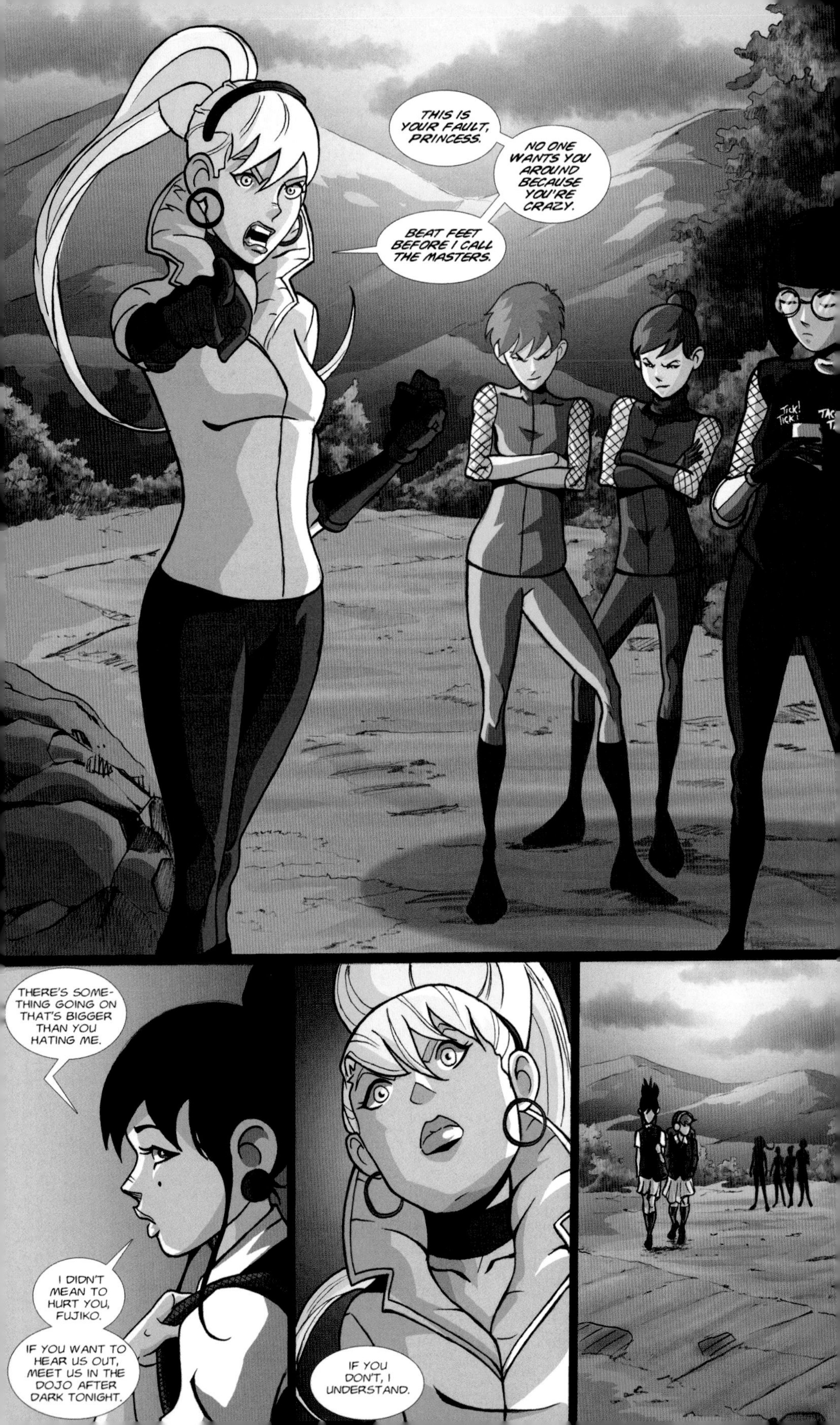
THIS IS YOUR FAULT, PRINCESS.
NO ONE WANTS YOU AROUND BECAUSE YOU'RE CRAZY.
BEAT FEET BEFORE I CALL THE MASTERS.
TICK! TICK!
THERE'S SOME-THING GOING ON THAT'S BIGGER THAN YOU HATING ME.
I DIDN'T MEAN TO HURT YOU, FUJIKO.
IF YOU WANT TO HEAR US OUT, MEET US IN THE DOJO AFTER DARK TONIGHT.
IF YOU DON'T, I UNDERSTAND.

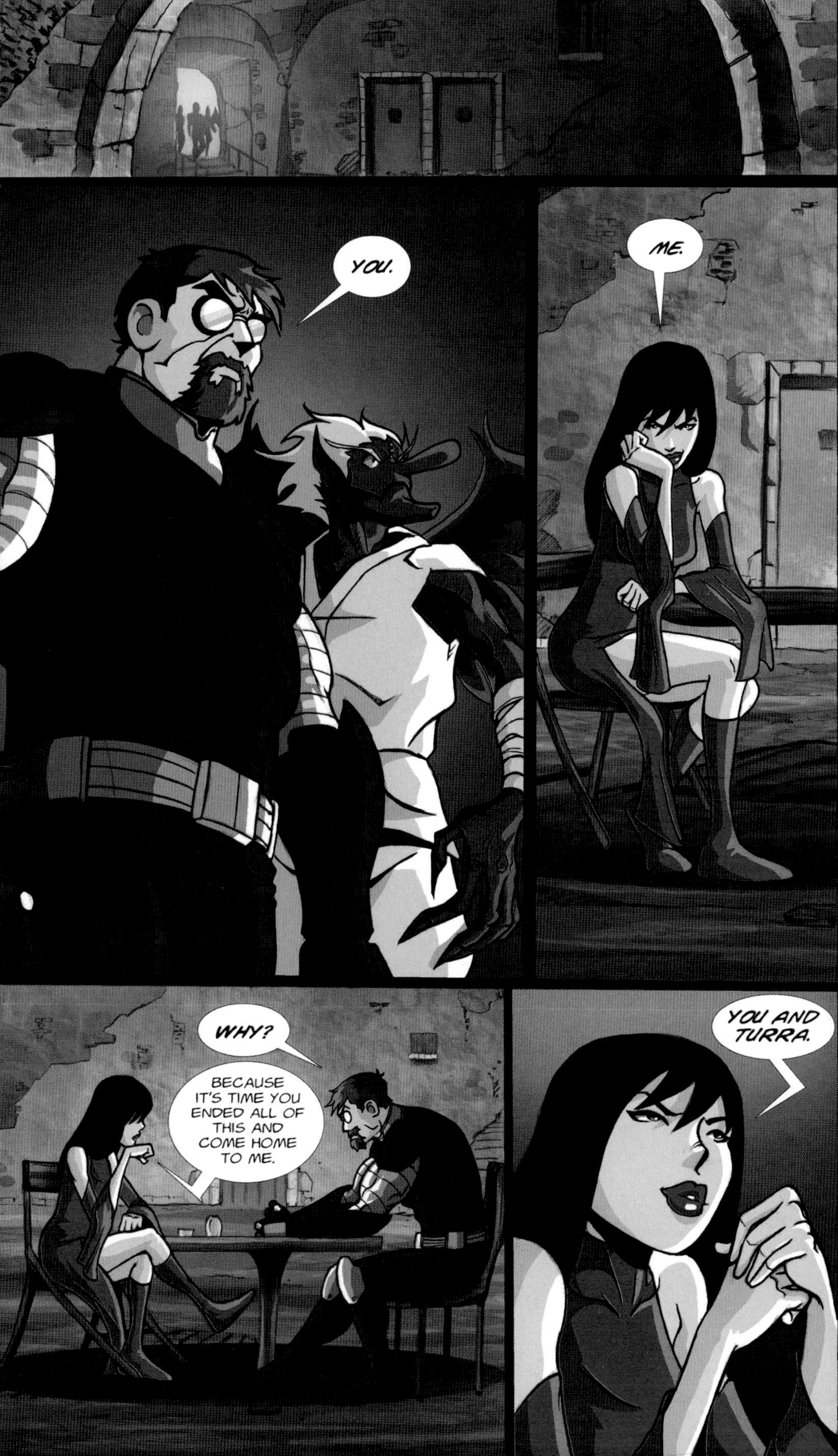
YOU.
ME.
WHY?
BECAUSE IT'S TIME YOU ENDED ALL OF THIS AND COME HOME TO ME.
YOU AND TURRA.

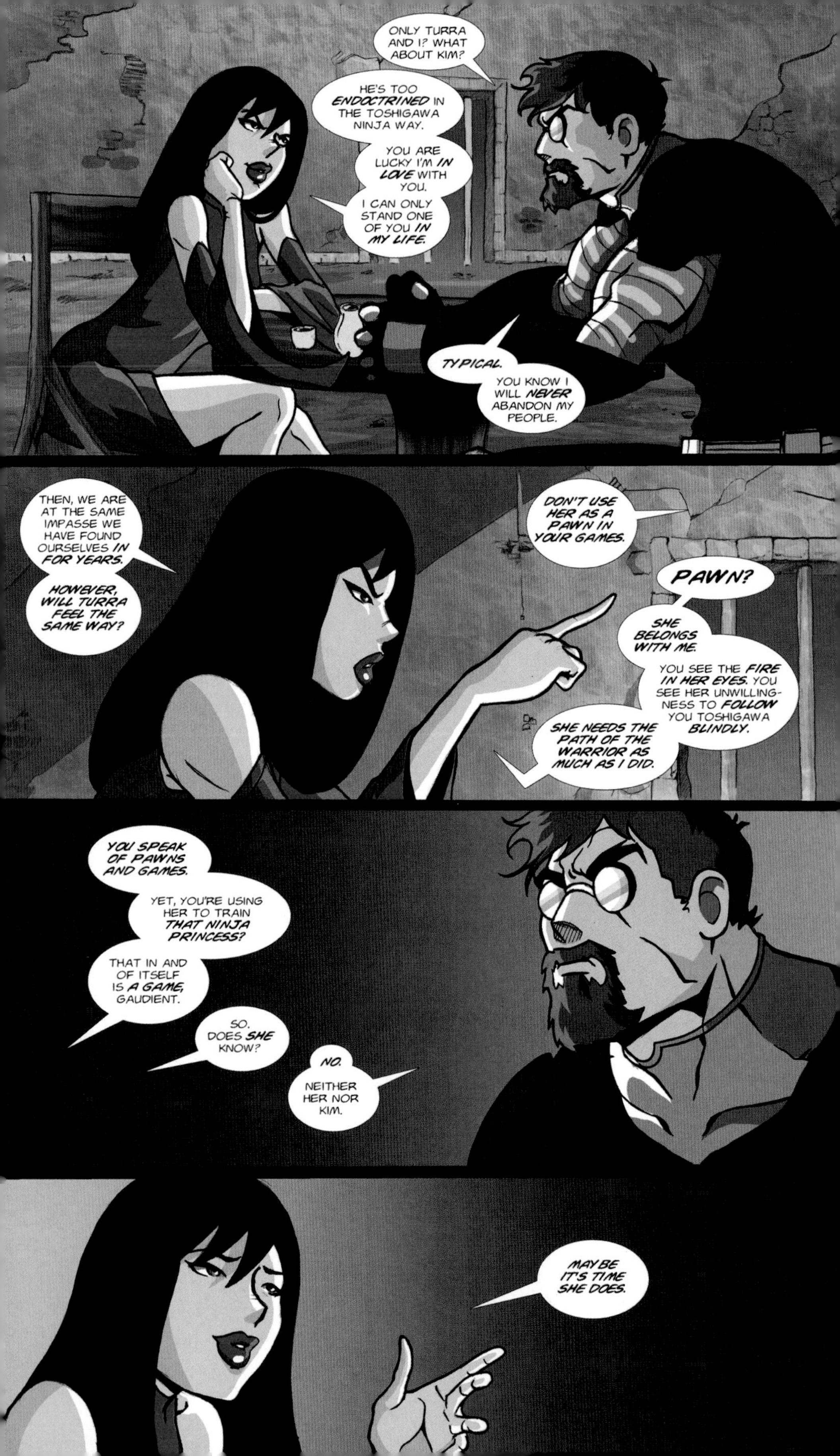
ONLY TURRA AND I? WHAT ABOUT KIM?
HE'S TOO ENDOCTRINED IN THE TOSHIGAWA NINJA WAY.
YOU ARE LUCKY I'M IN LOVE WITH YOU.
I CAN ONLY STAND ONE OF YOU IN MY LIFE.
TYPICAL.
YOU KNOW I WILL NEVER ABANDON MY PEOPLE.
THEN, WE ARE AT THE SAME IMPASSE WE HAVE FOUND OURSELVES IN FOR YEARS.
HOWEVER, WILL TURRA FEEL THE SAME WAY?
DON'T USE HER AS A PAWN IN YOUR GAMES.
PAWN?
SHE BELONGS WITH ME.
YOU SEE THE FIRE IN HER EYES. YOU SEE HER UNWILLINGNESS TO FOLLOW YOU TOSHIGAWA BLINDLY.
SHE NEEDS THE PATH OF THE WARRIOR AS MUCH AS I DID.
YOU SPEAK OF PAWNS AND GAMES.
YET, YOU'RE USING HER TO TRAIN THAT NINJA PRINCESS?
THAT IN AND OF ITSELF IS A GAME, GAUDIENT.
SO. DOES SHE KNOW?
NO.
NEITHER HER NOR KIM.
MAYBE IT'S TIME SHE DOES.

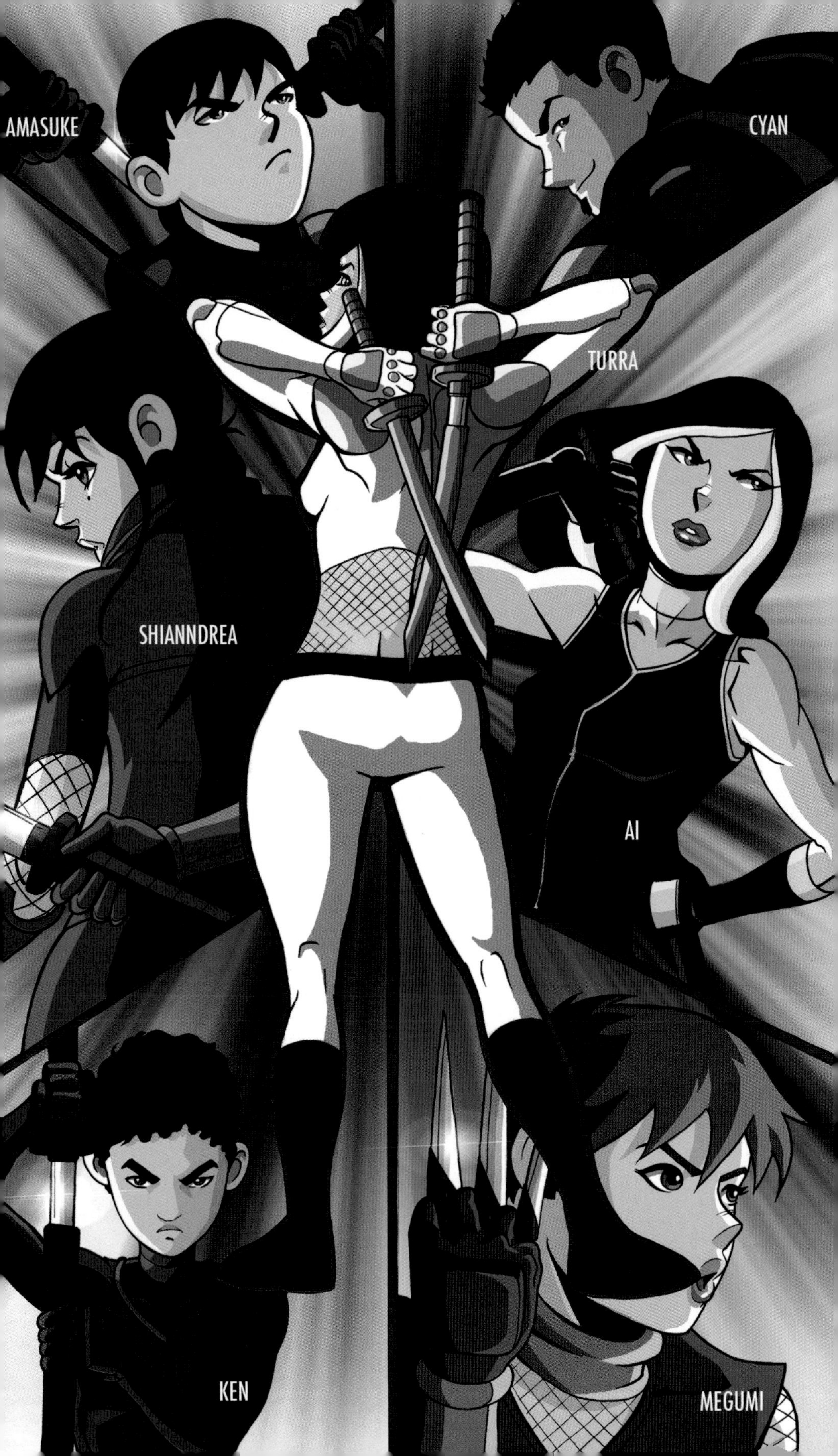
AMASUKE
CYAN
TURRA
SHIANNDREA
AI
KEN
MEGUMI

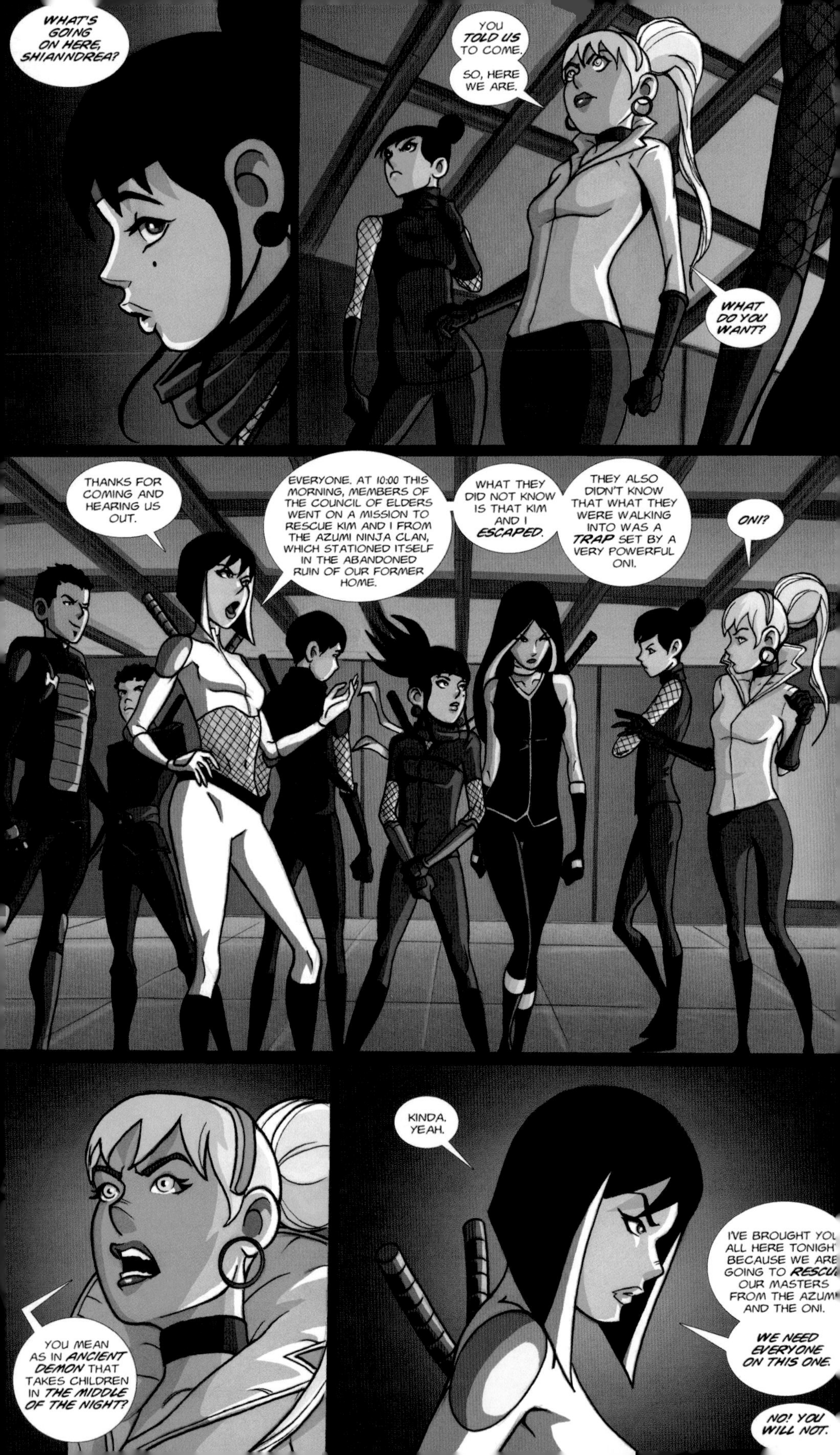
WHAT'S GOING ON HERE, SHIANNDREA?
YOU TOLD US TO COME.
SO, HERE WE ARE.
WHAT DO YOU WANT?
THANKS FOR COMING AND HEARING US OUT.
EVERYONE. AT 10:00 THIS MORNING, MEMBERS OF THE COUNCIL OF ELDERS WENT ON A MISSION TO RESCUE KIM AND I FROM THE AZUMI NINJA CLAN, WHICH STATIONED ITSELF IN THE ABANDONED RUIN OF OUR FORMER HOME.
WHAT THEY DID NOT KNOW IS THAT KIM AND I ESCAPED.
THEY ALSO DIDN'T KNOW THAT WHAT THEY WERE WALKING INTO WAS A TRAP SET BY A VERY POWERFUL ONI.
ONI?
YOU MEAN AS IN ANCIENT DEMON THAT TAKES CHILDREN IN THE MIDDLE OF THE NIGHT?
KINDA. YEAH.
I'VE BROUGHT YOU ALL HERE TONIGHT BECAUSE WE ARE GOING TO RESCUE OUR MASTERS FROM THE AZUMI AND THE ONI.
WE NEED EVERYONE ON THIS ONE.
NO! YOU WILL NOT.

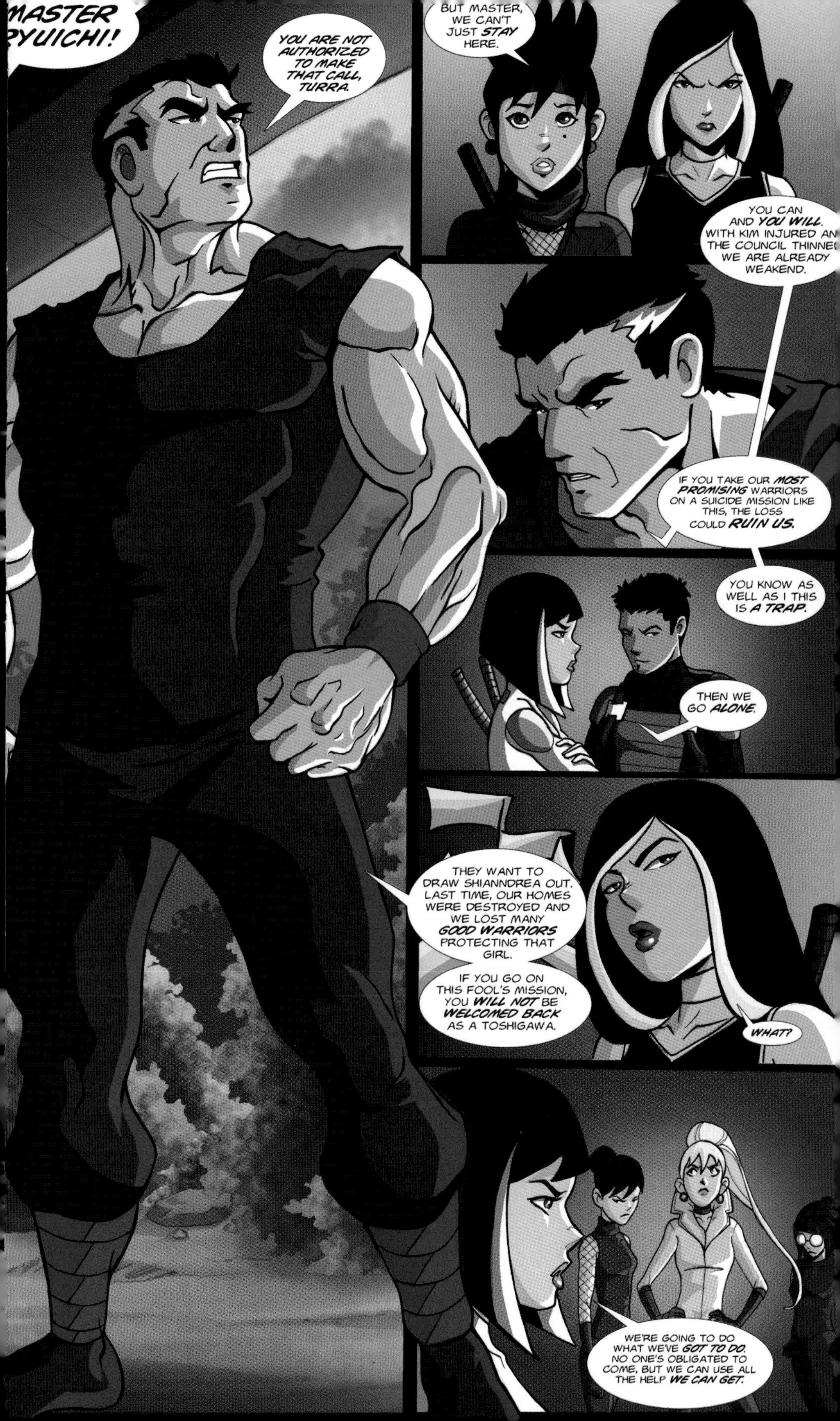
MASTER RYUICHI!
YOU ARE NOT AUTHORIZED TO MAKE THAT CALL, TURRA.
BUT MASTER, WE CAN'T JUST STAY HERE.
YOU CAN AND YOU WILL. WITH KIM INJURED AN THE COUNCIL THINNE WE ARE ALREADY WEAKEND.
IF YOU TAKE OUR MOST PROMISING WARRIORS ON A SUICIDE MISSION LIKE THIS, THE LOSS COULD RUIN US.
YOU KNOW AS WELL AS I THIS IS A TRAP.
THEN WE GO ALONE.
THEY WANT TO DRAW SHIANNDREA OUT. LAST TIME, OUR HOMES WERE DESTROYED AND WE LOST MANY GOOD WARRIORS PROTECTING THAT GIRL.
IF YOU GO ON THIS FOOL'S MISSION, YOU WILL NOT BE WELCOMED BACK AS A TOSHIGAWA.
WHAT?
WE'RE GOING TO DO WHAT WE'VE GOT TO DO. NO ONE'S OBLIGATED TO COME, BUT WE CAN USE ALL THE HELP WE CAN GET.

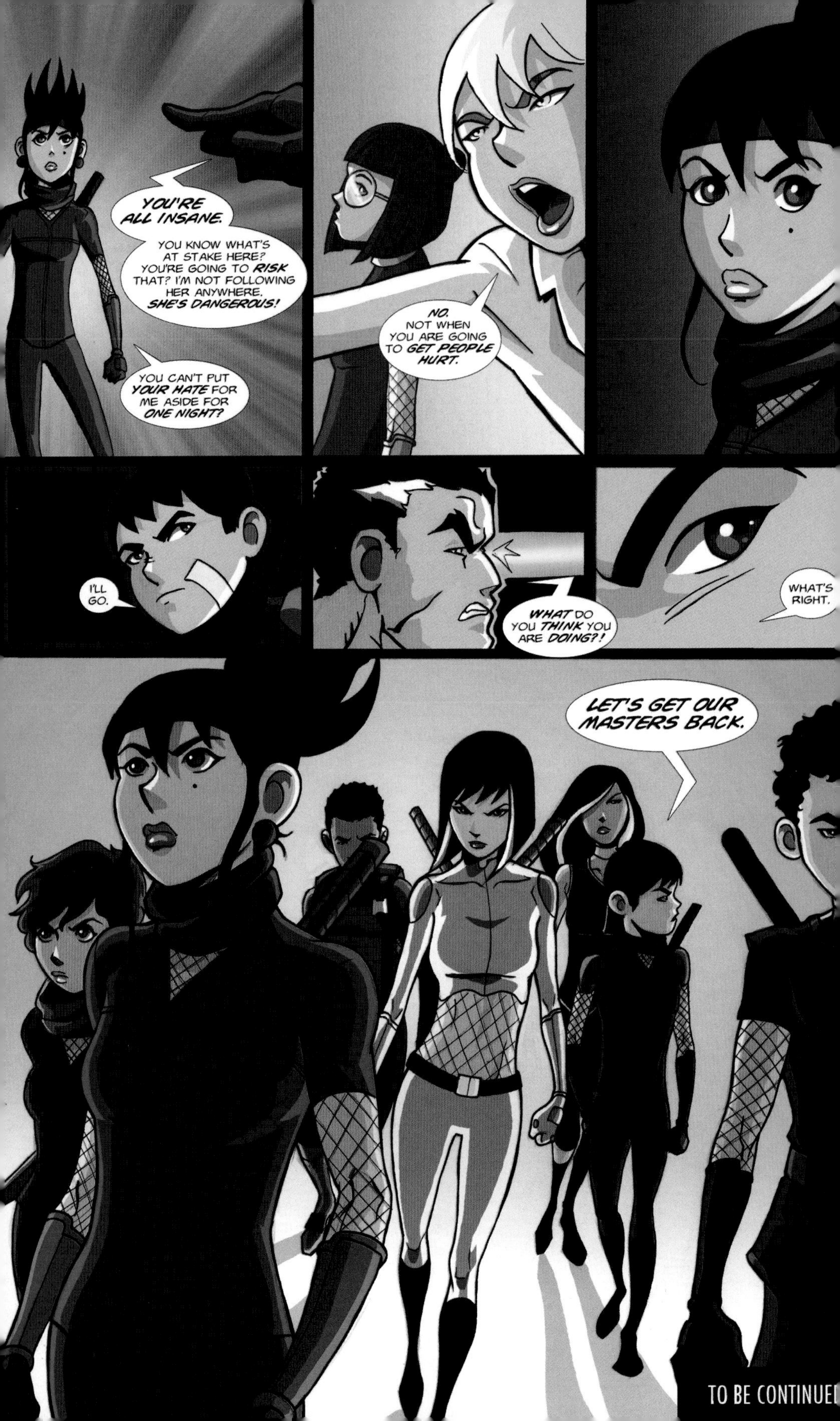
YOU'RE ALL INSANE.
YOU KNOW WHAT'S AT STAKE HERE? YOU'RE GOING TO RISK THAT? I'M NOT FOLLOWING HER ANYWHERE. SHE'S DANGEROUS!
YOU CAN'T PUT YOUR HATE FOR ME ASIDE FOR ONE NIGHT?
NO. NOT WHEN YOU ARE GOING TO GET PEOPLE HURT.
I'LL GO.
WHAT DO YOU THINK YOU ARE DOING?!
WHAT'S RIGHT.
LET'S GET OUR MASTERS BACK.
TO BE CONTINUED

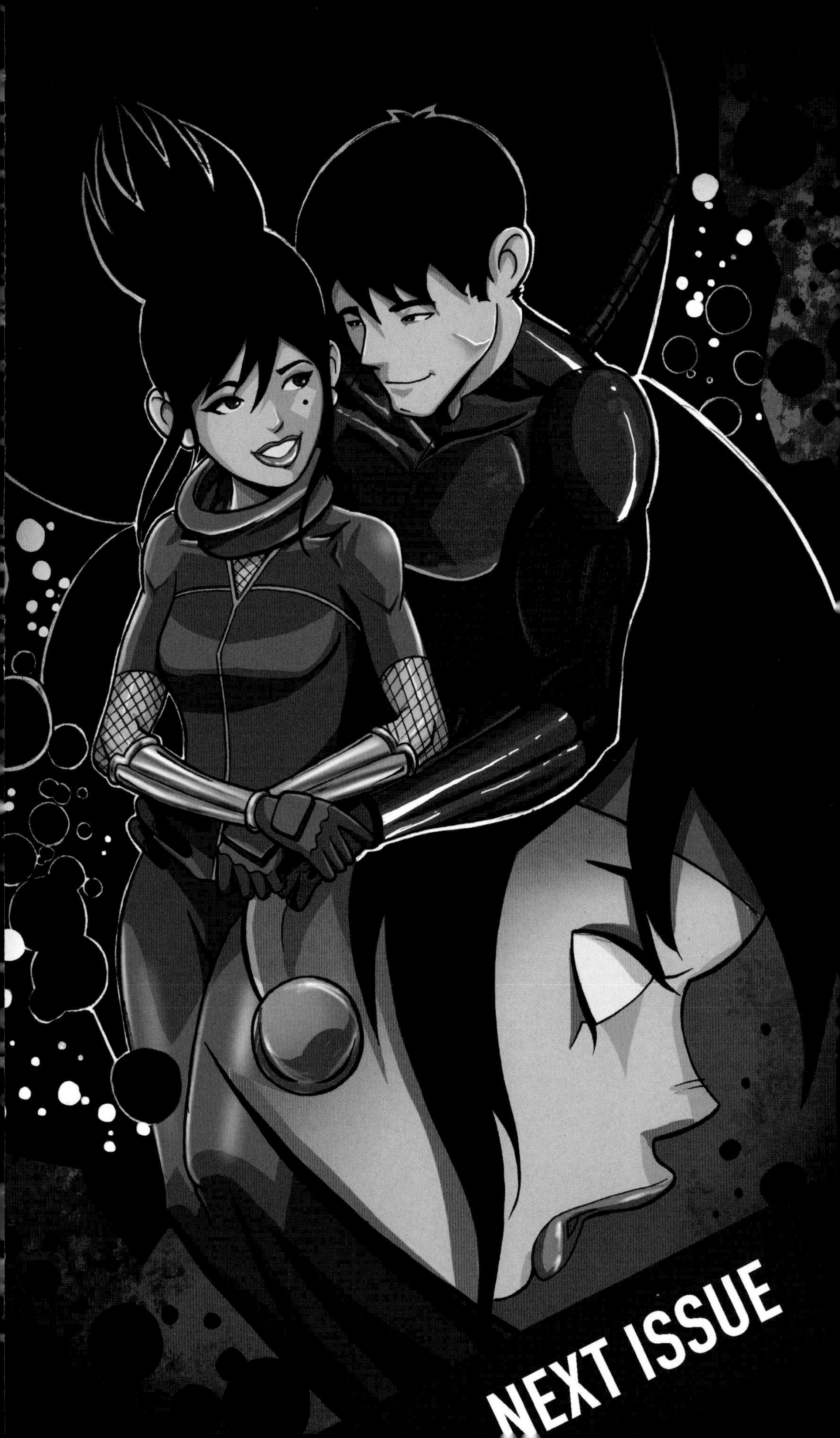
NEXT ISSUE

KENJI MAWADÉ

- *Age: 14*
- *Weapon: Blue Katana*
- *Likes: Video games, the latest techno-gadgets, Kamen Rid*
- *Dislikes: Spicy food*

Kenji, or Ken as his friends call him,
pretty interesting and mysterious backg
He is descendant of Yasuke, the first
mented African samurai. However,
American, Ken spends most of his life liv
any normal kid would: going to school,
homework, playing video games, partici
in dance offs, cosplaying at convention:
when summertime hits, his father takes
Japan to train with the Toshigawa Ninja C
honor family tradition. Ken considers t
version of summer camp.

Despite being a"part-time ninja", Ken's f
are glad to have him as part of the tea
ideas have led to upgrades on the team's
such as the addition of wrist mounted
pling hooks and knock-out darts.

Both Shianndrea and Ken dream of atte
and competing in EVO (the biggest fi
game tournament in America), somethi
two young ninja "train for" during their
time.

*I'm done playing. I thought we were going to
watch some Kamen Rider instead.*
-Ken

ON SECOND
THOUGHT, WHY
DON'T *YOU*
JOIN THEM?

WHACK!

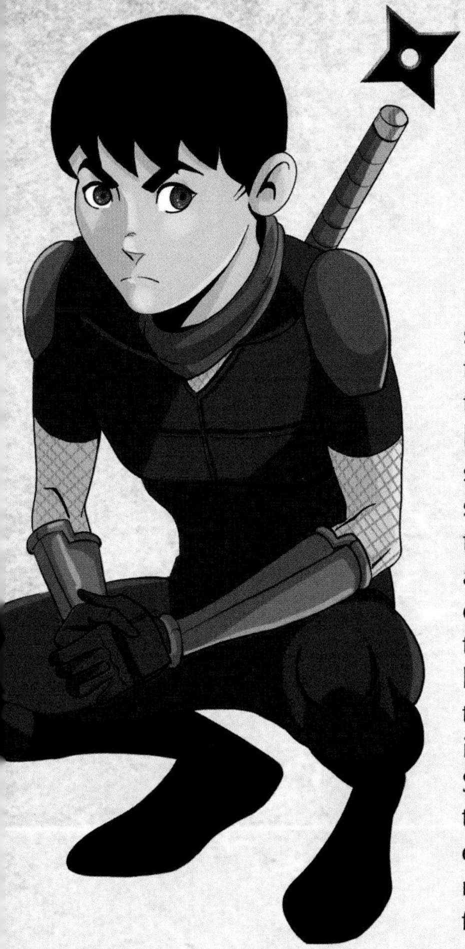

HAMASUKE GOZAN

- *Age: 15*
- *Weapon: Purple Katana*
- *Likes: Being in charge, being the best, maybe Shianndrea*
- *Dislikes: Coming in second, maybe Shianndrea*

Hamasuke Gozan is the ninja with a chip on his shoulder. He feels he has a lot to prove and a short time to do it in. While all of the other guys look up to Kim, Hamasuke despises him and longs to take his place as the dominant ninja in the clan. He is a skilled warrior. However, he feels his potential is stifled by the amount of attention Shianndrea gets from the other Masters. His jealousy fuels his rage and he often watches her from the shadows. His direct teacher, Master Ryuichi, has warned him that his fixation on Shianndrea will eventually lead him to ruin. But his true feelings hide a deep secret that could spell the end for Shianndrea if not kept in check. Secretly, Hamasuke has feelings for Shianndrea that constantly conflicts with his need to be the best. His confusion over his different emotions leads him into dark areas as he tries to make sense of the jealousy, anger, and love he feels for her.

Both of you need to follow MY lead. Just stay here, keep the bench warm for me and stay out of my way. That's what kunoichi do best anyway.
-Hamasuke

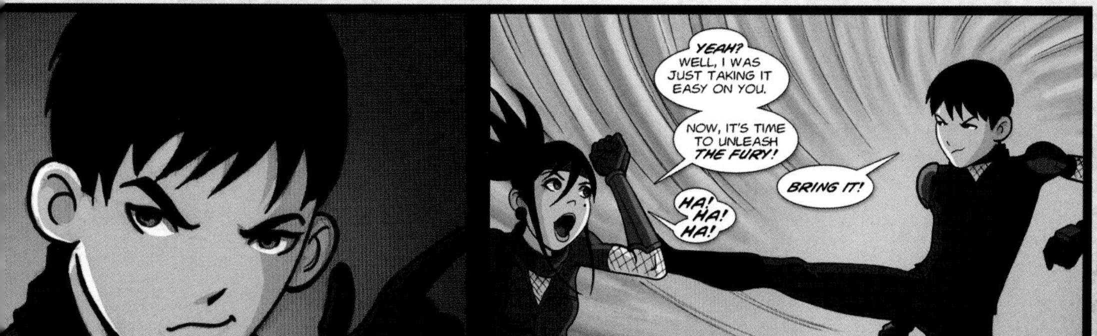
YEAH? WELL, I WAS JUST TAKING IT EASY ON YOU.
NOW, IT'S TIME TO UNLEASH THE FURY!
HA! HA! HA!
BRING IT!

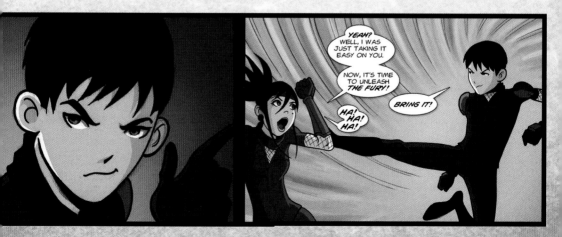

THE TOSHIGAWA COUNCIL OF ELDERS

✦ MASTER JUBEI

The eldest member of the Toshigawa Council of Elders, Jubei was once Master Gaudient and Terminus' (before he betrayed the clan) teacher. Shianndrea and Kristin (a 10 year old young ninja in the clan) both live with Gaudient, and he looks after them as if they where his daughters. Kind and full of knowledge, Jubei is the moral center for not only Shianndrea, but the entire clan.

✦ MASTER RYUICHI

Ryuichi is the second eldest of the Toshigawa Council of Elders. He was once a tracker for the Military, acting as a sort of double agent for the Toshigawa and the government. Because of this, he has seen the faults of both Emeperor Terminus and the Toshigawa Clan and believes that the clan has misplaced its faith in Shianndrea Toshigawa's supposed "abilities". He is Hamasuke's the direct instructor, and is also, unfortunately, the driving force of the young ninja's rivalry with the ninja princess.

✦ MASTER YUUKA

Master Yuuka is Ai's mother and the doctor of the Toshigawa Ninja Clan. She is the second youngest Master that sits on the Toshigawa Council of Elders and the only one that can "put Gaudient in his place".

✦ MASTER SHADOW

Not much is known about the Toshigawa Council of Elders member known only as Master Shadow. No one outside of the Council knows what he looks like under his hood and mask, or even his real name. He is an enigma inside of an enigma.

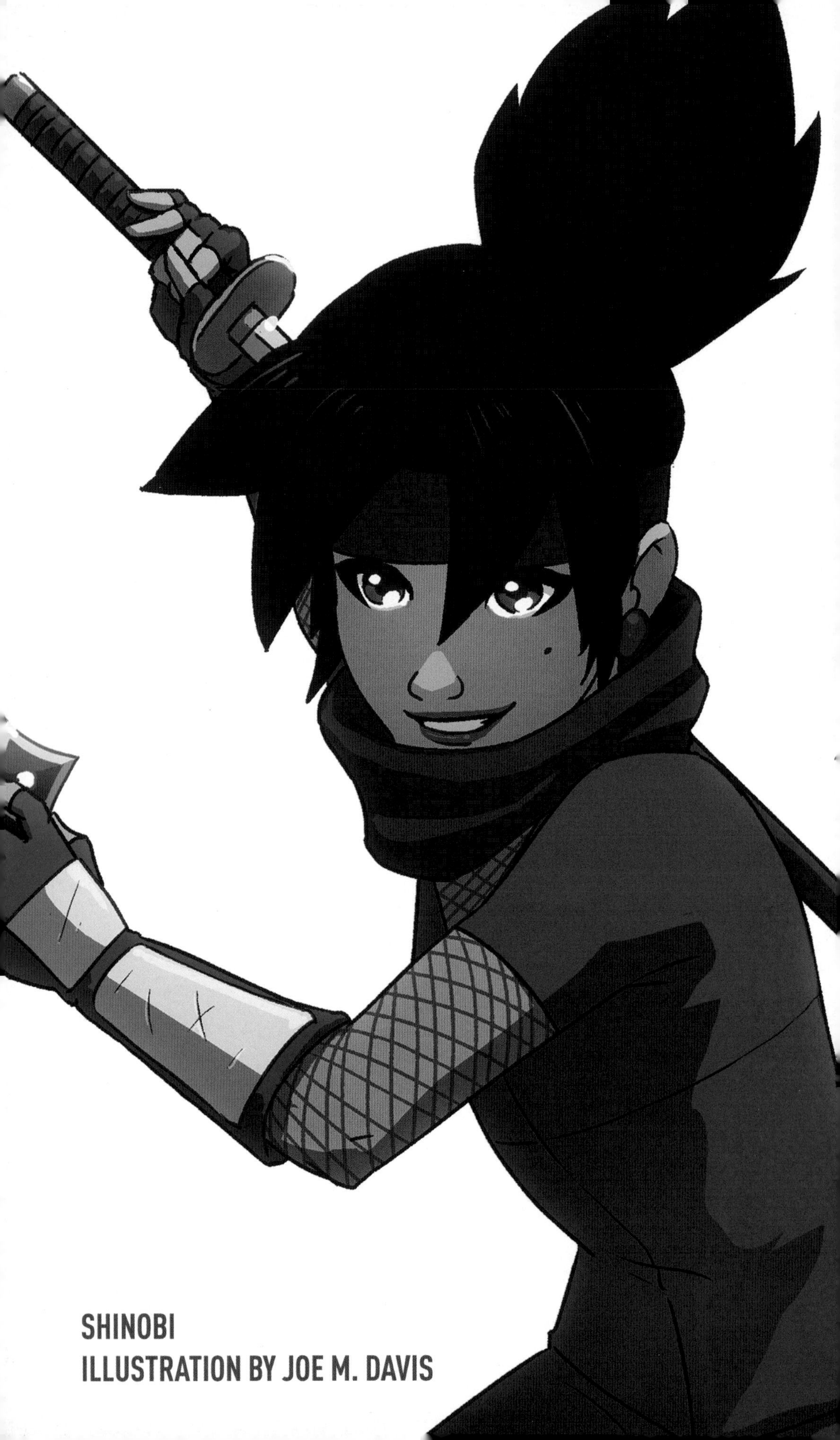

SHINOBI
ILLUSTRATION BY JOE M. DAVIS

SHINOBI 4

NINJA PRINCESS

THE LIGHTNING ONI

MARTHEUS WADE · JANET WADE · KEVIN WILLIAMS · GENE FAYNE

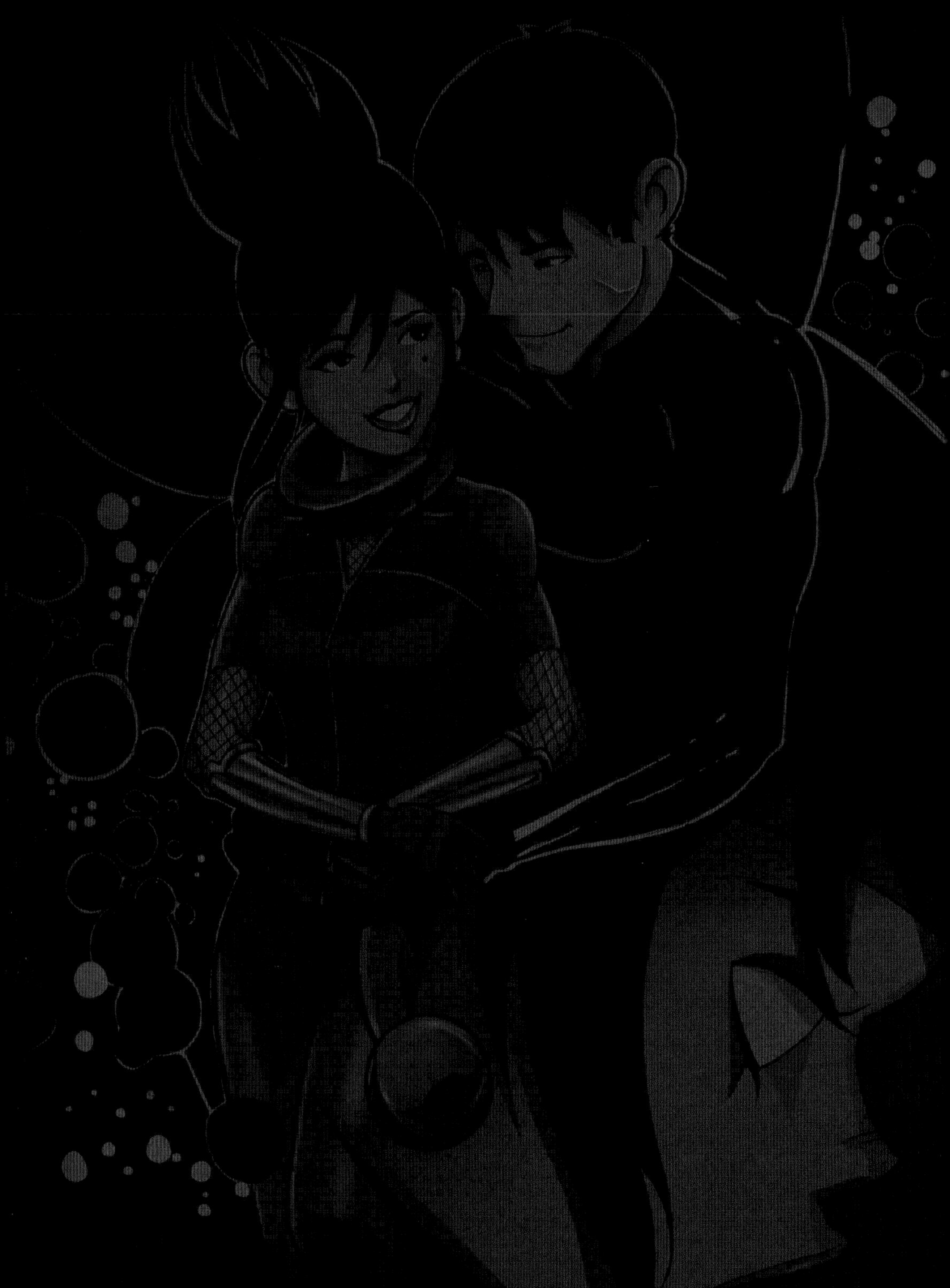

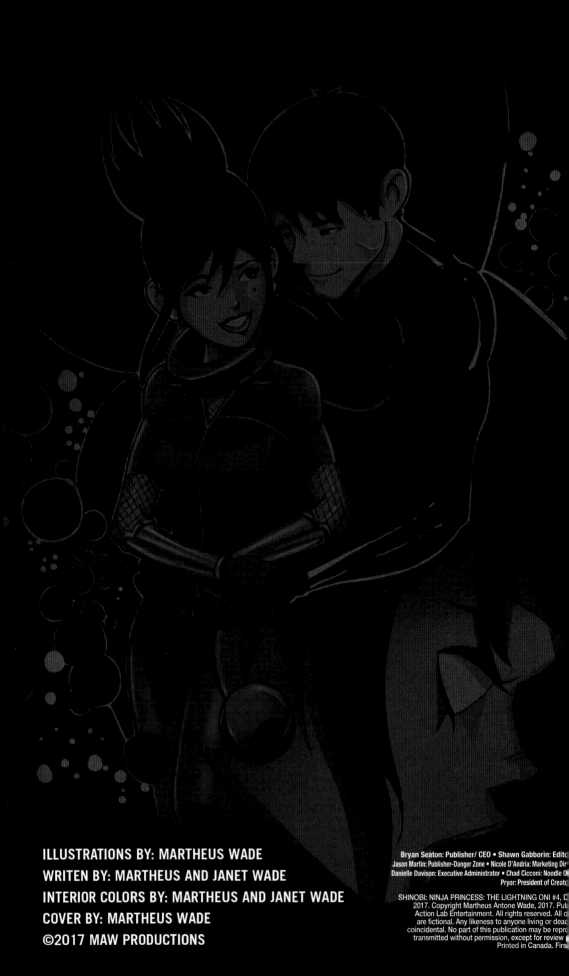

ILLUSTRATIONS BY: MARTHEUS WADE
WRITEN BY: MARTHEUS AND JANET WADE
INTERIOR COLORS BY: MARTHEUS AND JANET WADE
COVER BY: MARTHEUS WADE

Bryan Seaton: Publisher/ CEO • Shawn Gabborin: Edito
Jason Martin: Publisher-Danger Zone • Nicole D'Andria: Marketing Dir
Danielle Davison: Executive Administrator • Chad Cicconi: Noodle O
Pryor: President of Creato

D TOSHIGAWA STRONGHOLD

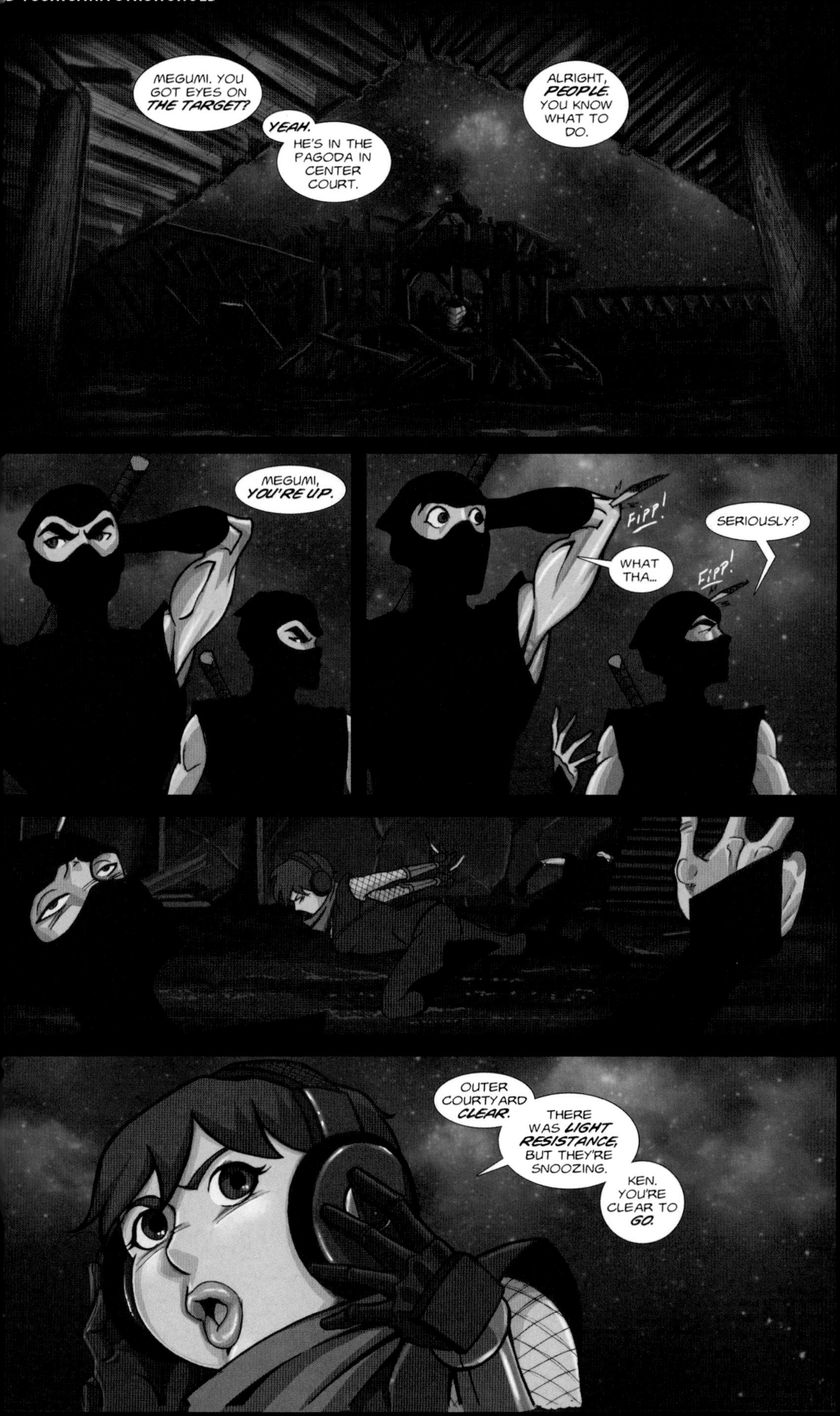
MEGUMI. YOU GOT EYES ON THE TARGET?
YEAH. HE'S IN THE PAGODA IN CENTER COURT.
ALRIGHT, PEOPLE. YOU KNOW WHAT TO DO.
MEGUMI, YOU'RE UP.
FIPP!
WHAT THA...
FIPP!
SERIOUSLY?
OUTER COURTYARD CLEAR.
THERE WAS LIGHT RESISTANCE, BUT THEY'RE SNOOZING.
KEN. YOU'RE CLEAR TO GO.

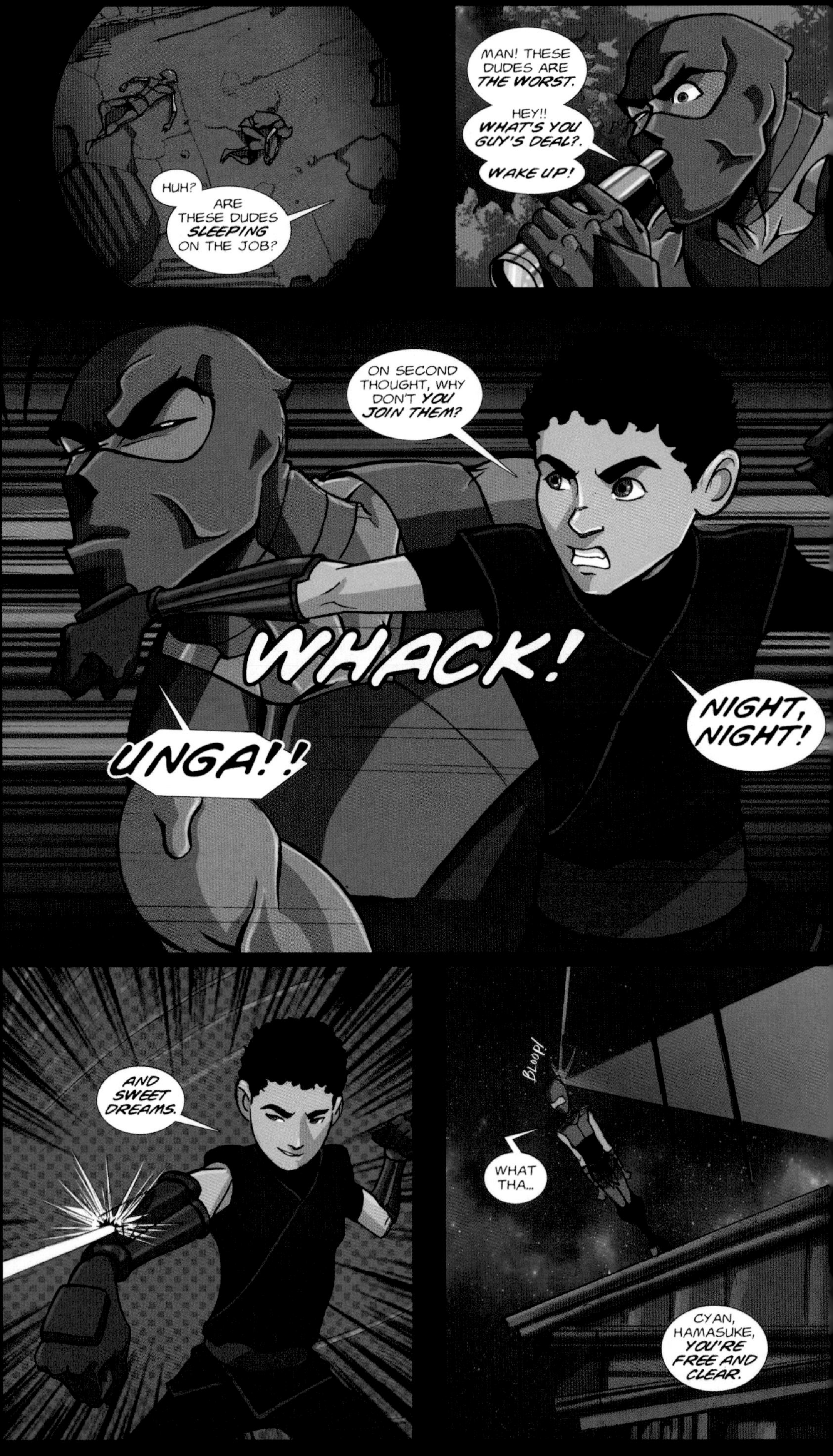
HUH?
ARE THESE DUDES SLEEPING ON THE JOB?
MAN! THESE DUDES ARE THE WORST.
HEY!! WHAT'S YOU GUY'S DEAL?.
WAKE UP!
ON SECOND THOUGHT, WHY DON'T YOU JOIN THEM?
WHACK!
UNGA!!
NIGHT, NIGHT!
AND SWEET DREAMS.
BLOOP!
WHAT THA...
CYAN, HAMASUKE, YOU'RE FREE AND CLEAR.

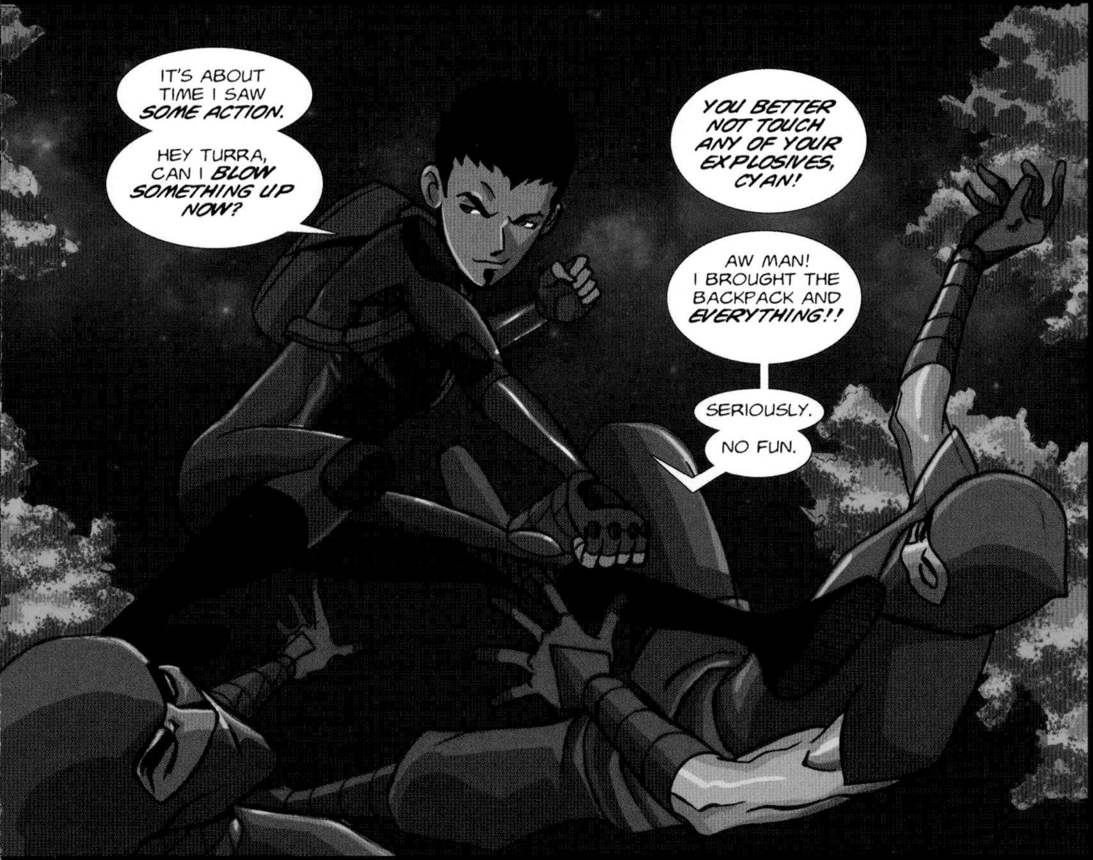
IT'S ABOUT TIME I SAW SOME ACTION.
HEY TURRA, CAN I BLOW SOMETHING UP NOW?
YOU BETTER NOT TOUCH ANY OF YOUR EXPLOSIVES, CYAN!
AW MAN! I BROUGHT THE BACKPACK AND EVERYTHING!!
SERIOUSLY.
NO FUN.

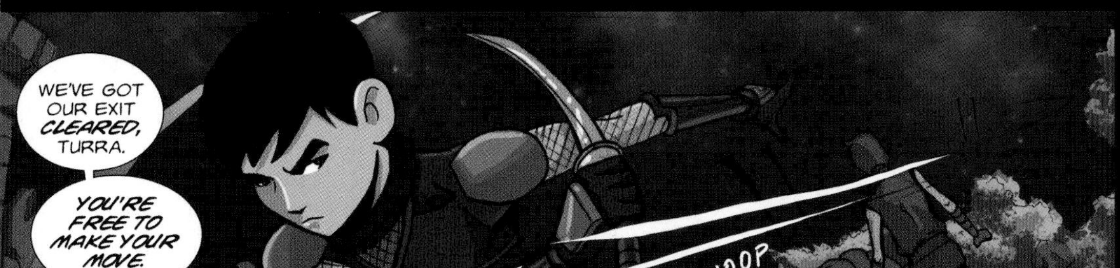
WE'VE GOT OUR EXIT CLEARED, TURRA.
YOU'RE FREE TO MAKE YOUR MOVE.
SWOOP

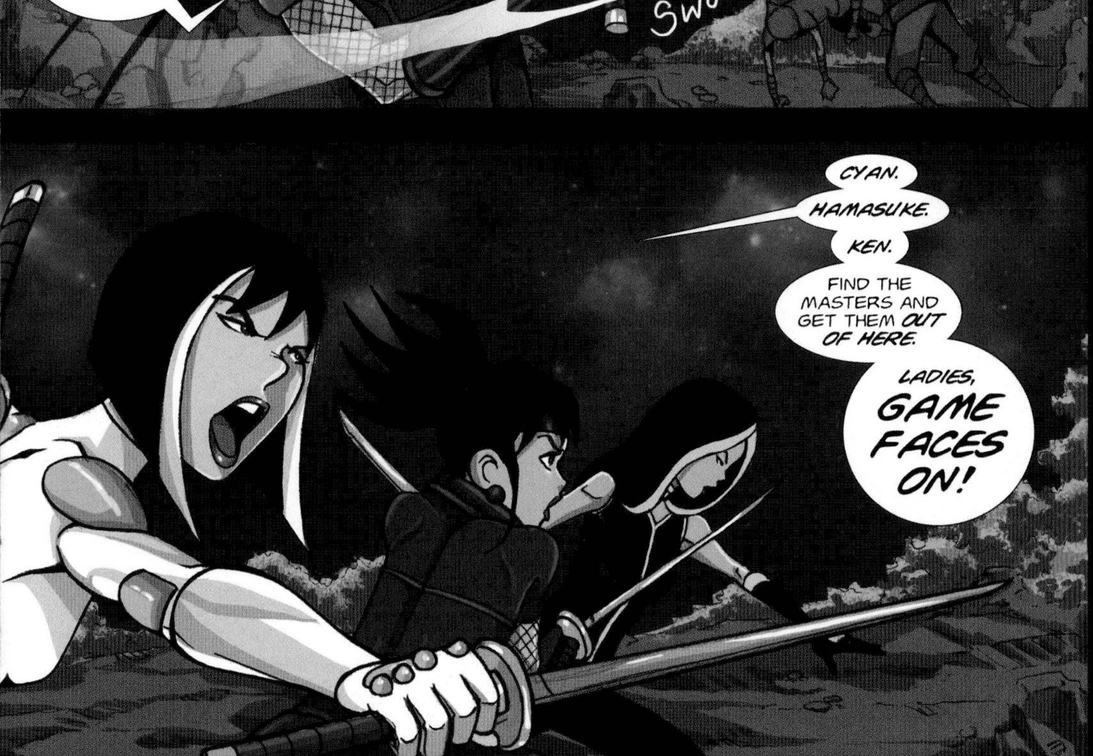
CYAN.
HAMASUKE.
KEN.
FIND THE MASTERS AND GET THEM OUT OF HERE.
LADIES, GAME FACES ON!

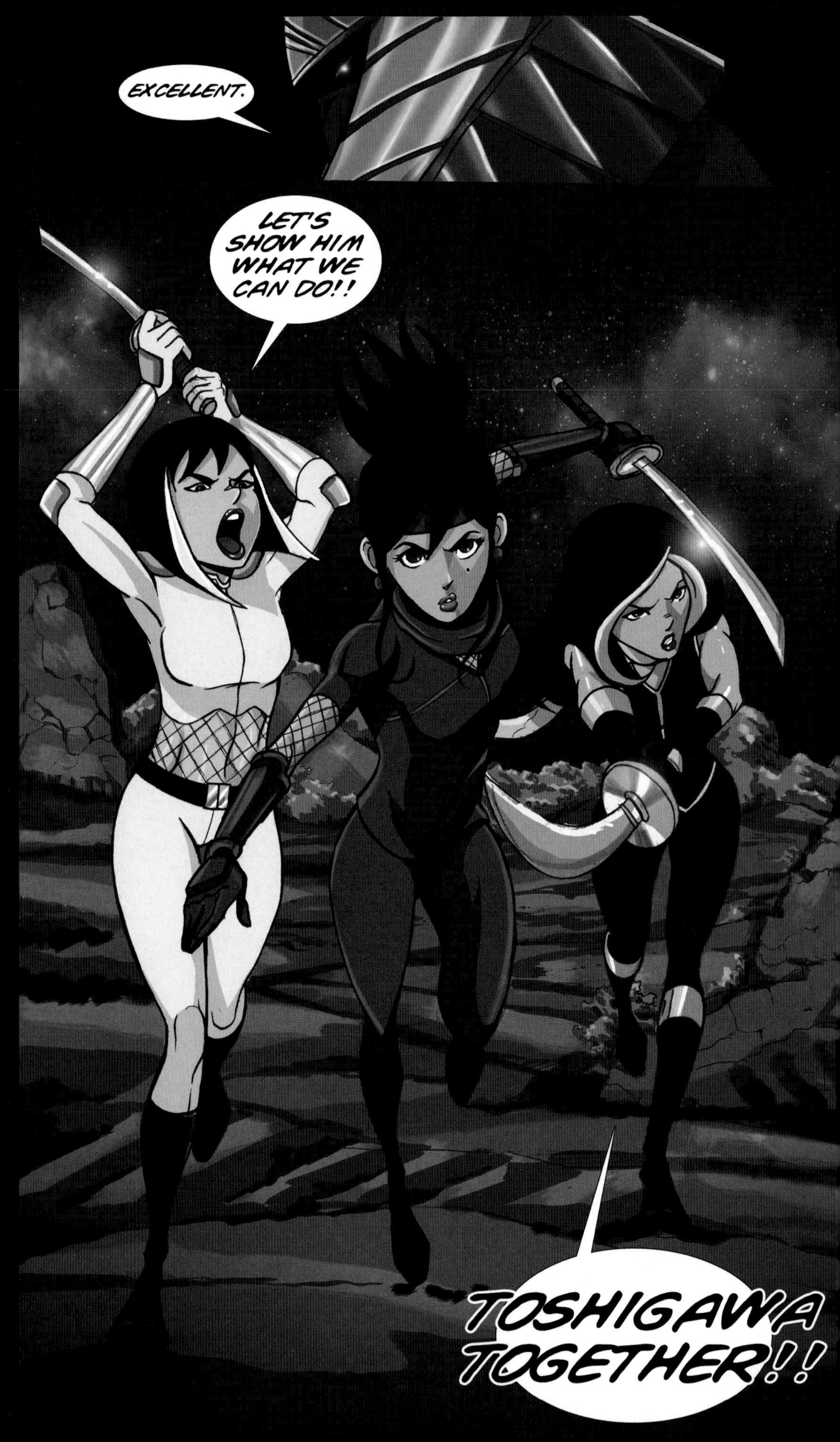
EXCELLENT.
LET'S SHOW HIM WHAT WE CAN DO!!
TOSHIGAWA TOGETHER!!

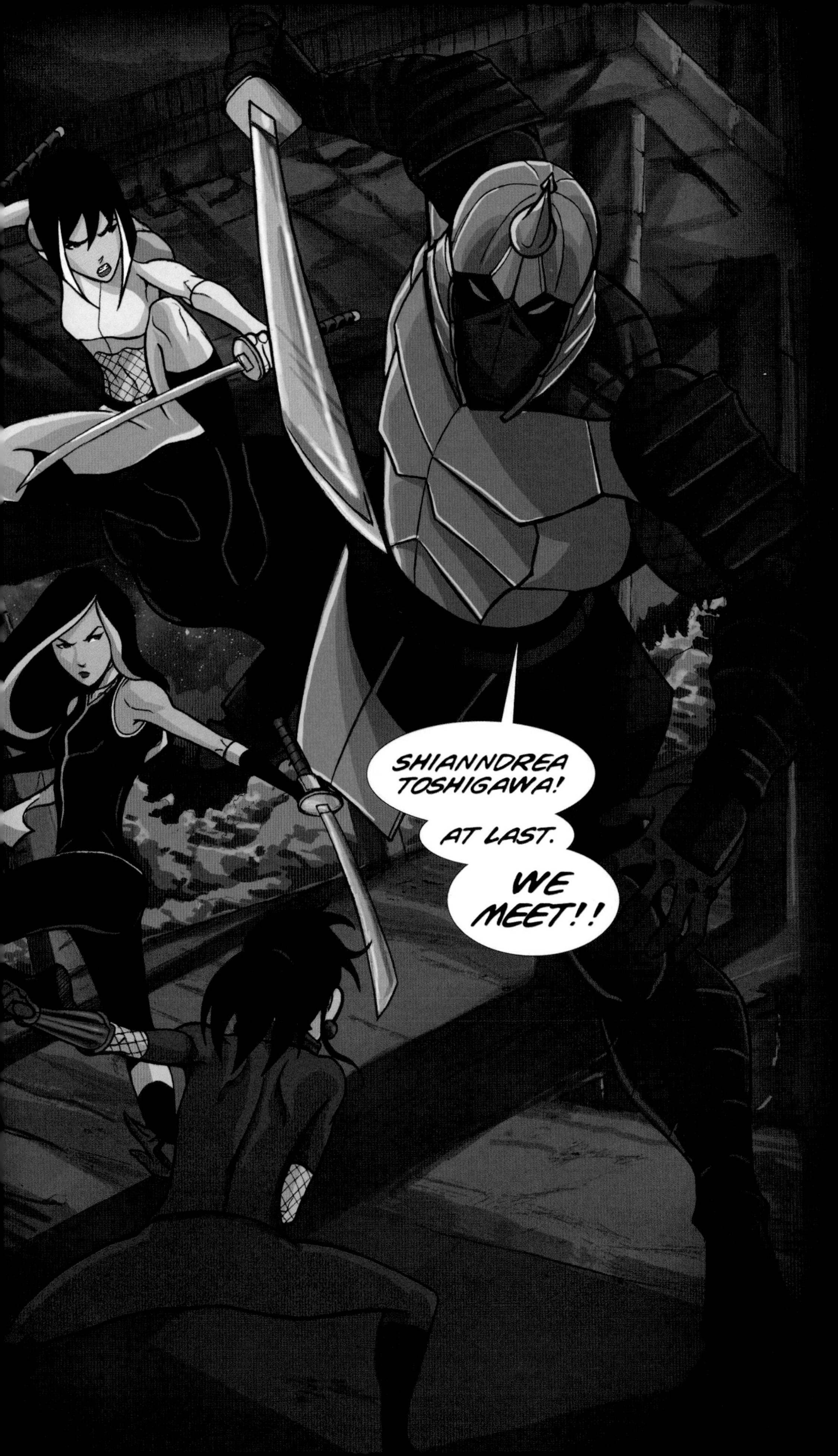
SHIANNDREA TOSHIGAWA!
AT LAST.
WE MEET!!

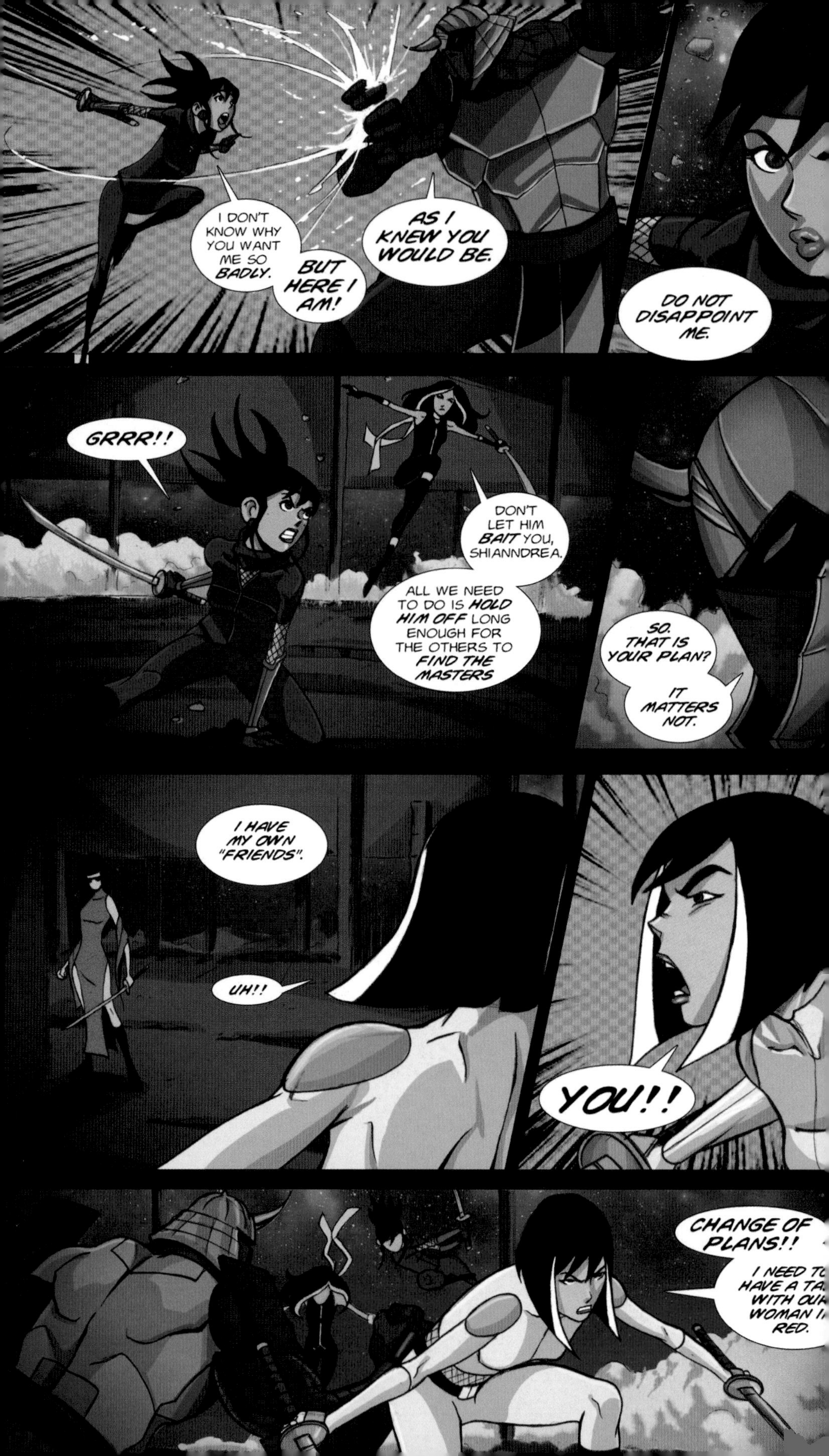
I DON'T KNOW WHY YOU WANT ME SO BADLY.
BUT HERE I AM!
AS I KNEW YOU WOULD BE.
DO NOT DISAPPOINT ME.
GRRR!!
DON'T LET HIM BAIT YOU, SHIANNDREA.
ALL WE NEED TO DO IS HOLD HIM OFF LONG ENOUGH FOR THE OTHERS TO FIND THE MASTERS
SO. THAT IS YOUR PLAN?
IT MATTERS NOT.
I HAVE MY OWN "FRIENDS".
UH!!
YOU!!
CHANGE OF PLANS!!

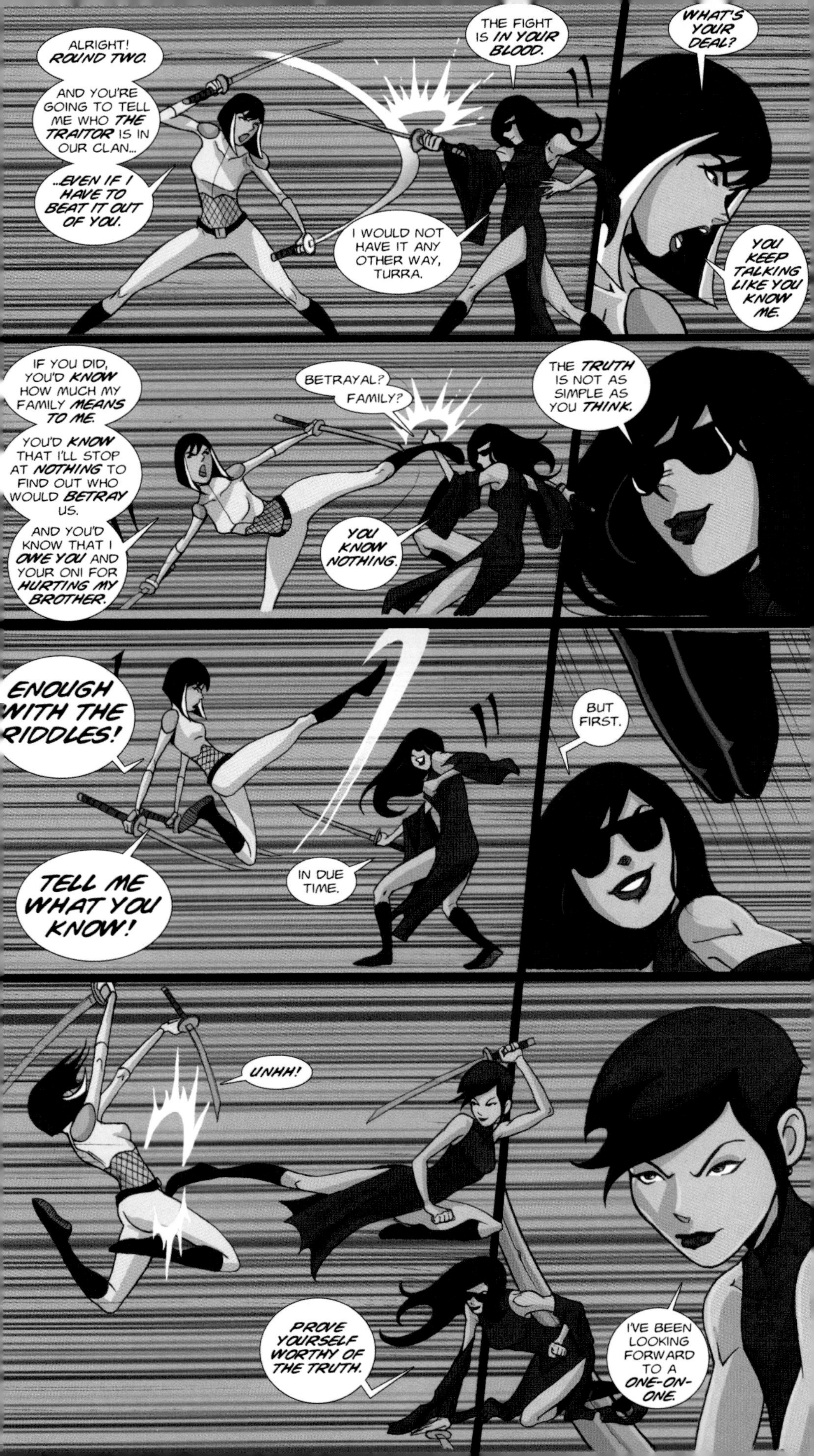
ALRIGHT! ROUND TWO.
AND YOU'RE GOING TO TELL ME WHO THE TRAITOR IS IN OUR CLAN...
...EVEN IF I HAVE TO BEAT IT OUT OF YOU.
THE FIGHT IS IN YOUR BLOOD.
I WOULD NOT HAVE IT ANY OTHER WAY, TURRA.
WHAT'S YOUR DEAL?
YOU KEEP TALKING LIKE YOU KNOW ME.
IF YOU DID, YOU'D KNOW HOW MUCH MY FAMILY MEANS TO ME.
YOU'D KNOW THAT I'LL STOP AT NOTHING TO FIND OUT WHO WOULD BETRAY US.
AND YOU'D KNOW THAT I OWE YOU AND YOUR ONI FOR HURTING MY BROTHER.
BETRAYAL?
FAMILY?
YOU KNOW NOTHING.
THE TRUTH IS NOT AS SIMPLE AS YOU THINK.
ENOUGH WITH THE RIDDLES!
TELL ME WHAT YOU KNOW!
IN DUE TIME.
BUT FIRST.
UNHH!
PROVE YOURSELF WORTHY OF THE TRUTH.
I'VE BEEN LOOKING FORWARD TO A ONE-ON-ONE.

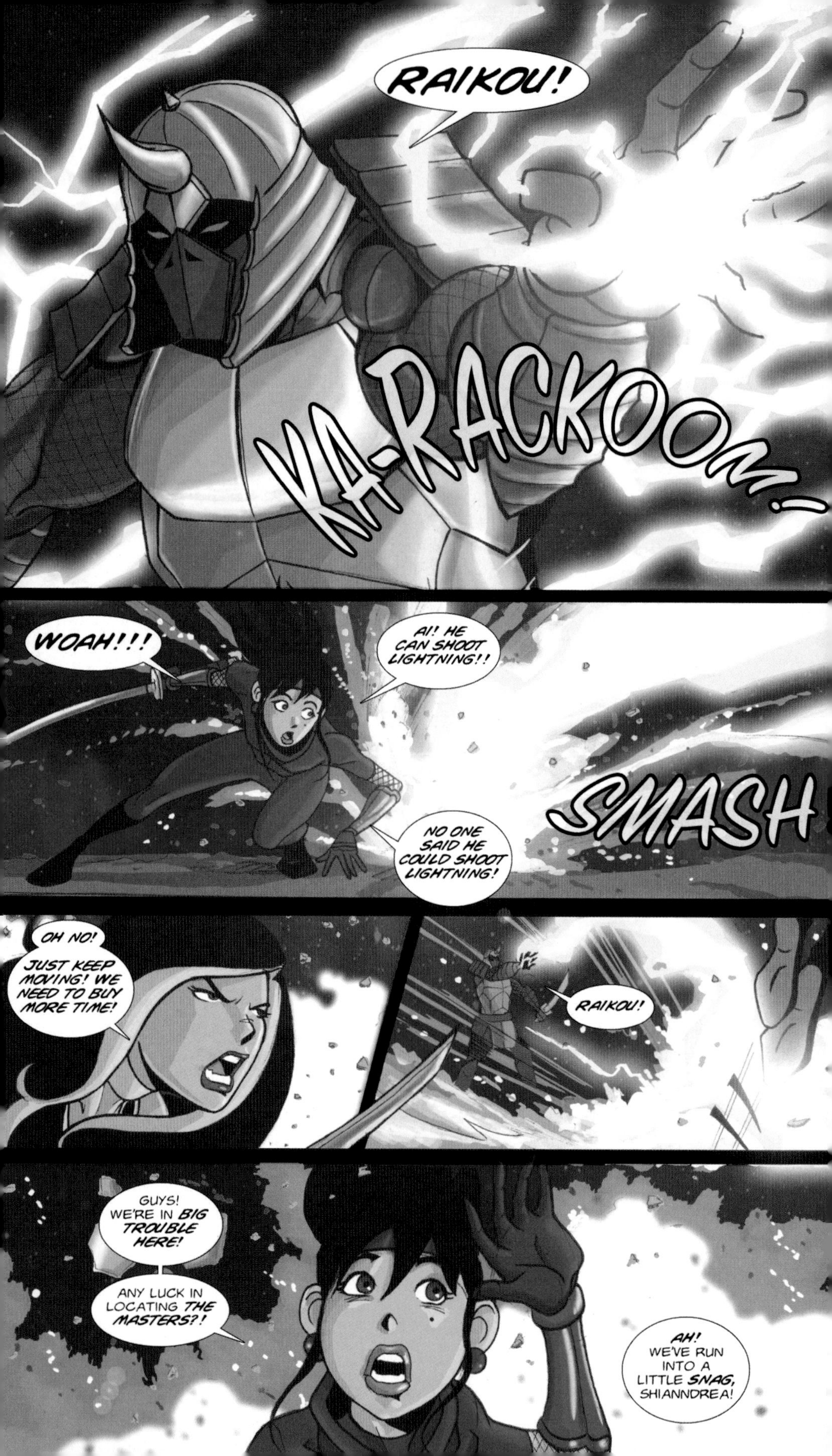
RAIKOU!
KA-RACKOOM!
WOAH!!!
AI! HE CAN SHOOT LIGHTNING!!
SMASH!
NO ONE SAID HE COULD SHOOT LIGHTNING!
OH NO!
JUST KEEP MOVING! WE NEED TO BUY MORE TIME!
RAIKOU!
GUYS! WE'RE IN BIG TROUBLE HERE!
ANY LUCK IN LOCATING THE MASTERS?!
AH! WE'VE RUN INTO A LITTLE SNAG, SHIANNDREA!

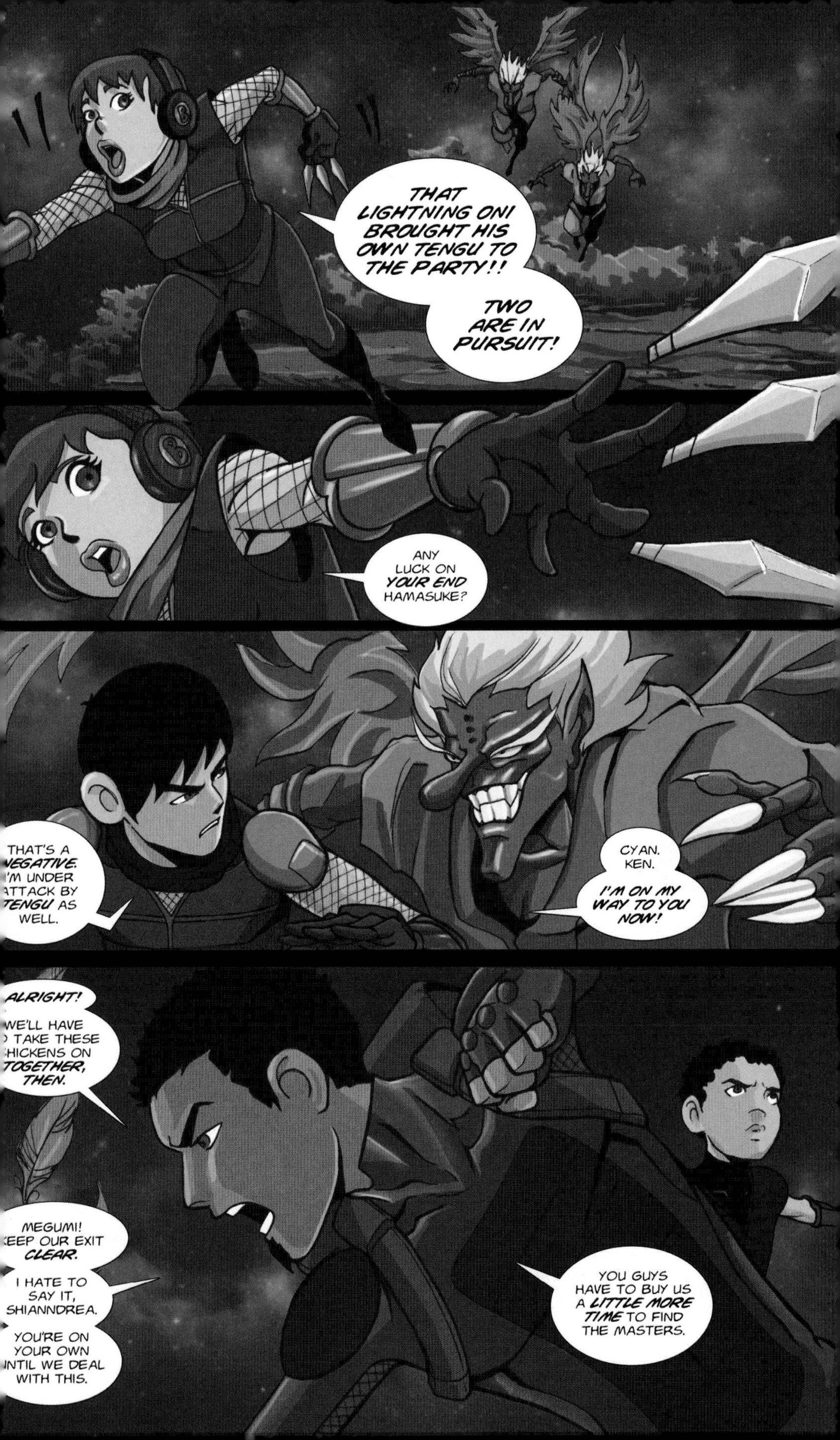
THAT LIGHTNING ONI BROUGHT HIS OWN TENGU TO THE PARTY!!
TWO ARE IN PURSUIT!
ANY LUCK ON *YOUR END* HAMASUKE?
THAT'S A *EGATIVE*. 'M UNDER TTACK BY *ENGU* AS WELL.
CYAN. KEN.
I'M ON MY WAY TO YOU NOW!
LRIGHT!
E'LL HAVE TAKE THESE HICKENS ON *OGETHER, THEN.*
MEGUMI! EEP OUR EXIT *CLEAR*.
I HATE TO SAY IT, SHIANNDREA.
YOU'RE ON YOUR OWN NTIL WE DEAL WITH THIS.
YOU GUYS HAVE TO BUY US A *LITTLE MORE TIME* TO FIND THE MASTERS.

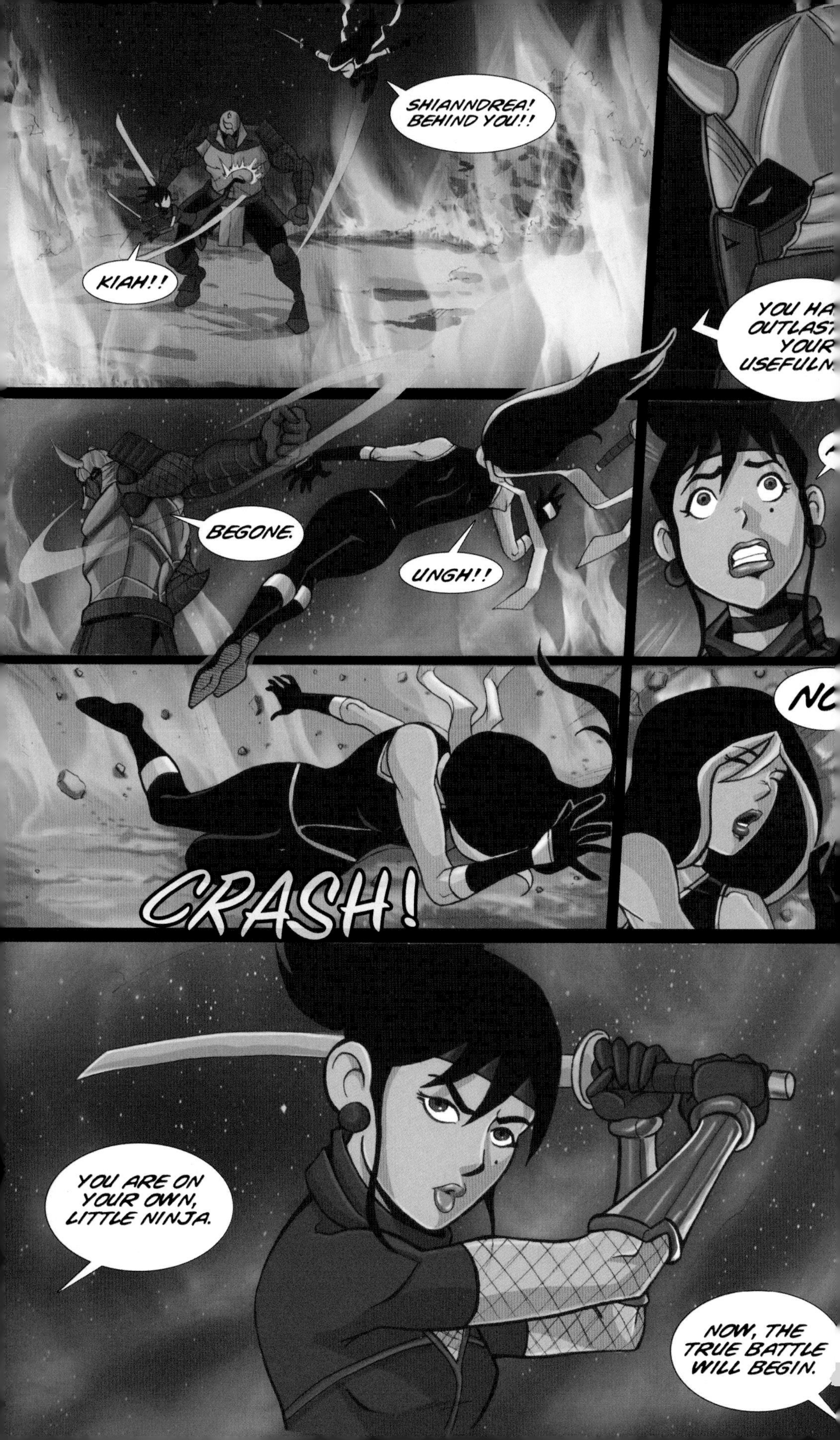
SHIANNDREA! BEHIND YOU!!
KIAH!!
YOU HA
OUTLAST
YOUR
USEFULN
BEGONE.
UNGH!!
CRASH!
N
YOU ARE ON YOUR OWN, LITTLE NINJA.
NOW, THE TRUE BATTLE WILL BEGIN.

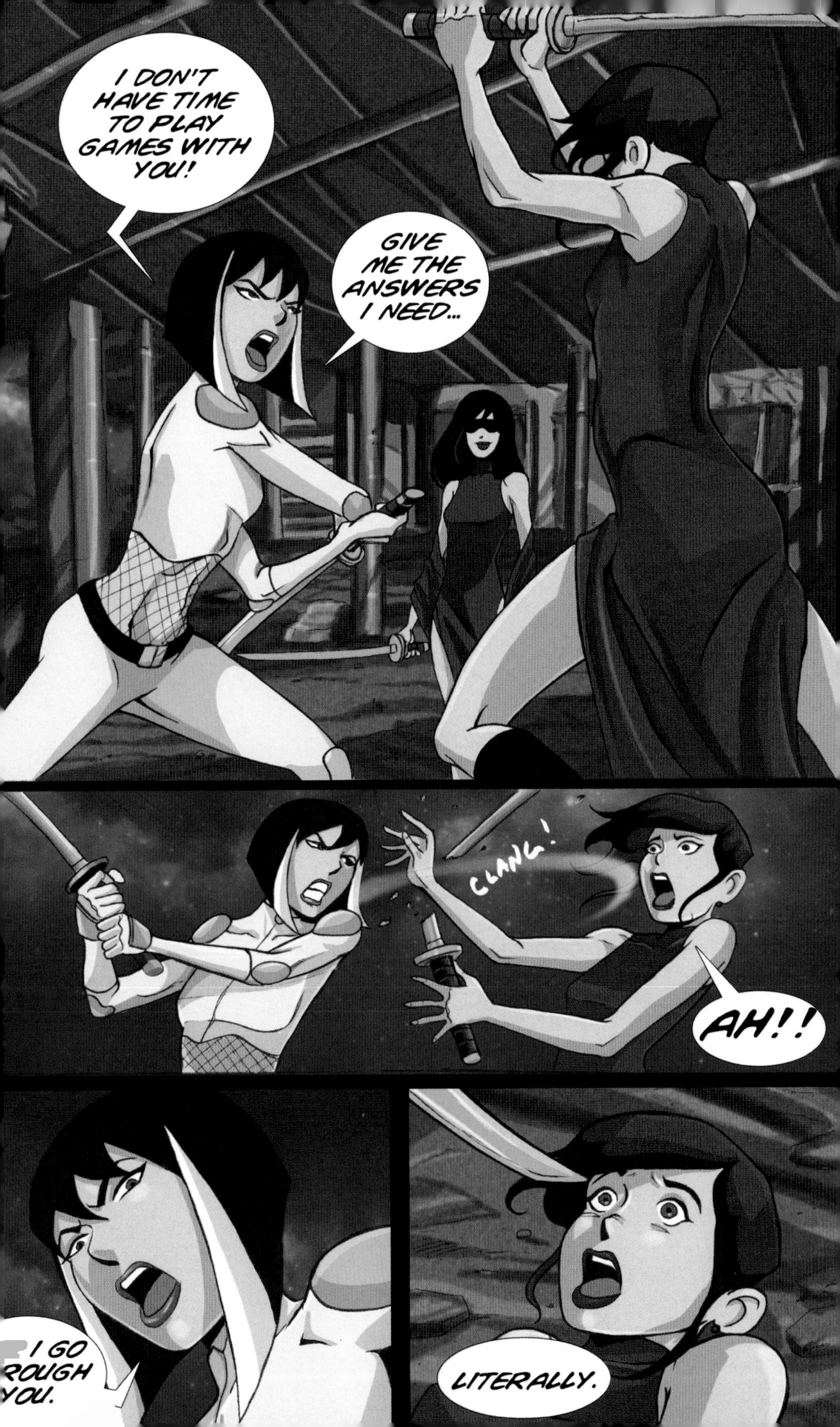
I DON'T HAVE TIME TO PLAY GAMES WITH YOU!
GIVE ME THE ANSWERS I NEED...
CLANG!
AH!!
I GO ROUGH YOU.
LITERALLY.

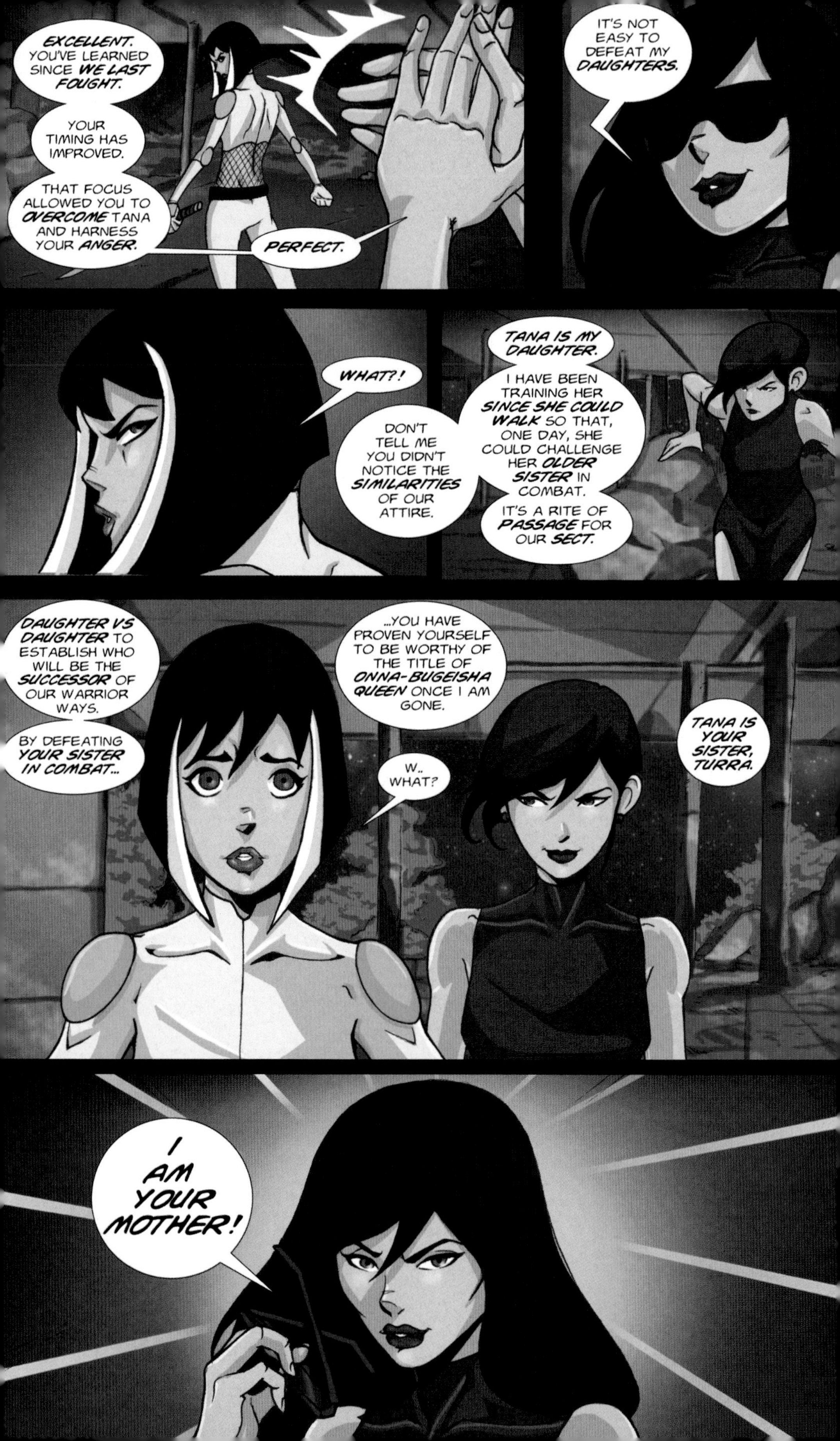
EXCELLENT. YOU'VE LEARNED SINCE WE LAST FOUGHT.
YOUR TIMING HAS IMPROVED.
THAT FOCUS ALLOWED YOU TO OVERCOME TANA AND HARNESS YOUR ANGER.
PERFECT.
IT'S NOT EASY TO DEFEAT MY DAUGHTERS.
WHAT?!
DON'T TELL ME YOU DIDN'T NOTICE THE SIMILARITIES OF OUR ATTIRE.
TANA IS MY DAUGHTER.
I HAVE BEEN TRAINING HER SINCE SHE COULD WALK SO THAT, ONE DAY, SHE COULD CHALLENGE HER OLDER SISTER IN COMBAT.
IT'S A RITE OF PASSAGE FOR OUR SECT.
DAUGHTER VS DAUGHTER TO ESTABLISH WHO WILL BE THE SUCCESSOR OF OUR WARRIOR WAYS.
BY DEFEATING YOUR SISTER IN COMBAT...
...YOU HAVE PROVEN YOURSELF TO BE WORTHY OF THE TITLE OF ONNA-BUGEISHA QUEEN ONCE I AM GONE.
W.. WHAT?
TANA IS YOUR SISTER, TURRA.
I AM YOUR MOTHER!

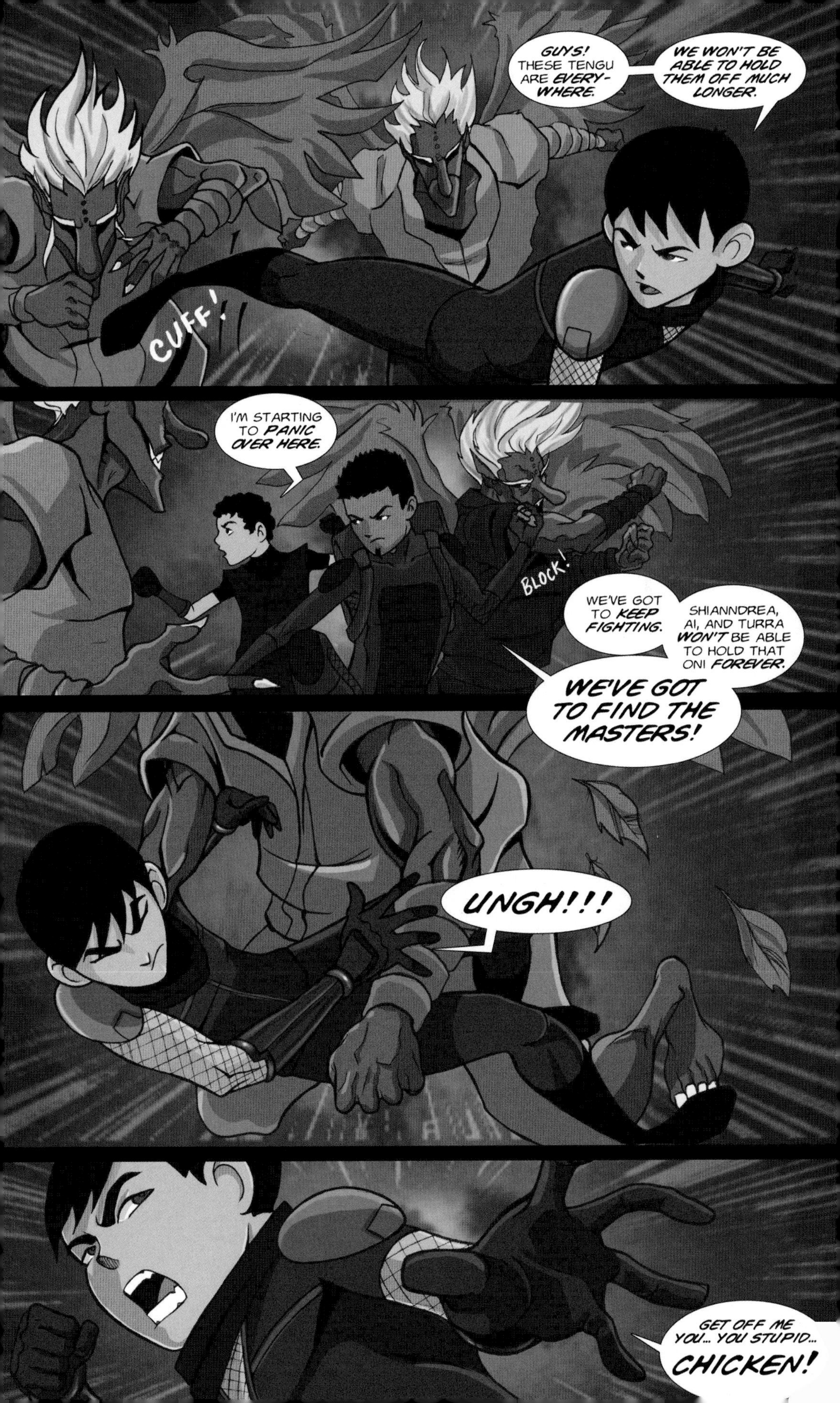
GUYS! THESE TENGU ARE EVERY-WHERE.
WE WON'T BE ABLE TO HOLD THEM OFF MUCH LONGER.
CUFF!
I'M STARTING TO PANIC OVER HERE.
BLOCK!
WE'VE GOT TO KEEP FIGHTING.
SHIANNDREA, AI, AND TURRA WON'T BE ABLE TO HOLD THAT ONI FOREVER.
WE'VE GOT TO FIND THE MASTERS!
UNGH!!!
GET OFF ME YOU... YOU STUPID... CHICKEN!

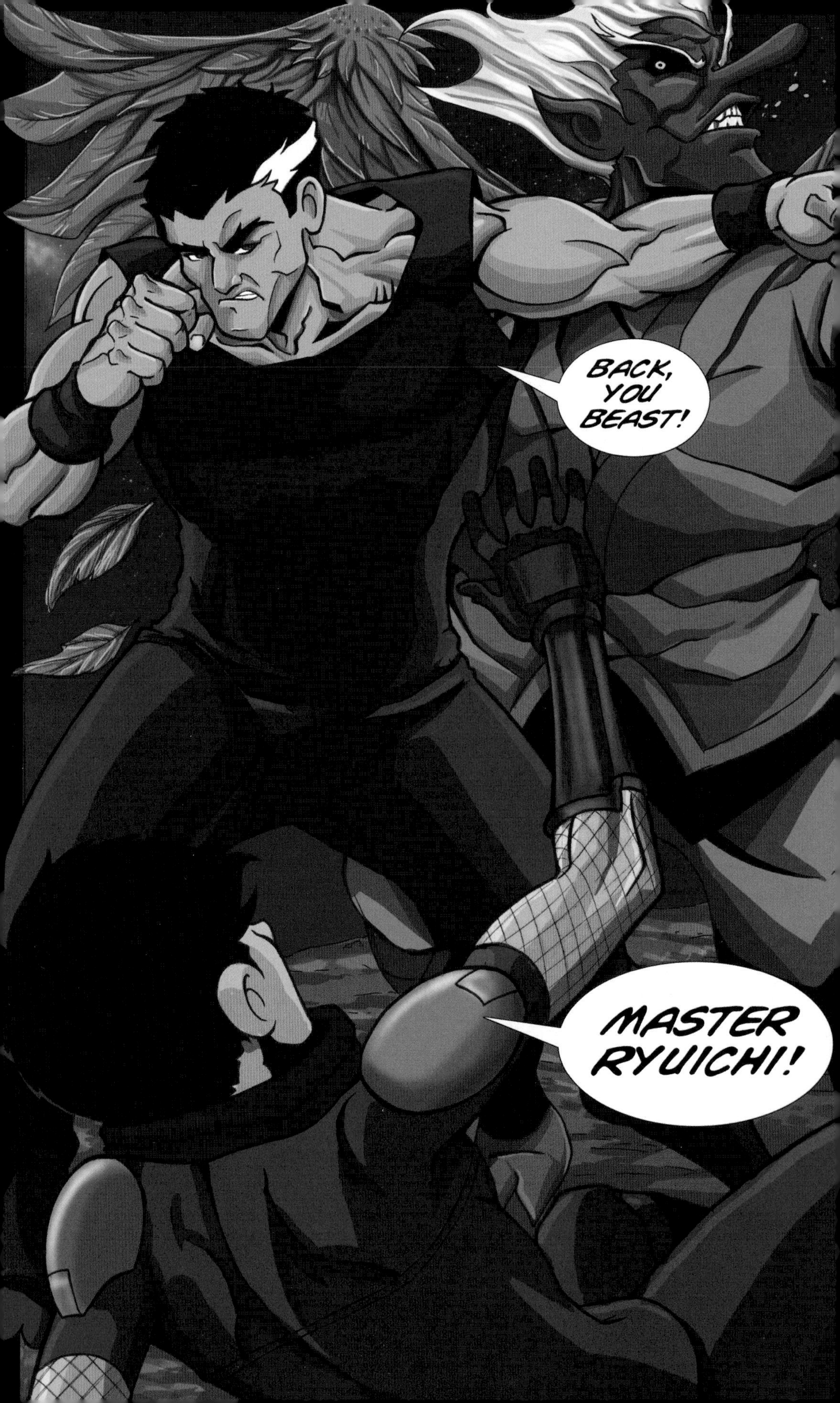
BACK, YOU BEAST!
MASTER RYUICHI!

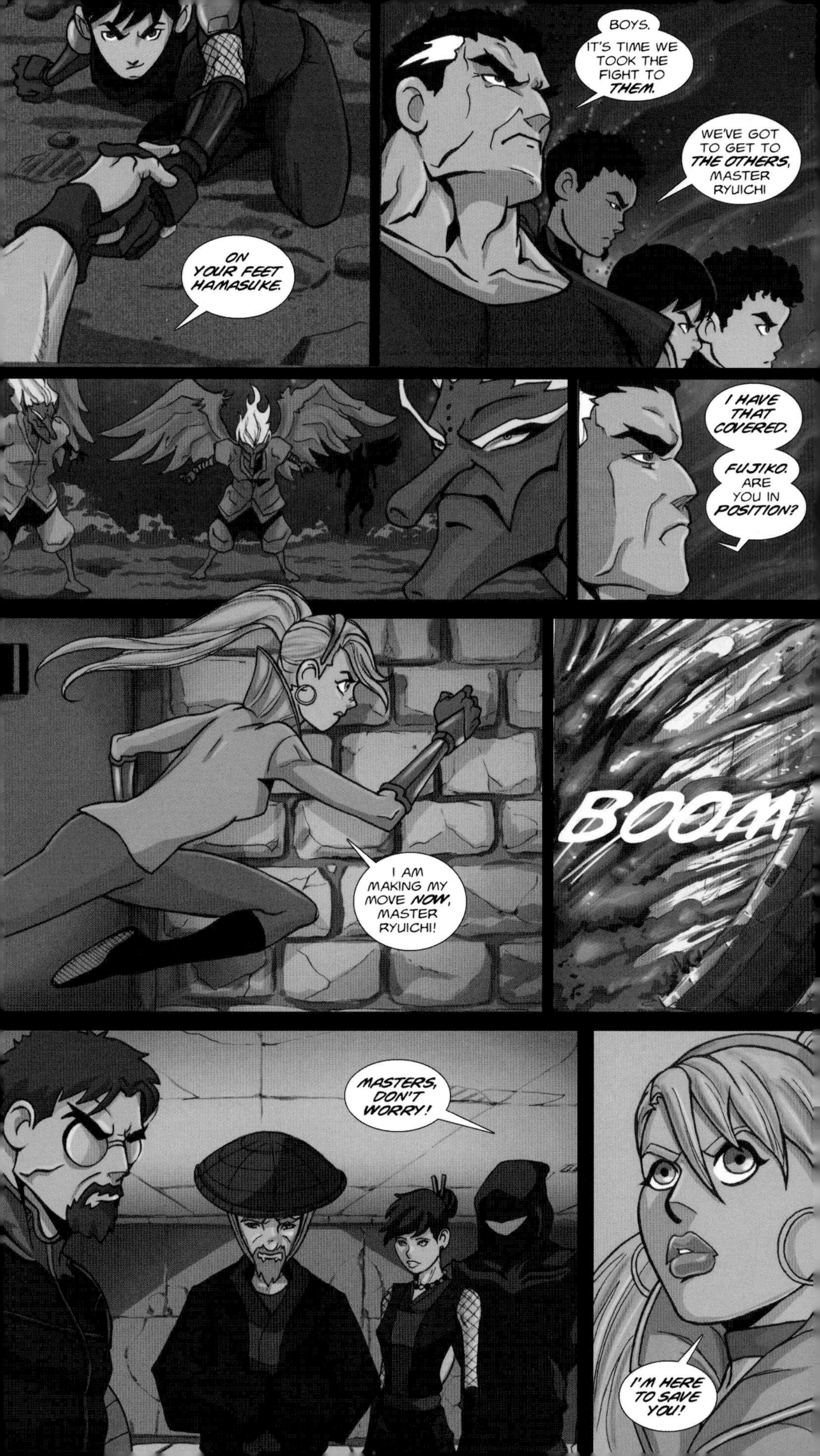
ON YOUR FEET HAMASUKE.
BOYS. IT'S TIME WE TOOK THE FIGHT TO *THEM*.
WE'VE GOT TO GET TO *THE OTHERS*, MASTER RYUICHI
I HAVE THAT COVERED.
FUJIKO. ARE YOU IN *POSITION?*
I AM MAKING MY MOVE *NOW*, MASTER RYUICHI!
BOOM
MASTERS, DON'T WORRY!
I'M HERE TO SAVE YOU!

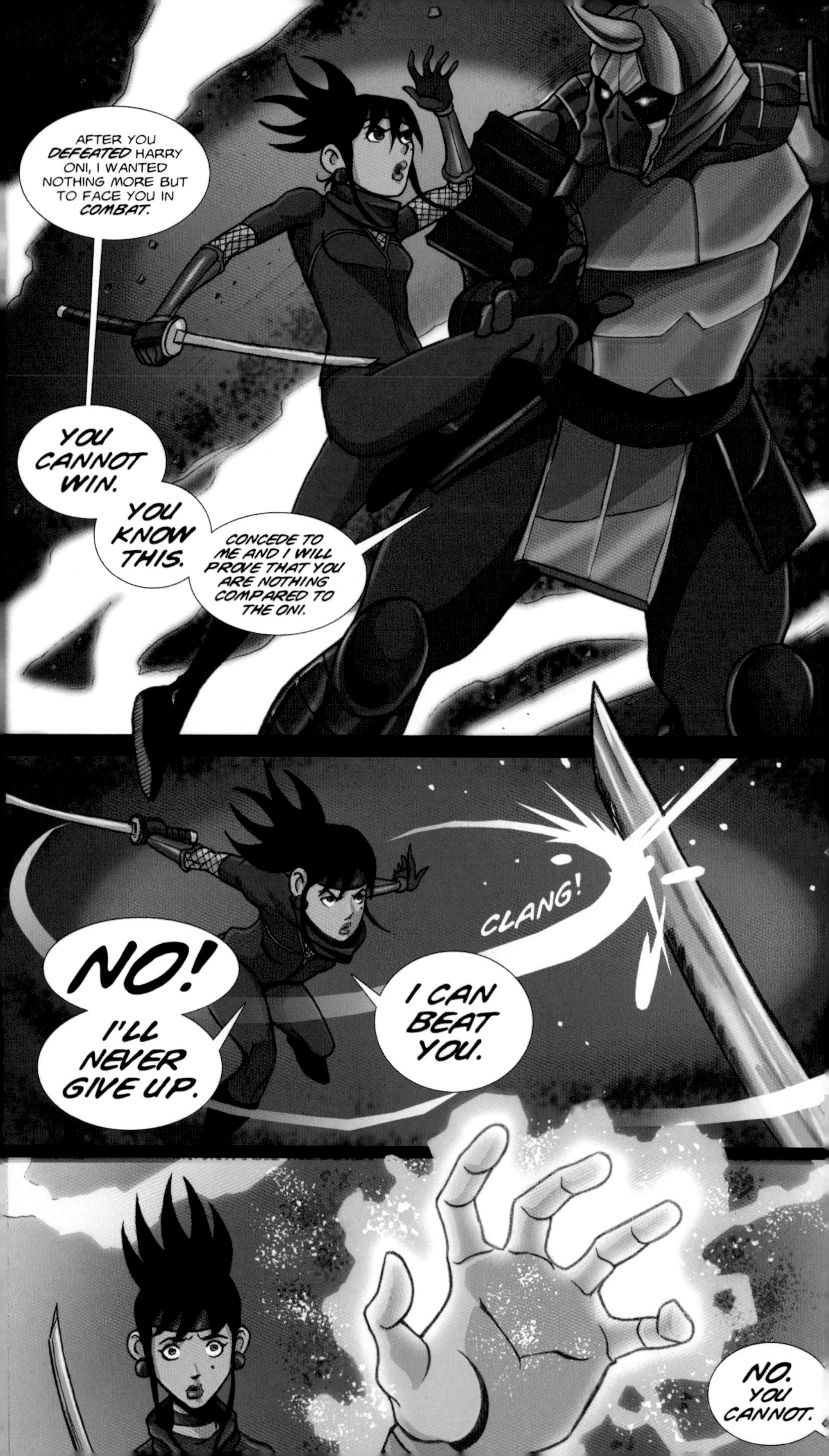
AFTER YOU DEFEATED HARRY ONI, I WANTED NOTHING MORE BUT TO FACE YOU IN COMBAT.
YOU CANNOT WIN.
YOU KNOW THIS.
CONCEDE TO ME AND I WILL PROVE THAT YOU ARE NOTHING COMPARED TO THE ONI.
CLANG!
NO!
I'LL NEVER GIVE UP.
I CAN BEAT YOU.
NO. YOU CANNOT.

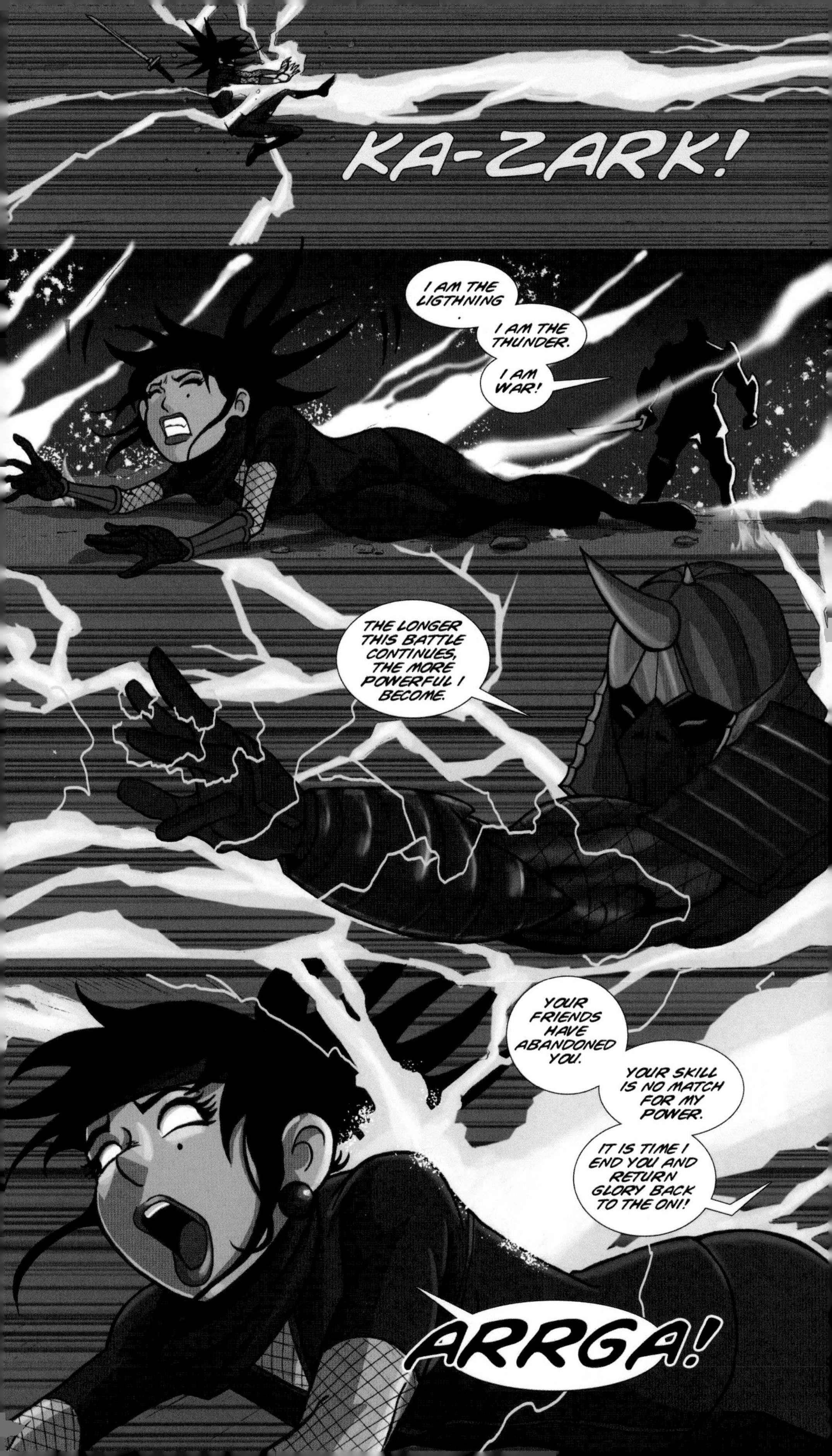
KA-ZARK!
I AM THE LIGTHNING.
I AM THE THUNDER.
I AM WAR!
THE LONGER THIS BATTLE CONTINUES, THE MORE POWERFUL I BECOME.
YOUR FRIENDS HAVE ABANDONED YOU.
YOUR SKILL IS NO MATCH FOR MY POWER.
IT IS TIME I END YOU AND RETURN GLORY BACK TO THE ONI!
ARRGA!

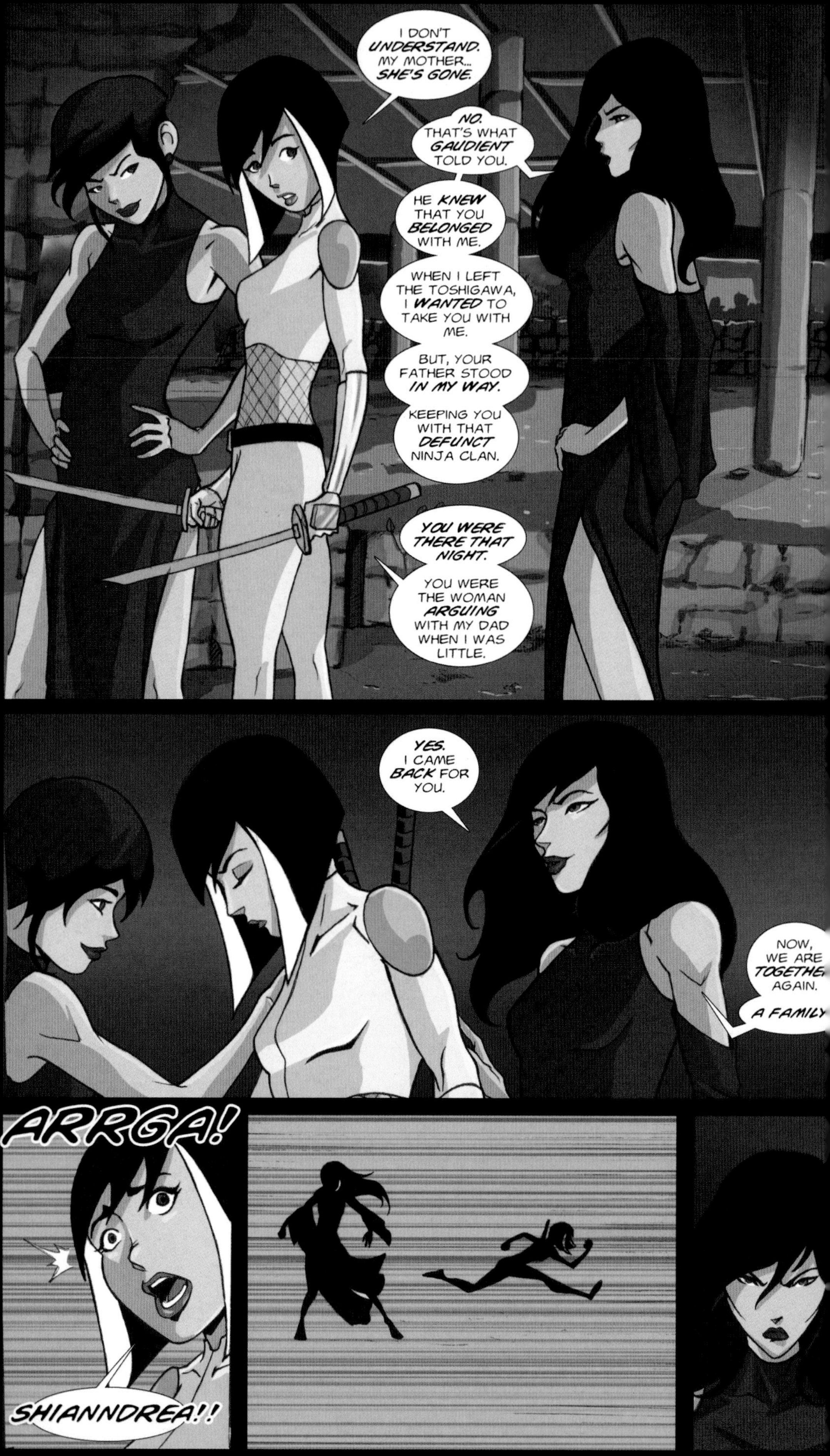

I DON'T UNDERSTAND. MY MOTHER... SHE'S GONE.
NO. THAT'S WHAT GAUDIENT TOLD YOU.
HE KNEW THAT YOU BELONGED WITH ME.
WHEN I LEFT THE TOSHIGAWA, I WANTED TO TAKE YOU WITH ME.
BUT, YOUR FATHER STOOD IN MY WAY.
KEEPING YOU WITH THAT DEFUNCT NINJA CLAN.
YOU WERE THERE THAT NIGHT.
YOU WERE THE WOMAN ARGUING WITH MY DAD WHEN I WAS LITTLE.
YES. I CAME BACK FOR YOU.
NOW, WE ARE TOGETHE
AGAIN.
A FAMIL
ARRGA!
SHIANNDREA!!

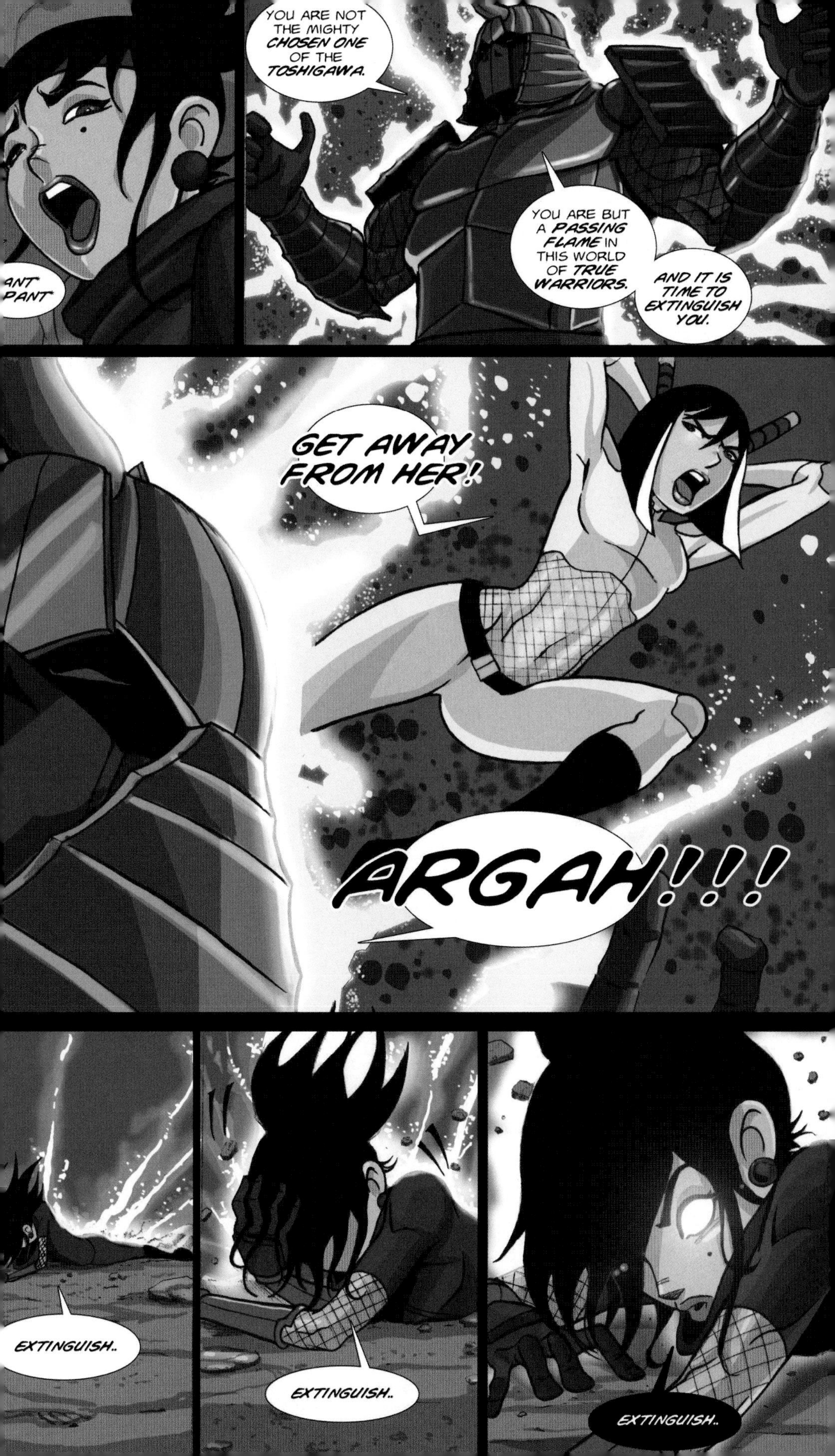

ANT* PANT*
YOU ARE NOT THE MIGHTY CHOSEN ONE OF THE TOSHIGAWA.
YOU ARE BUT A PASSING FLAME IN THIS WORLD OF TRUE WARRIORS.
AND IT IS TIME TO EXTINGUISH YOU.
GET AWAY FROM HER!
ARGAH!!!
EXTINGUISH..
EXTINGUISH..
EXTINGUISH..

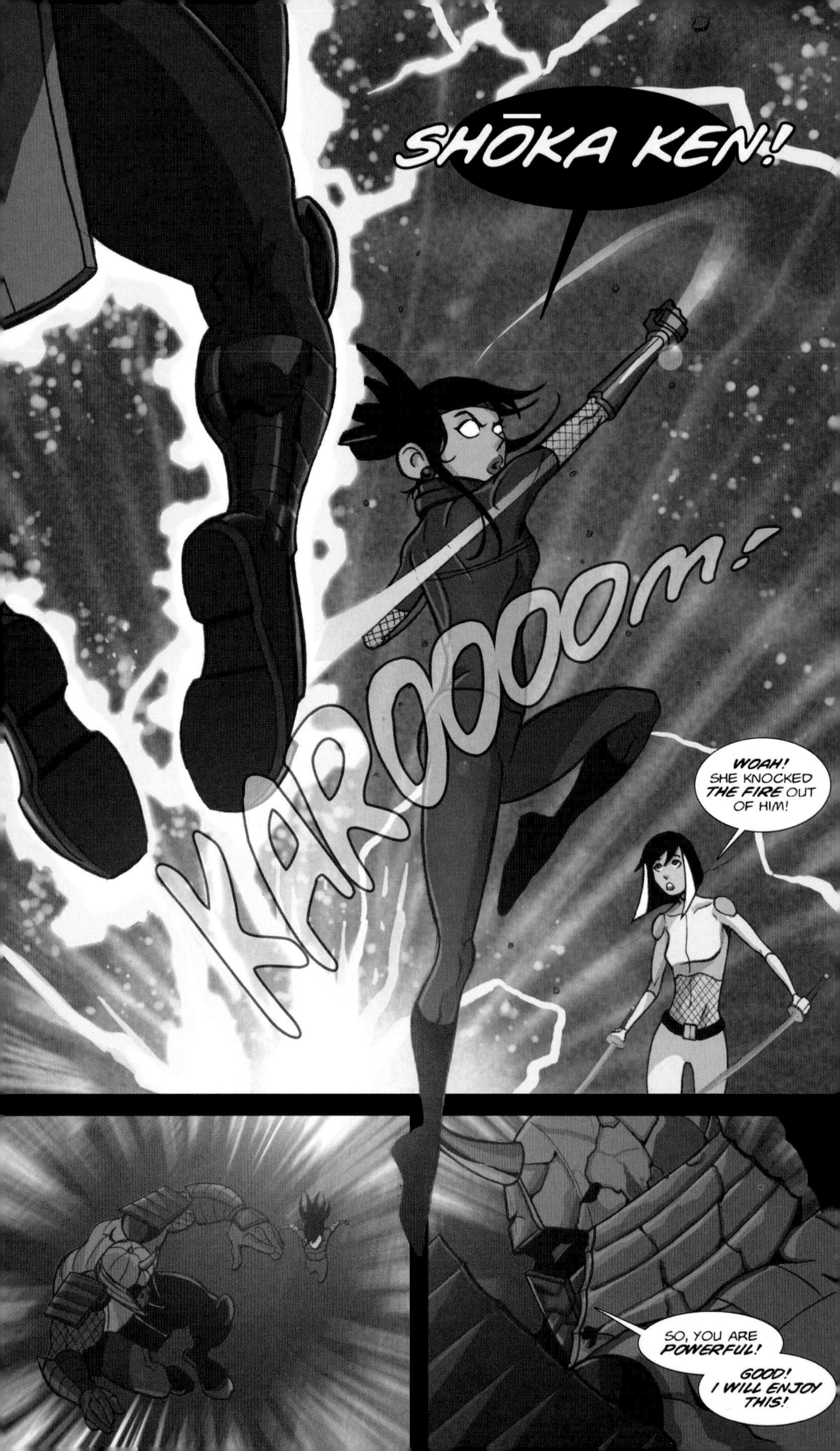

SHŌKA KEN!
KAROOOOOM!
WOAH! SHE KNOCKED THE FIRE OUT OF HIM!
SO, YOU ARE POWERFUL!
GOOD! I WILL ENJOY THIS!

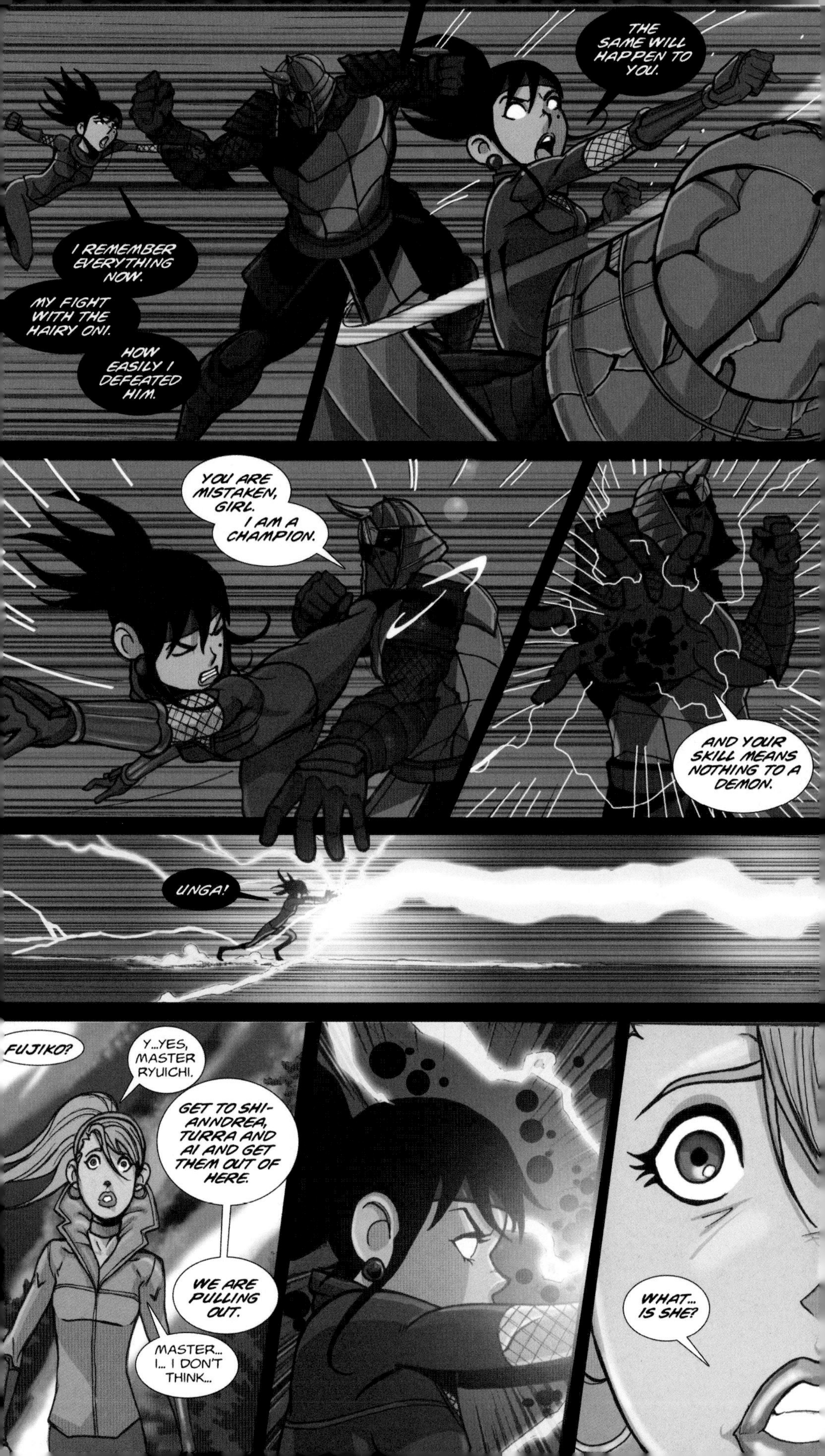
I REMEMBER EVERYTHING NOW.
MY FIGHT WITH THE HAIRY ONI.
HOW EASILY I DEFEATED HIM.
THE SAME WILL HAPPEN TO YOU.
YOU ARE MISTAKEN, GIRL. I AM A CHAMPION.
AND YOUR SKILL MEANS NOTHING TO A DEMON.
UNGA!
FUJIKO?
Y...YES, MASTER RYUICHI.
GET TO SHI-ANNDREA, TURRA AND AI AND GET THEM OUT OF HERE.
WE ARE PULLING OUT.
MASTER... I... I DON'T THINK...
WHAT... IS SHE?

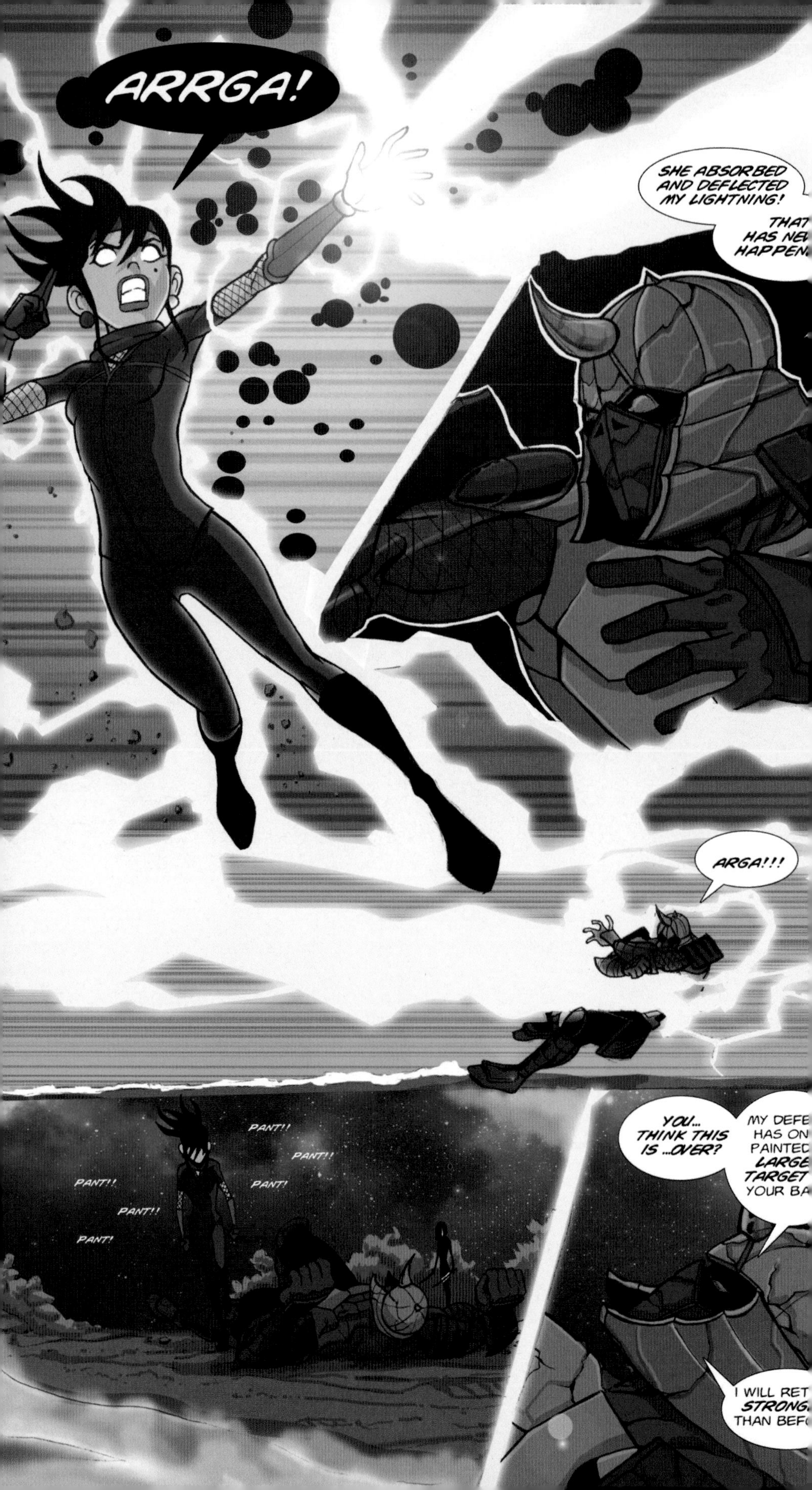
ARRGA!
SHE ABSORBED AND DEFLECTED MY LIGHTNING!
THAT HAS NEV HAPPEN
ARGA!!!
PANT!!
PANT!!
PANT!!
PANT!
PANT!!
PANT!
YOU... THINK THIS IS ...OVER?
MY DEFE HAS ON PAINTED LARGE TARGET YOUR BA
I WILL RET STRONG THAN BEF

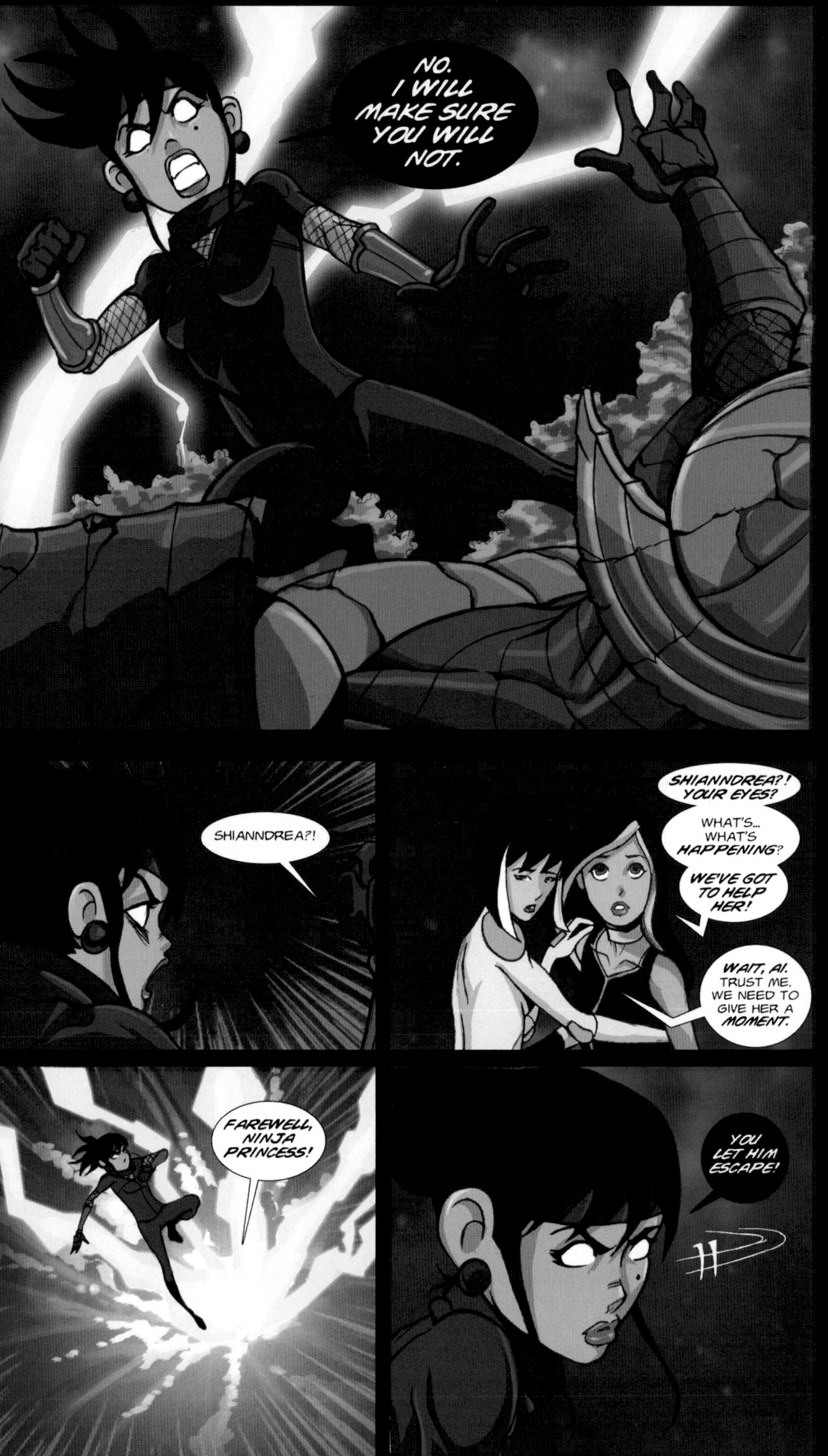
NO. I WILL MAKE SURE YOU WILL NOT.
SHIANNDREA?!
SHIANNDREA?! YOUR EYES?
WHAT'S... WHAT'S HAPPENING?
WE'VE GOT TO HELP HER!
WAIT, AI. TRUST ME. WE NEED TO GIVE HER A MOMENT.
FAREWELL, NINJA PRINCESS!
YOU LET HIM ESCAPE!

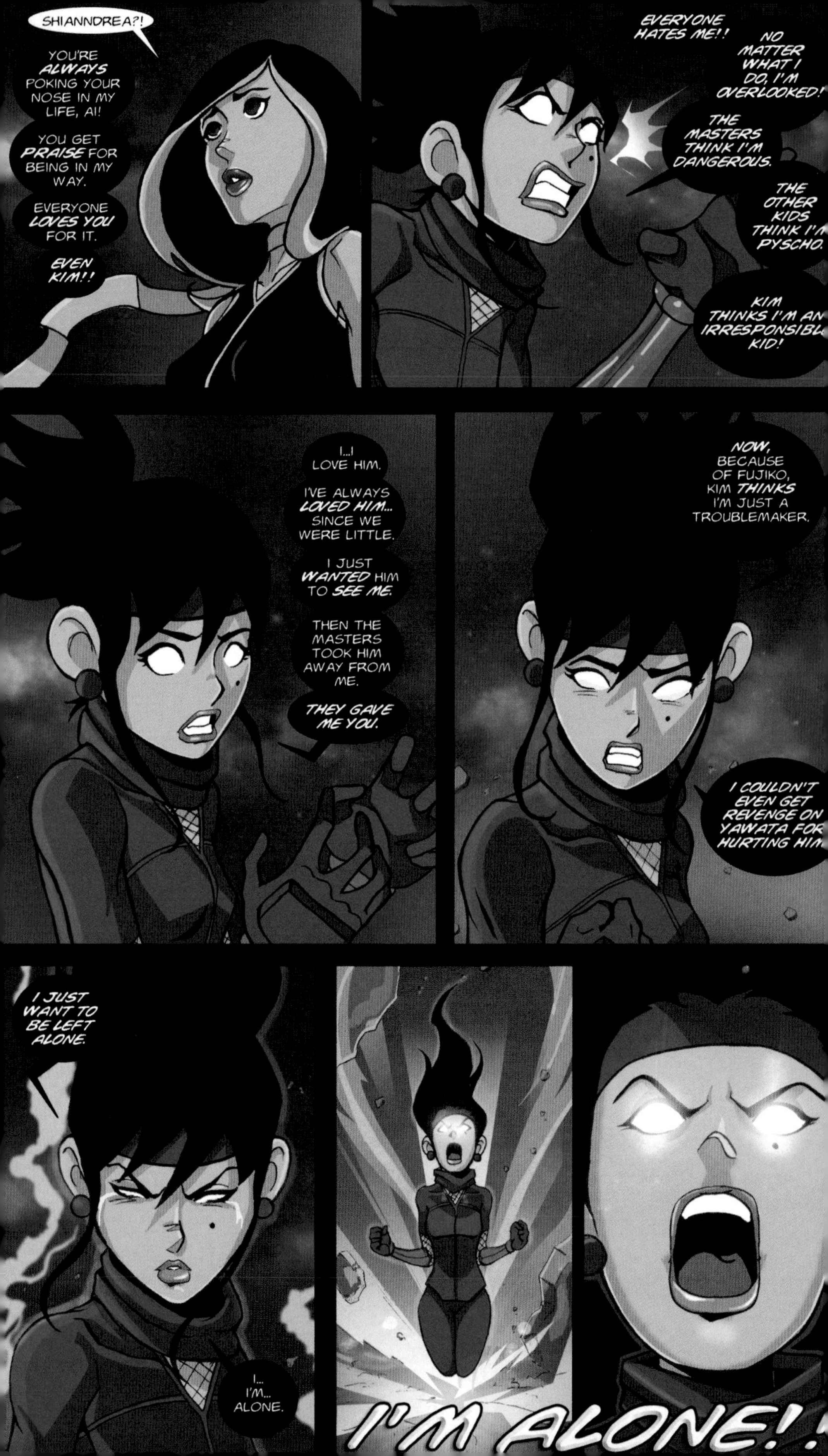

SHIANNDREA?!
YOU'RE ALWAYS POKING YOUR NOSE IN MY LIFE, AI!
YOU GET PRAISE FOR BEING IN MY WAY.
EVERYONE LOVES YOU FOR IT.
EVEN KIM!!
EVERYONE HATES ME!!
NO MATTER WHAT I DO, I'M OVERLOOKED!
THE MASTERS THINK I'M DANGEROUS.
THE OTHER KIDS THINK I'M PYSCHO.
KIM THINKS I'M AN IRRESPONSIBLE KID!
I...I LOVE HIM.
I'VE ALWAYS LOVED HIM... SINCE WE WERE LITTLE.
I JUST WANTED HIM TO SEE ME.
THEN THE MASTERS TOOK HIM AWAY FROM ME.
THEY GAVE ME YOU.
NOW, BECAUSE OF FUJIKO, KIM THINKS I'M JUST A TROUBLEMAKER.
I COULDN'T EVEN GET REVENGE ON YAWATA FOR HURTING HIM
I JUST WANT TO BE LEFT ALONE.
I... I'M... ALONE.
I'M ALONE!!

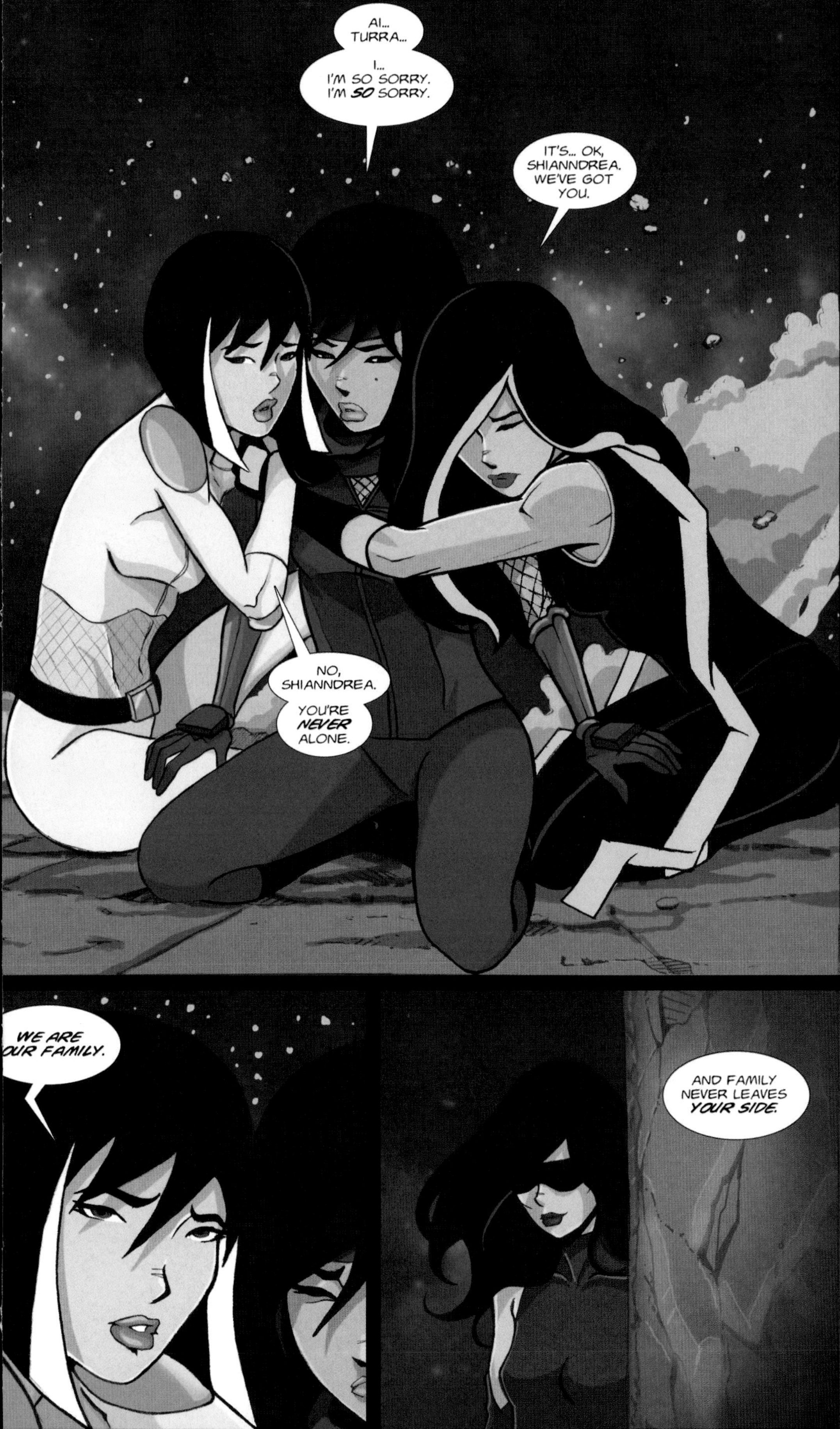
AI... TURRA... I... I'M SO SORRY. I'M ***SO*** SORRY.
IT'S... OK, SHIANNDREA. WE'VE GOT YOU.
NO, SHIANNDREA. YOU'RE ***NEVER*** ALONE.
WE ARE
UR FAMILY.
AND FAMILY NEVER LEAVES ***YOUR SIDE.***

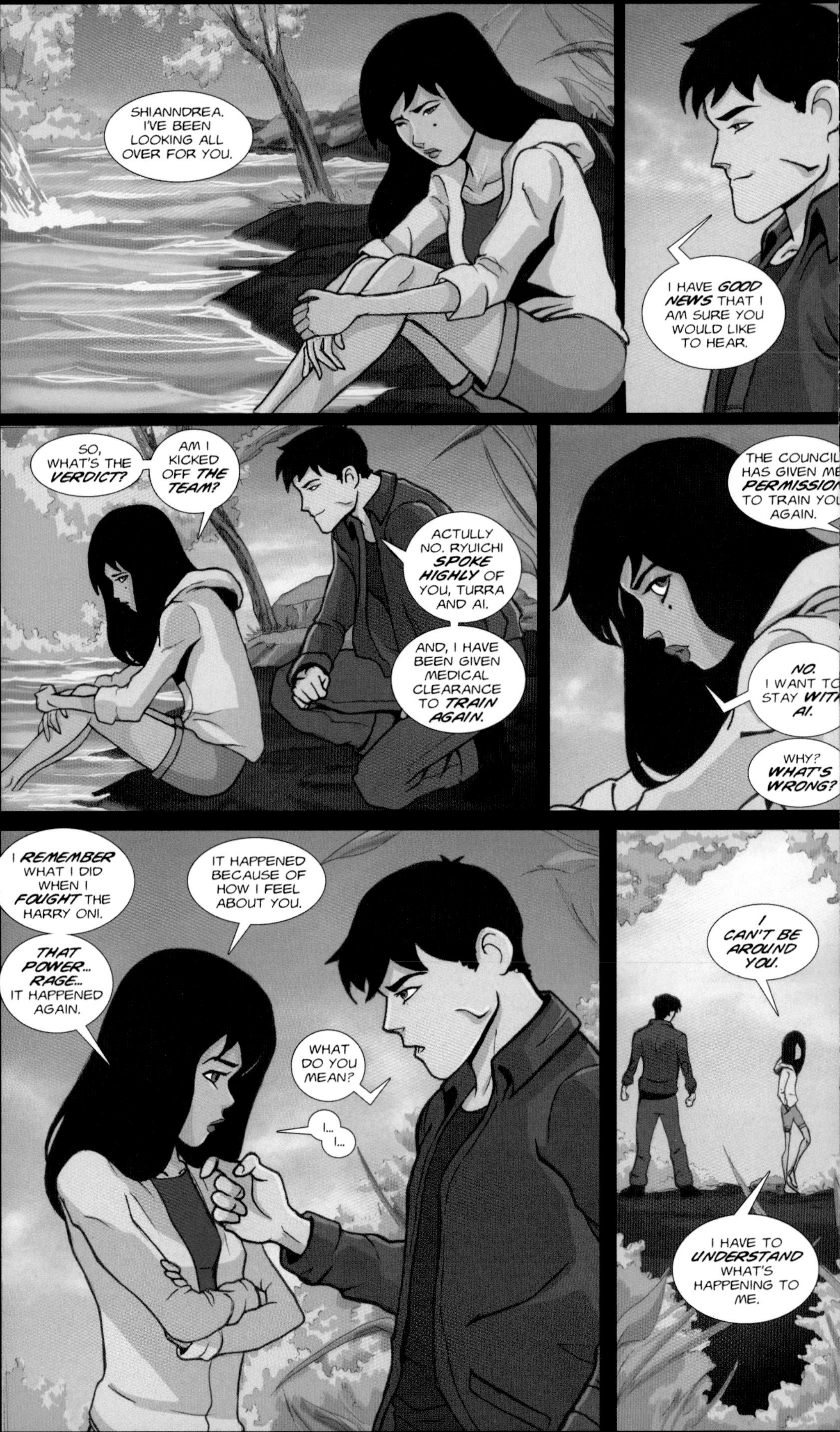
SHIANNDREA. I'VE BEEN LOOKING ALL OVER FOR YOU.
I HAVE GOOD NEWS THAT I AM SURE YOU WOULD LIKE TO HEAR.
SO, WHAT'S THE VERDICT?
AM I KICKED OFF THE TEAM?
ACTULLY NO. RYUICHI SPOKE HIGHLY OF YOU, TURRA AND AI.
AND, I HAVE BEEN GIVEN MEDICAL CLEARANCE TO TRAIN AGAIN.
THE COUNCIL HAS GIVEN ME PERMISSION TO TRAIN YOU AGAIN.
NO. I WANT TO STAY WITH AI.
WHY? WHAT'S WRONG?
I REMEMBER WHAT I DID WHEN I FOUGHT THE HARRY ONI.
THAT POWER... RAGE... IT HAPPENED AGAIN.
IT HAPPENED BECAUSE OF HOW I FEEL ABOUT YOU.
WHAT DO YOU MEAN?
I... I...
I CAN'T BE AROUND YOU.
I HAVE TO UNDERSTAND WHAT'S HAPPENING TO ME.

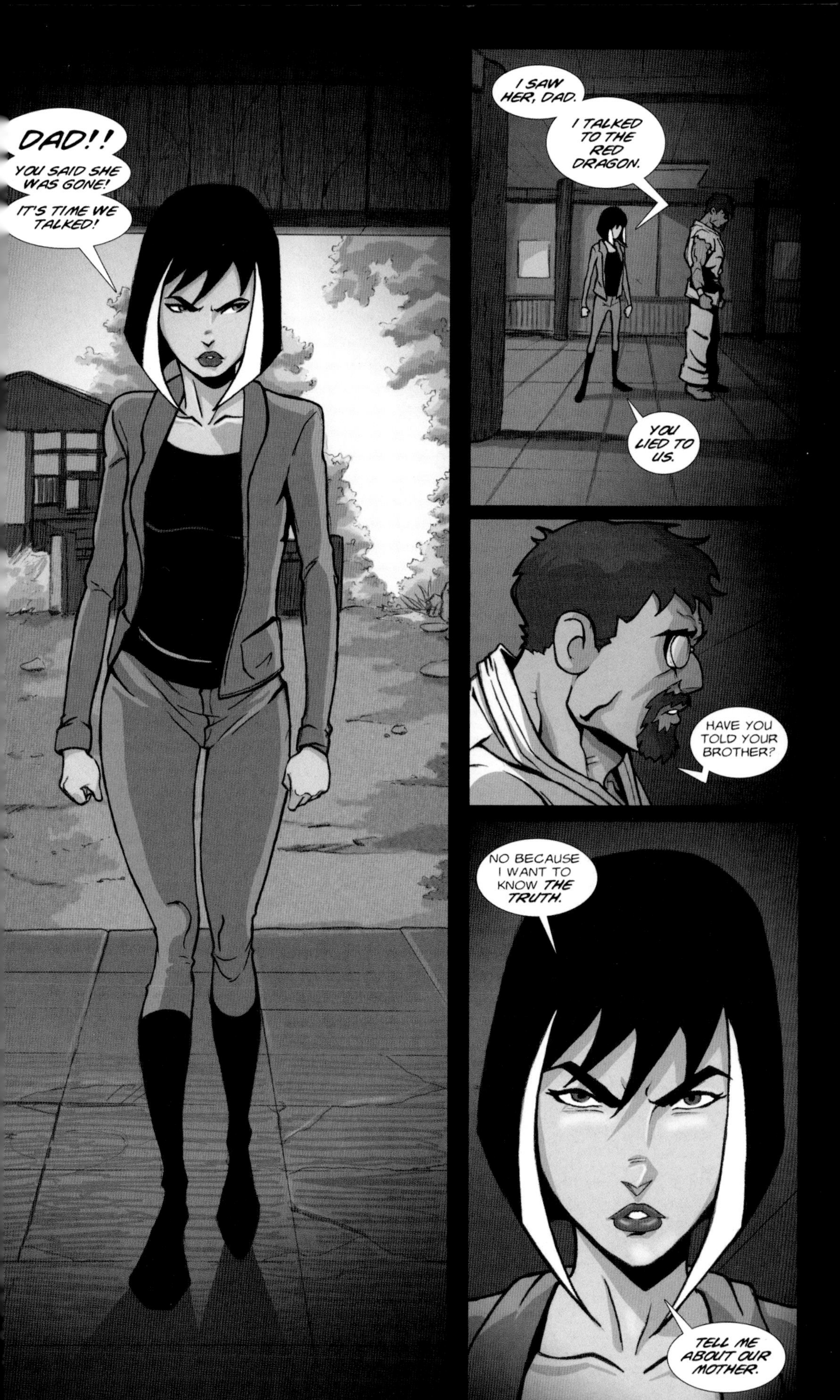
DAD!!
YOU SAID SHE WAS GONE!
IT'S TIME WE TALKED!
I SAW HER, DAD.
I TALKED TO THE RED DRAGON.
YOU LIED TO US.
HAVE YOU TOLD YOUR BROTHER?
NO BECAUSE I WANT TO KNOW THE TRUTH.
TELL ME ABOUT OUR MOTHER.

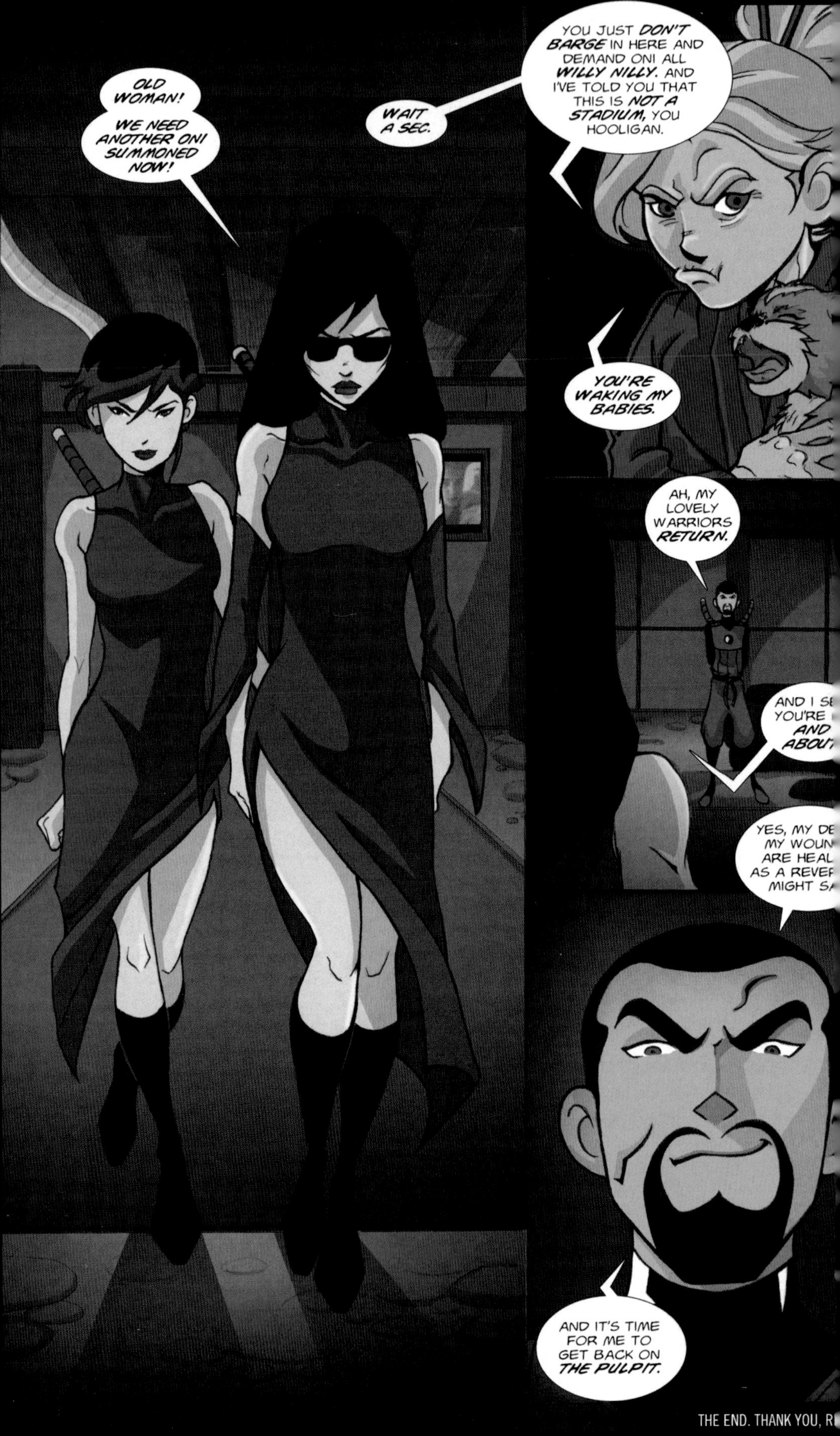
OLD WOMAN!
WE NEED ANOTHER ONI SUMMONED NOW!
WAIT A SEC.
YOU JUST DON'T BARGE IN HERE AND DEMAND ONI ALL WILLY NILLY. AND I'VE TOLD YOU THAT THIS IS NOT A STADIUM, YOU HOOLIGAN.
YOU'RE WAKING MY BABIES.
AH, MY LOVELY WARRIORS RETURN.
AND I SE
YOU'RE
AND
YES, MY DE
MY WOUN
ARE HEAL
AS A REVER
MIGHT S
AND IT'S TIME FOR ME TO GET BACK ON THE PULPIT.

THE END. THANK YOU, R

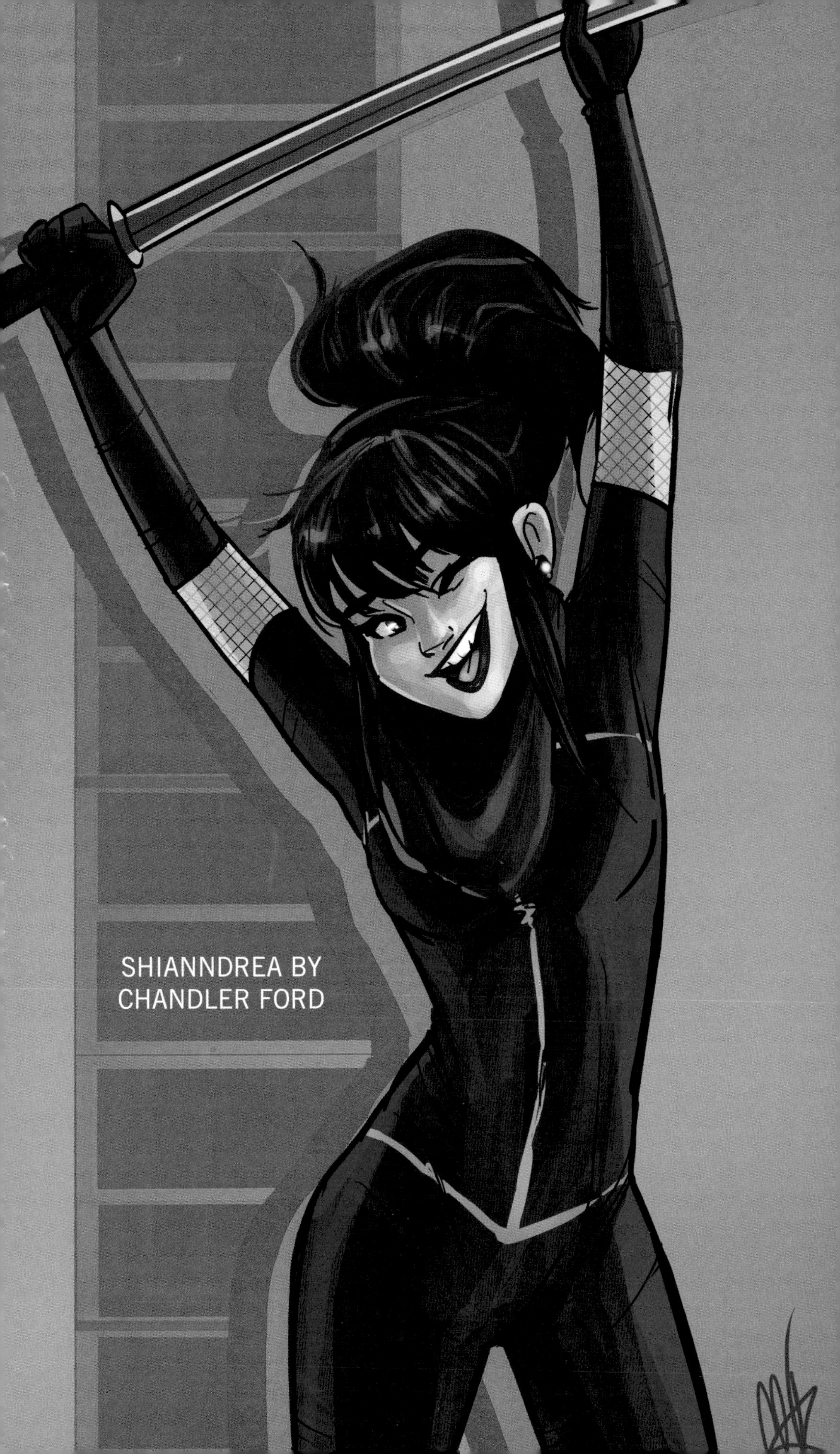

SHIANNDREA BY
CHANDLER FORD